Delhi

Raza Rumi is a writer and development professional from Pakistan. Currently, he is affiliated with the Jinnah Institute, a public policy think tank in Islamabad. He also edits the *Friday Times* every week, writes columns for leading Pakistani newspapers and journals, and is a well-known commentator on politics and culture.

Earlier, Raza worked as a governance expert for the Asian Development Bank, the United Nations Mission in Kosovo and the Government of Pakistan. This is his first book.

Impressions of a Pakistani Traveller

Raza Rumi

HarperCollins *Publishers* India

First published in India in 2013 by
HarperCollins *Publishers* India

P-ISBN: 978-93-5029-418-5
E-ISBN: 978-93-5029-998-2

4 6 8 10 9 7 5 3

HarperCollins *Publishers*
A-75, Sector 57, Noida, Uttar Pradesh 201301, India
1 London Bridge Street, London, SE1 9GF, United Kingdom
Hazelton Lanes, 55 Avenue Road, Suite 2900, Toronto, Ontario M5R 3L2
and 1995 Markham Road, Scarborough, Ontario M1B 5M8, Canada
25 Ryde Road, Pymble, Sydney, NSW 2073, Australia
195 Broadway, New York NY 10007, USA

Typeset in 11/14.9 Bell MT
by Jojy Philip, New Delhi 110 015

Printed and bound at
Manipal Technologies Ltd., Manipal

For my parents
Bilquis and Sheikh Riaz Ahmed

Contents

Preface

I have always wanted to be an author. This, an unintended and unplanned book, is my first attempt at trying to be one. And while not unaccustomed to writing per se, I must confess I was quite unsure how the book would shape up until the publisher gave her approval to the initial draft.

Delhi by Heart was written between 2007 and 2009 as a testament to my discovery of Delhi and its multilayered history. By no means is this venture an academic one, nor is it a journalist's 'contemporary' account. It is in many ways an internalized dialogue with a bit of research and occasional interviews. In other ways, it is a great leap into the unknown.

As a Pakistani who was born into textbook nationalism, the process of viewing the 'other' and what separated us from British India in 1947 has been an arduous one. I grew up and lived in a milieu that conditioned me to resent India, especially its role in dismembering the Pakistani state in 1971. At the same time, I also lived in the semi-schizophrenic state of being part of the 'enemy' landscape. The cultural references, historical threads and many other bonds were far too strong. These bonds became stronger as I went abroad for my studies and befriended many Indians in a neutral territory. A Kashmiri Pandit, a Calcutta-based Punjabi and many a Dilli-wala humanized the vision that had been imposed on me. Unlearning was a rare gift that I am tremendously thankful for. I think my Indian friends must have gone through a similar process when we were twenty-somethings attempting to understand the world.

My second meeting with Indians took place when I worked in Kosovo as part of the UN peacekeeping mission during 2000–02. As an officer of the administrative service, the Indian civil servants in Kosovo were my friends and there was far too much in common between us, given how we were all, at the end of the day, cogs in unwieldy post-colonial states to be ignored or wished away. My entry into the Asian Development Bank in 2002 again brought me in contact with dozens of Indian colleagues, their spouses and families, who represented another variant of India's multitudinal reality.

It was during those days that I arrived in Delhi for work. There were frequent visits as a staffer of an international organization, and the work entailed interaction with different segments of Delhi society. This was also the time when I was fascinated by the city and that is when the idea of this book first took root. However, writing it as a full-time civil servant was not easy. In 2008, my life took another turn when I decided to treat myself to a well-deserved sabbatical, returned to Pakistan, and started a career in journalism and freelance policy work. I was free to travel and open to meeting more people; it was during this period that I discovered the countless, interconnected worlds that exist across the border.

Since then I have also been part of several peace initiatives, both on the Track II diplomacy side as well as cultural cooperation between the two countries. Therefore, the seeming chaos in the organization of this book and its occasionally rambling tone are reflective of diverse influences, scattered notes and raw memories. As I read the draft before it went to the publishers I could not help notice how awestruck I appeared in some of my initial reactions, especially in the early days, and instead of changing them I have let the original emotion remain.

Delhi has undergone several changes over the past few years. People and places have changed too. The book might seem a little dated at places but I would like to remind the readers that it was written several years ago. Updating it would have been a bit unfair to the spirit in which it was authored.

By no means is this an exhaustive travel guide. These are impressions of a foreigner—an 'outsider'—who has obviously selected moments and histories of his liking and penned them down. In that sense, I admit its partiality and perhaps a sense of incompleteness. I do fervently hope that my views are appreciated as that of a faint voice that wants to transcend boundaries and borders and reject the ills of jingoism spun by nation-state narratives, which permeate our troubled consciousness. I hope also that it will be received by readers on both sides in its true spirit.

1

The City and I

Under the overcast Delhi sky, I turn my face towards the monsoon breeze. The faint scent of champa flowers seems hauntingly familiar. Somewhere within I am plagued by the fact that this, my very first trip to Delhi, is an official one. But with more visits, coming ashore has become more and more easy. I am never tired of coming to Delhi.

It is a Saturday, my first day in the city. I am without a guide-book—I have always been averse to these travel instruments. I did not want to use the hotel tourism services either. They are expensive and soulless, herding travellers into a minibus with maverick guides spouting oriental phraseology. As a Pakistani I feel that I am not lonely on planet Delhi.

My earliest memory of the city is mingled with the image of the Hazrat Nizamuddin shrine dedicated to the Sufi saint, Hazrat Nizamuddin Auliya, and discovering a muse that now seems a little prearranged by the stars—not that I have ever believed in the immutability of destiny or of preordained occurrences. I dig for the little scrap of paper hidden somewhere in my laptop bag. I find a little note with the name 'Sadia Dehlvi' and then a telephone number. I have a femme fatale image of Sadia stuck in my memory from Khushwant Singh's book, *Women and Men in my Life* and, of course, from knowing the family of her late Pakistani husband, a man much older than her who loved her with cavernous passion. My questions on the telephone are routine—what is the best time to go to the shrine, how do I get there, etc. She tells me I should go there around the time of maghreb.

A yellow-black Ambassador taxi takes me to the shrine. We go through the shady boulevards of Chanakyapuri, the posh diplomatic enclave of Delhi. It feels remarkably like another serene neighbourhood of Lahore, my home town, especially when the monsoon rains have washed away layers of dust that clings to the trees during the arid heat of Delhi's summers.

Accident of history turned Delhi into a sacred space for Muslims during the medieval period. Its centrality as the cultural heartland for South Asia's Muslim past is well known. It emerged as a grand city during many years of Muslim rule to be known as the 'city of cities'. Much of contemporary north Indian cuisine, manners and language evolved within the precincts of Delhi.

The legendary twenty-two Sufis sleeping under its urban mass turned the city and its environs into an unmatched place of reverence. Termed as 'Little Mecca'[1] by medieval and colonial *tazkiras* of the subcontinent, Delhi's primacy as the Sufi capital was unchallenged except by Ajmer, cited as 'Little Medina'[2] by the biographers of Khwaja Moinuddin Chishti. And in medieval times, this was best summed up by these lines in a *mathnawi* of Khusrau:

> Noble Delhi, shelter of religion and treasure
> It is the Garden of Eden, may it last forever.
> A veritable earthly Paradise in all its qualities
> May Allah protect it from calamities.
> If it but heard the tale of this garden,
> Mecca would make a pilgrimage to Hindustan.[3]

Apart from the spiritual solace they provide, the tombs of Muslim emperors and saints in Delhi can be seen as transitional spaces between the temporal and afterworld of Muslims. But more significantly, they are markers of Muslim identity in India. Grave visitations and associated events turn into informal statements of local communal memory and the substantive content of such personal and communal statements as well.

In Pakistan, with Delhi and Ajmer having been lost to the arbitrary line drawn by Radcliffe, Lahore was to acquire this status in the new Muslim state. Data Darbar, the shrine of Ali Hujweri, in Lahore, is now the equivalent of Little Mecca and Little Medina in India.

These jumbled thoughts surface and disappear as Delhi's tombs merge with the chaos of the city traffic.

Delhi's international airport is named after the late prime minister Indira Gandhi, famous for her parentage, mourned for her tragic assassination and reviled for the Emergency she imposed on a stubborn democracy. For a second, the name made me a little nervous because of her trumpeted role in 'breaking' Pakistan. Pakistani sensibilities can be offended easily, especially when you are brainwashed about the 'other'. The Haj Terminal, an appeasement carrot for the Muslim minority, is boldly displayed among the signages. This, of course, comes as a surprise to a sceptical Pakistani.

When I first visited the Indira Gandhi International Airport, its lifeless architecture and shoddy facilities nearly shocked me (the new terminal, T3, was a later development). In contrast, Lahore's glitzy airport named after the poet Allama Iqbal, with swanky interiors and polished floors, speaks of the Pakistani elite's quest for grandeur. Immigration queues are long with languishing non-resident Indians and foreign tourists. But, for a Pakistani, it is an entry into a highly guarded domain protected by quirks of history and ideology rife with suspicion. Pakistanis need to report at a separate counter to fill up a rather banal form detailing where in India one intends to visit, and that one has to inform the government if there is a change in the duration of stay. Of late, Pakistanis are viewed as terrorists; I am sure the feelings are mutual at Pakistani airports too.

I encounter a colonial anachronism—a specific form for Pakistani nationals, entailing a process reminiscent of the snail-paced era of Raj officialdom. But it is not all that unpleasant. The immigration officials are helpful, but only after the usual barrage of questions and visa inquiries. The Sikh gentleman at the counter hears my Punjabi and his attitude undergoes a noticeable change from curtness towards familiarity; he immediately asks me where I am from. He tells me that his parents were from 'western' Punjab. I find it difficult to conceptualize the west and the east of what I have known all my life as the Punjab.

Deep down, I am excited and terrified and stand in a world that hitherto existed only in books, discussions and images. A part of me also inappropriately remembers the poem of a Pakistani poet, Neelma Naheed Durrani:

> I have come to see the city
> Longing for which my elders left this world
> In their graves, in Lahore's Mominpura graveyard
> My father and grandfather must be saying joyfully
> Our daughter has gone to our city, Amritsar.

Well, here is a son and this is not Amritsar, does it make any difference?

My mother's family migrated from Amritsar and I knew what it meant to her elder sister, a better part of whose childhood and adult life were spent in that holy town also known for its thriving commerce. But memory can be treacherous. Amritsar was remembered in the golden sunlight of memory that constantly brightened my aunt's existence. I had promised her at the dawn of the new millennium that we would travel to Amritsar. Her husband's family had little interest in revisiting the city as the burden of relocation was solely hers. She died a few years before the wait for my luggage in front of this conveyor belt.

Ah, this luggage. If not picked up in time, it turns into a lifelong trial.

Navigating through Delhi's traffic, I reach Mathura Road in less than an hour. Very soon, I wade into a distinctly medieval ambience—labyrinthine alleys, crowds of beggars and street vendors, a distinct bazaar atmosphere. As I walk towards the Hazrat Nizamuddin shrine, I spot a board pointing towards Ghalib's mazar. This is a traditional Muslim area—there are several advertisements offering pilgrimage packages to Mecca and Ajmer, identifying places where Pakistani currency can be exchanged and many signboards are in Urdu. The stereotype of the marginalized Indian Muslim seems somewhat obvious here. I try not to notice all that and walk around until Ghalib's tomb appears. Having being fixated on Ghalib and his poetry for the better part of my life, I am a little disappointed by the matter-of-factness of the place. Even though the tomb has recently been renovated after a court order, it is still a little bit of a disappointment. Ironically, on the signage, 'Ministry of Tourism' is more visible than the name 'Ghalib', and addition of the latter looks almost like an apologetic afterthought.

Nevertheless, the area retains a unique atmosphere and the structure surrounding the tomb appears intriguing. I am late and rush to Hazrat Nizamuddin's dargah. I am as much a victim of 'shrine commerce' as the next person and the scent of desi roses (a native variety known for its crimson hue and heady scent) wafts up until I find my way to the tomb.

The narrow lanes and hugely crowded alleys open up into a set of courtyards linked to each other. Inside the dargah compound, calm prevails despite the growing number of visitors. Surrounded by old buildings and congested houses, the tombs of Amir Khusrau and Hazrat Nizamuddin Auliya keep the twelfth century intact in the heart of a teeming metropolis. This is a sort of homecoming even though I do not belong. The predominantly Muslim locality reminds me that this part of the city is at the core of my cultural heritage. For a second I am not an alien even though I have filled in the form some hours ago under a law that regulates foreigners of Pakistani origin. I am there yet not there. Elemental yet separate.

The sajjadah-nashins of the tomb have mastered the art of making one's entire experience commercial. There are issues of maintenance of the dargah, arrangements for regular langars for the poor, but over time, this has turned into an industry by itself. Among other things, we share this curse with the dargahs of Lahore. Thus, I have to guard myself from solicitations and offers of intermediation with the saints. This offer can quickly metamorphose into intimidation if not tackled with indifference. So I just walk straight and look for Sadia.

Incidentally, the place where Hazrat Nizamuddin Auliya's tomb is located is not where he established his *khanqah.* When he arrived in Delhi, he had ambitions of becoming a qazi. However, the spiritual world of the Sufis, especially the Chishtiya order, attracted him, and soon he joined Baba Fariduddin Ganj-e-Shakar's khanqah in Ajodhan, Punjab (now in Pakistan). After spending a few years with Baba Farid, he returned to Delhi as a Chishti ambassador and made his home near the River Jamuna, about a kilometre east of the present-day dargah. This is where he prayed, meditated, and attracted the inhabitants of Delhi. The place has changed, and as I find out later, relegated to the footnotes of history books.

I ask around for the tomb of Amir Khusrau, Hazrat Nizamuddin Auliya's most prominent devotee, who lies buried close to his beloved saint. The convention is that you have to first pay your respects to Khusrau before offering your salaam to the saint. I have been an unabashed admirer of Khusrau since I became familiar with Urdu and Persian poetry. Sadly though, his contribution to the evolution of Urdu and modern Hindustani is still under-acknowledged. He was truly avant-garde, using modern idiom and imagery in medieval India.

Amir Khusrau's domed marble tomb dates back to the early sixteenth century. Intricate red sandstone jalis displaying the refined nuances of Mughal aesthetics enclose the room with the tombstone reportedly constructed by a Mughal courtier. The illustrious keeper of the dargah, Hasan Nizami, in the early twentieth century, unearthed the dates in Persian etched on the sandstone. The marble jalis, however, cannot be fully cleaned, given that they have been whitewashed over the centuries and now embrace hundreds of coloured threads that devotees tie through the fine filigree to fulfil their fleeting wishes.

Overawed by the mood of this setting, I wait for Sadia. What a place this must have been, given the deep effect it had on language and multicultural interfaith communication and the evolution of north Indian musicology.

Sadia and I meet outside Hazrat Nizamuddin's tomb, where a qawwali is being performed in the courtyard and hundreds of people of diverse faiths—Hindus, Muslims and Sikhs—are present. While I imbibe the mellow notes of a taan prior to a full-scale performance, Sadia introduces me to the local sajjadah-nashin; Sadia and her eccentric, lovable mother are lifelong devotees and know everyone here.

That this first meeting was going to turn into a deep friendship was not known to me till later. It was from the very start a hit, as we clicked with the very first joke about Muslims. To recall the little epitaph to our conversation, 'Yes, we are at liberty to joke about ourselves,' what is better than the ability to be irreverent about one's own self? And this is what Sadia and I share as we were to discover in due course. We sit with the affable, plump shrine keeper, Pir Hasnain, who offers us masala chips and a much needed cup of tea. Being Pakistani, I am the recipient of extraordinary attention from the visitors at his gaddi. I get a sense of what is likely to come—questions about my exotic Pakistani identity, questions about Musharraf, jihad and other stereotypes that occupy the Indian mind pedalled by the media. I pander to this discourse as far as possible until I can take it no more, reminding myself that Pakistani textbook representations of the wily, untrustworthy Hindu are mirror images of this syndrome.

Pir Hasnain ushers me into the tomb and I follow the motions. There is extended dua and I am presented with a chadar (in fact, the chadar is tied around my head much to the envy of many other visitors). There is an intrinsic profundity in the small space. The interior of the tomb is quiet, despite the human traffic. My senses are heavy. I wonder if it has to do with the climate or my own psychological disposition at the time.

I am overwhelmed by the feeling that the place is incredibly enchanting. It is a magical kingdom bereft of symbols of worldly power and one which weaves a spell of peace and forgetting.

The qawwali resumes after the maghreb prayers and the place echoes with the lyrics:

> Colour me in your hue, my love,
> You are my master, oh beloved of the Almighty;
> Colour me in your hue.
> My scarf and the beloved's turban,
> Both ought to be dyed in the hue of spring ...

The evening turns into a 'happening' inside the dargah compound. The sheer number of people loitering about, sitting, praying and crying is mind-boggling. Shrines are metaphors of the complexity of human woes and desires. Here, the thronging multitudes wish to connect without conditions, free of orthodoxy's linear world view of conformity and suffering for penance, a psychosocial arena reflecting joys and sorrows in a single space where strangers appear to be familiar and the solemn air subsumes inner agitations.

To me, Hazrat Nizamuddin's compound is the ultimate metaphor of Delhi and its lost past. From the medieval tombs of the Mughals—Princess Jahanara, Atagah Khan, Emperor Akbar's minister, and the unfortunate Emperor Mohammad Shah Rangeela—to contemporary concrete rooms and hideous taps, this was the essence of what I had imagined Delhi to be. Apart from the Sufi trappings, this place could offer a captivating look through the rusty windows of history, sociology and music.

At the end of the first day's spiritual excursion, I discover that Sadia and I share the same gateway to Islam. Our respective ancestors were converted by the same wandering 'shams' of Multan. Apa, my grandmother's amazing sister, would have loved to meet Sadia and hear her own version of her family history. Apa told me it was to Benares where our ancestors were heading before they were converted by a wandering Sufi. I too, like my ancestors, have to go to the shores of the Ganga to complete that truncated journey of my Hindu forefathers—a sojourn that was interrupted by a hiatus of six centuries.

But I am not in Benares, I am in Delhi or at least halfway there. Alas, these are not the ethereal shores of the Ganga but the banks of the dirty Jamuna. I am comforted that along its downstream course, the Jamuna merges with the Ganga somewhere near Allahabad.

Old Lahore's Shah Alam was inhabited mostly by Hindus. Named after the Mughal Emperor Shah Alam, this neighbourhood was akin to Delhi's walled city. Also known as 'Shahalmi' in Punjabi, this locality suffered colossal rioting, plunder and near annihilation during Partition as most of the houses and buildings were set ablaze. My paternal grandmother's family lived there too. They left their house for a Muslim locality and by the time they returned after the bloodbath, most of the neighbours had left including the extended family of Sorayya, the legendary actor. The grey swirl of the ashes of burning houses mixed with dust made everything invisible. But buried in the thick air that traumatized the narrow alleys, there must have been some euphoria somewhere, for now there was a new country for India's Muslims.

Bibiji, my paternal grandmother, and her elder sister, Apa, were almost synonymous with Shahalmi during most of my childhood years. In the 1960s, Bibiji, with her children, had moved to an emerging posh suburb called Model Town that is now famous for its association with Pakistan's former prime minister Nawaz Sharif, who built luxury bungalows and upgraded Model Town. But Bibiji could not get the sheher, which literally meant 'city' but in this case, the 'old city' out of her system, making feeble excuses each week to travel to the walled city. Sometimes it was to buy better-quality spices such as crisp cumin seeds and at other times it would be an 'urgent' need to see her doctor who lived there. The witty doctor, Abdullah, was more of a friend to my grandmother than a physician.

Bibiji would pack her little basket for an emotional picnic in Shahalmi and I would trail her on the street till she had no option but to take me along. We would ride a bus, sometimes to Rang Mahal and then take a tonga to Shahalmi. The entire journey was a fascinating series of stops, halts, haggling and finding your way into Old Lahore's labyrinth. Tongas would not go beyond the entrance of the Shahalmi gate; one had to dismount and trundle along the time-frozen lanes to get to Apa's house.

Apa was an Old Lahore agony aunt of sorts, seeking and furnishing advice, offering emotional succour or reciting folk stories, anecdotes and Urdu couplets in her thick Lahori accent. In this accent, the 'r's and the 'd's were pronounced in a peculiar way that made me laugh. So conversations with Apa, however serious, had this little humour tagged on like the lovable noise of old gramophones.

Apa was my gateway to the past. My parents were more interested in inculcating an urbane, post-colonial idiom in our lives—correct Urdu and English, contemporary table manners, westernized etiquette. But Apa, as I slept on her grand old bed, would narrate tales of the Shahalmi that was, and of her long-lost neighbours.

It was on this bed that, at the age of eight, I learnt how our Hindu ancestors had been converted by a wandering dervish named Shams Sabzwari, erroneously confused with Rumi's master Shams Tabrez; how he was the beacon of a new egalitarian faith and lifestyle that evidently attracted my surely caste-challenged ancestors. So we were Sheikhs and precisely, Shamsi Sheikhs.

The elusive Shah Shams Sabzwari is also claimed by the Ismailis as their celebrated *dai*. His life, like that of his namesake, the fabled Shams who changed Rumi's life, remains a mystery. What is known for certain is that he arrived in Multan, in southern Punjab, and joined the other saints living there. The year of Shah Shams's death, or in Sufi parlance, his reunion with the beloved creator, is recorded, courtesy his tomb in Multan, as 1276.

Shams's collection of poetry tells us that he spent his early years in a medieval Persian town called Sabzwar and travelled widely. He is supposed to have roamed around India and converted many people in Kashmir, Sindh, Gujarat and Little Tibet before moving to Punjab, where Sufi mythology holds that he performed the miracle of restoring someone to life.

This is when Apa's narrative would move into an intimate fictional mode. I remember that dark winter night when the old high ceiling turned into a canvas for my imagination. Apa had a longish rendition of how her forefathers had set out from Lahore on a pilgrimage to Benares. Halfway there, their caravan was looted and the poor families found shelter in the humble khanqah of Shah Shams. They stayed there for a few weeks until they resumed their journey. But during those lingering medieval days and nights, the miracles and conduct of the saint inspired the Lahore travellers to investigate the saint-master's foreign, mysterious faith more closely. Some low-caste Hindus found the freedom to chant the name of Ram that they could not perhaps do near a Brahmin.

The Lahoris set out again for Benares. But the magnetism of Shams pulled them back to him. They never did reach Benares. A mass conversion took place and an expansive, invisible, loving and sometimes stern God filled their spiritual space. I remember how the dark emptiness of Apa's room became my metaphor of an amorphous, fathomless God. Apa was perhaps unaware that in the nineteenth century, Ghalib, the Turk-Muslim poet who lived in Delhi, had stayed in Benares for a month and that he, in some ways, circled the narrative of religious identities.

From this discreet moment in the lives of my imagined distant family, began a generational devotion, like that of countless other families, to khanqahs and shrines. Over the centuries, the temporal powers of sultans and emperors were seen to be getting blurred by the lasting legacy of Sufi saints who came to India. This was also the time when Amir Khusrau was experimenting with a new language. He wrote, 'Though Hindus do not believe in the religion in which we do, in many matters they and we believe in the same thing.'[4] And his beloved master, Hazrat Nizamuddin Auliya was attracting the population of Delhi and beyond to the inclusive vision of the Chishti Sufis. Thus, my childhood visions of Delhi were that of mysterious environs with sultans and their lashkars moving about, shrines and tombs warming up to devotees and a grand cultural mingling.

Apa, however, had no respect for the linearity of historical annals. She would jump nimbly to the Partition telling me how her friends and neighbours fled Shahalmi and how, by the time she returned to a burnt mohallah, all the neighbours had left. She had never been so jolted in her life as when she saw those empty homes, some of them burnt and others looted. She had also lost her jewellery, mortgaged with the legendary moneylender, Bhulaki Mal Shah. She would remember with some sorrow how her dowry had been gobbled up by Partition and bequeathed to the Hades of history and politics.

A faceless, nameless ghost thus lived in Apa's house. She sort of nurtured it and, since no one was interested, locked it in her teakwood almirah to guard her empty ivory-inlayed jewellery box and a copy of the family tree that uncomfortably harked back to a Hindu name. Poor Apa, the brief spell of illness before she died made her a trifle delusional. She would mutter the names of her childhood friends ending with 'Kumari' or 'Devi'. These names sounded distant to my extended cousins who tended her during her last days; these were also stereotypical textbook names that were heard on TV, when an attempt at cultural amity was beamed via unregulated Doordarshan programmes, Doordarshan being the national Indian television channel.

When I was thirteen, I took Bibiji and Apa to have passport-sized pictures taken for Indian visas. There were no relatives, no split families. This was a yearning to revisit the shrines of Delhi and Ajmer. Ironically, my father's employment with a state institution ended up as a big hurdle in our visa quest.

Bibiji died, her longing unfulfilled.

> The seven climes are in its every lane
> Does Delhi have its equal anywhere?[5]

I was twenty years old when I visited India for the first time and arrived in Bombay. I was an excited backpacker and this my gateway to our enemy land, an enemy meticulously inserted into our mental landscape through school curricula and textbooks. Thanks to a spirited history teacher at school and direct interaction with Indian students in London, India and Indianness acquired a nuanced status in my consciousness that defied the textbook enemy-ness. However, this brief visit to Bombay, mostly spent hanging out with some upper-middle-class kids, fun as it was, failed to quell my desire to visit Delhi.

Delhi was not just the capital of India or the repository of Mughal monuments. There was a deeper and more far-reaching symbolism in my journey towards it. This was to be a kind of inner voyage, a milestone that had to be achieved given that the road was proverbially long and potholed by upheavals of history.

Reclaiming one's past is messy business. Whilst scores of milestones of pre-Pakistan history survive and live in my country, the sudden chopping off of an entity known as 'British India' and the creation of two new states based on ideology, power and politics, have led to half a story made invisible—a mythical ploy, such as the taking away of the vision of one eye or putting a little divider in the middle of the brain. It makes up a story that the other half can read but never comprehend fully.

In Punjabi folklore and Sufi poetry there is a river to be crossed—a fictionalized boundary of sorts. This crossing is the test of endurance, of love and life. This ancient mythical river rarely has a destination and holds mysterious dangers, but it is eternal. At the same time, the river's inner boundary defines home. Life on the other side can be vaguely forbidding. However, it is the fascination with the unknown that prompts the crossing of this river. As a young civil servant I could never get a visa.

Standing on the other side of history, it wasn't clear to me where I wanted to be. To reach Delhi, the threshold of twenty-two Sufis or to discover the ground where Indraprastha was built? Or was it an odyssey to the seat of the Islamicate that ruled India for no less than a thousand years? Was this crossing to end in Mir and Ghalib's Delhi or Lutyens's architectural feat for the new seat of the British Empire? Indeed, the possibilities of Delhi were infinite and more so for those who may endeavour to unearth the layers of history. Where else in the world could a conurbation of mystics exist under the ground that still bears the marks of Indraprastha, the prehistoric mythical capital?

So it took me fifteen years to get to Delhi.

Exhausted and exhilarated, I return to my hotel—just a single day and what a fabulously minute introduction to Delhi's soul! As I look outside the glass window at the expanse of Lutyens's Delhi and some other modern structures hidden by thick green foliage, I realize that Hazrat Nizamuddin is just a fraction of this vast metropolis that is trying hard to forget its past. It is tragic that most of Delhi has turned its back on Hazrat Nizamuddin. The peculiarity of Delhi's evolution is that it is a tale of forgetting and moving on with the march of history.

Taking advantage of the Sunday and since my work-related meetings did not start before midday, I return to the Nizamuddin Basti. I am irritated with my posh and plush room; how could I be staying here when there are places far more enticing? This is what I resent most about luxury hotels in developing countries—the sense of disconnectedness and lack of character wilfully designed by highly paid designers who end up mocking what seems real.

My thoughts in a jumble, I catch a taxi to Hazrat Nizamuddin. It is early morning and the otherwise cluttered roads are free, and I find myself simply merging with the glorious morning—the trees, the tombs and roads, everything looks serene. I manage to see some of the striking symbols of the 'New' Delhi—the India Gate, imposing, wide boulevards signifying the grandeur of the Raj and the distinctive hybrid architecture with its colonial bungalows.

My great-grandfather, Dr Allah Bux, was in Delhi in December 1911. The occasion was the Third Royal Durbar to commemorate the coronation of King George V and Queen Mary as emperor and empress of India. A lone porcelain mug with an unflattering portrait of the king survives in the family silver. It has the words 'Delhi Durbar' inscribed on it and rests in complete disharmony with the other objects on the shelf.

Dr Bux, an employee of the Jammu and Kashmir state medical service, had emigrated from Lahore in the late nineteenth century. He only returned to Lahore after his retirement in the 1930s. Prior to this final relocation, he had travelled across India. His medical education was in Calcutta and his employment took him to splendid Kashmir where he served as a medical professional in Srinagar, Baramulla, Sopore, Shopian and so on—places that are now infamous for violence and bloodletting in the name of nationalism, liberation, secularism and, of course, Islam.

Nearly a century later, at a little gathering in Delhi, his great-grandson was destined to find out how several empty spaces in Kashmir had turned into collective graveyards and there were only a few homes that had not confronted the taste of death or at least its fearful imminence.

Dr Bux owed his attendance at the Durbar to being part of the entourage of the maharaja of Kashmir. He was dressed in a special tailor-made suit, mingled with many a sahib and even held a cigar. But cigar smoking was alien to him. He choked a little and hated the acrid aftertaste. However, the glory of the Durbar did enchant him. For several years, Dr Bux had been visiting Delhi mainly to pay his respect to the saints but this was a different kind of event. It had nothing of the dargah ambience or culture, and to him the Red Fort now glowed with the radiance of imperial power that represented both modernity and the echoes of the shrieks of hundreds and thousands who died or were dispossessed after the 1857 Mutiny or the mythologized 'War of Independence' at the same location. Ruling princes, nobles and the socially engineered gentry of India were present to offer obeisance to the sovereigns. In keeping with the pomp of their predecessors, the royals also made an appearance for public darshan at the marble jharoka of the Red Fort. Dr Bux was one of the half a million or more attendees of this event, though his employment enabled him to be in the exclusive part of the crowd.

The Delhi Durbar of 1911 bestowed on Delhi its due place by announcing the shifting of the capital from Calcutta. Thus, the seat of the Empire had once again shifted. Millions were spent on this occasion while famine ravaged the areas surrounding Delhi. Dr Bux had no idea perhaps; he was coming from Kashmir and he was no revolutionary.

After his return to Lahore, this connection with Kashmir came to an end and the family retreated into its Lahori world. But his visits to the Delhi and Sirhind[6] shrines continued. My father, as a child, accompanied his father and grandfather and had faint memories when I would ask him questions. However, what had been immediate and accessible in the early 1940s now required passports and visas. This discontinuity was nothing compared to what millions experienced and struggled, combined with the painful journey of forgetting.

But I hold no bitterness. My personal experience is not stained by bloodletting. I do not even remember the 1971 war and I condemned the Kargil adventure like several others in the subcontinent. I still feel that the connection can be restored and broken threads picked up where they were left off by my ancestors.

I notice the Sabz Burj (Green Dome) standing rather oddly in the middle of the road. Nobody really knows whose tomb it is. Also known as the Neela Gumbad, it stands awkwardly on a green patch at the intersection of Lodi Road and Mathura Road, very close to Nizamuddin Basti. I stop near the intersection, get rid of the taxi and walk up the few steps that culminate on a platform where the tomb rests.

Its structure is quite Central Asian, octagonal in shape much like the tombs in Multan, Pakistan. The eight sides are alternately wide and narrow and each has a recessed arch adorned with a pattern of chiselled plaster and glazed tiles. Its now ruined appearance fails to conceal what a beauty it must have been. Built in the earlier half of the sixteenth century, it was later used as a police post under British rule. The Archaeological Survey of India took control of the structure after Independence and undertook its conservation, giving the dome its current blue look as opposed to the original green I had read somewhere. I cannot help wondering why the Islamic green was made into blue. Conspiracy theories come to the surface but I have no time to waste. The wristwatch stares at me and I push myself away from the tower even though I want to go in. Despite the gate being locked, I do get a brief glimpse inside. The ceiling is ornamented with faded and typically Persian geometric designs in red and blue.

Hazrat Nizamuddin Auliya was born around the year 1243 and lived for nearly eighty-two years. Originally from Badayun (located in north-central Uttar Pradesh), he moved to Delhi with his mother in 1274 for better education. However, once in Delhi, he moved from place to place for eleven years until he settled in Ghiyaspur which was later renamed Nizamuddin after him, situated outside the main city, where the messy basti stands today.

This settlement, Nizamuddin, grew organically around his khanqah and later his tomb. Ghiyaspur, at that time, a jungle on the banks of the Sitari, an offshoot of the Jamuna, was identified as a quiet place to meditate and continue with the *tariqa*. Initially, Hazrat Nizamuddin lived in a hut with a thatched roof amid fisherfolk. Later, his devotees and some nobles helped build the khanqah for him. The khanqah still exists. Subsequent kings continued to embellish and add to his tomb, creating the web of buildings and facilities that define his dargah today.

The Nizamuddin Basti presents the face of the quintessential

Muslim ghetto of today's India. Congested, unkempt and stinking in parts, it retains a medieval air. Here is a burqa-clad woman and there, shops selling meat with hundreds of flies buzzing around. But its architectural gems juxtaposed with rickshaw-walas, vendors and beggars make it an amazing amalgam of the old and the new with tradition refusing to leave the cultural canvas.

Trails of the old and infirm meet the eye as one walks towards the dargah. The narrow warren-like alleys are colourful; fresh desi rose petals and incense are sold in overcrowded stalls, and sometimes, hard to miss, the sewage hits you hard. The arches, steps and even some of the walls are old.

The basti, circumambulating like concentric circles around the dargah boasts several structures of historical and cultural significance. For instance, towards the west of it is the red sandstone Jamat Khana Mosque constructed in the fourteenth century. It is a composite structure of three domes over three bays, the central one being the largest. One cannot miss the marble lotus buds that fringe the mosque's arches, which are designed in such a manner that the square bays appear octagonal.

The octagonal shape has a particular significance. In Islamic architecture, this shape is a symbol of ascent to heaven by the Prophet and by man. The octagonal structure is a step in the mathematical series going from a square (symbolizing fixity of the earthly manifestation) to a circle (symbolizing the perfection of heaven). Traditional baptismal fonts are also of this shape. However, in the tombs erected for saints, the lower part is square with an octagonal drum inserted as a transition between the cube and the dome, to symbolize the saint as the link between man and God. The octagonal structure of Jerusalem's Dome of the Rock became the model for domed sanctuaries and saints' tombs from Morocco to China.

Within the basti, there is a now filthy but lovingly designed baoli, now almost a septic tank, closed to the public. The young men of the settlement had used it as a communal swimming pool. It was built during the reign of Sultan Feroze Tughlaq. His predecessor Ghiyasuddin Tughlaq disliked the saint Hazrat Nizamuddin and had forbidden the construction of the baoli. But the medieval labour union, which was also working on Ghiyasuddin's fort, chose to build the baoli at night using oil lamps for illumination. Oral records suggest that the sultan was furious at this defiance and ordered that shops should not sell oil to the people of Ghiyaspur.

Legend speaks of a miracle connected to this decree. Hazrat Nizamuddin instructed one of his favourite disciples to use the water from the baoli to light the lamps and it is said that the water began to burn as oil. This disciple was no other than the one who is buried far from the basti in a locality that is now known as Chirag Dilli after his title of Hazrat Chiragh Dilli (Delhi's Lamp).

I walk back from the dargah, halting at the Chaunsath Khambe (sixty-four pillars), another monument behind Ghalib's mausoleum. This lonesome structure, built centuries after Hazrat Nizamuddin's time, is Mirza Shamsuddin's tomb. Shamsuddin was the brother of Mirza Aziz Kokantash and their mother was the foster-mother of Emperor Akbar. The monument, simple and squarish in design, was built by Akbar. I am amazed at how a few hundred metres were turning into time-travel steps. Centuries are covered with one's humdrum visual experience.

The wine-loving Ghalib's mazar now faces the Indian Tableeghi Jamat's *markaz* where you see Muslim brethren, drunk on piety, loitering about. Tableeghis have grown in number and influence both in Pakistan and Bangladesh. The markaz, as I discover during subsequent visits, is also a place with its own story. The site of this present-day centre of Islamic puritanism was once a garden named Baghicha-e-Anarkali. This garden with a stunning pavilion was built by two rich Delhi nobles, the brothers, Mir Taqi and Mir Naqi. Once upon a time, the Sitari stream, branching off from the Jamuna, would lazily flow and nurture this garden. This was also a place where riverine commerce took place and these brothers must have built the set-up for a few moments of leisure amidst their businesses. Known as bangla, this must have been a modern structure in the nineteenth century. Under the rule of Bahadur Shah Zafar, the last Mughal, this place came under official control and a mosque known as 'Banglewali Masjid' was built.

And now, this structure hosts the offices and living quarters of pious and preachy Muslims who do not necessarily share the eclecticism offered by the Sufi environs. But then, Muslims are not homogeneous as a community and nurture all shades of beliefs and cultural practices. Indeed, the basti houses a disparate community that, as a whole, appears to have withdrawn unto itself and is reeling under a psychological siege defying generalizations. Nizamuddin Basti seems to have closed its ranks to the outside world, including modernity and education.

The basti, however, awakens from its slumber during the urs celebrations of Hazrat Nizamuddin and Amir Khusrau. Known as Mahboob-e-Ilahi (Beloved of God), Hazrat Nizamuddin Auliya's pull has lasted for centuries. The basti is also the arena where the hallmark Indo-Islamic cuisine developed and Urdu or Hindustani as the lingua franca of northern India originated and blossomed into what we speak and hear from Delhi to Lahore and from Karachi to Lucknow.

As I pass by the kulcha tandoor, I ponder over the culinary influences that Central Asians and Turks brought to India and whether the global clientele of the ubiquitous 'Indian' restaurants is aware that the kababs and naans they just ordered once took birth in this dilapidated basti. In Nizamuddin, meat reigns supreme. And sweets—kulfis and jalebis among others—are the essential endings to a meal (I hear jalebis were invented in Nizamuddin too; however, many say that jalebis did exist in ancient India). Several dishes, now served in dhabas and makeshift restaurants, were once the secretly guarded intellectual property of the cooks of the sultans and Mughals. Over the centuries, these recipes have reached the commoners with the increasing availability and affordability of ingredients.

The music of the basti takes on myriad shapes—from Bollywood songs to Nusrat Fateh Ali Khan's global stardom and the self-conscious and increasingly popular South Asian Sufi music. The qawwal families living here have contributed to the meandering journey of Indian classical music, sometimes singing the melodies of Tansen of Akbar's court and at others, the khayal.

The basti is a relic but neither abandoned nor ruined. It breathes with real people largely dependent on the cash economy generated by thousands of devotees across India. Dargah worship thus remains a source of livelihood for the basti; it is an unwitting continuation of a community and its culture, striking for its quaintness and heart-rending for its marginality.

Hazrat Nizamuddin's dargah compound, encompassing years of Sufi tradition, open to all, irrespective of caste, creed, religion, or class, (though not always gender), twenty-four hours a day, continues to challenge Hindu and Muslim orthodoxies. It was deviant then and it is deviant now; a bit odd in today's age of Islamism and Hindutva. In medieval Delhi, where dominant Hindu practices must have been defined by caste hierarchies and exclusion, Hazrat Nizamuddin was the refuge of the lowly. Even as the Muslim clergy with its supremacist and mainstream discourse was justifying the sultanate rule, Hazrat Nizamuddin and his circle of Chishti saints were creating a parallel history through their acceptance of people without labels and religious identities.

Ghiyaspur, the ancestral basti, grew to be an alternative society. Hazrat Nizamuddin Auliya maintained a noticeable distance from the power politics of the court. Demonstrating a simple lifestyle, his patronage of music and assimilation of local and foreign traditions took him closer to the people of Delhi and outside. Thus the khanqah, and later his shrine, assumed the status of a personal space for healing and fulfilment. This is why this sanctuary is still visited by thousands of ordinary and, often, afflicted souls. The feeling that I am an outsider here bites the dust as the magic of the place uncannily makes me feel at home.

However, the irony of the present cannot go unnoticed. The time-warped basti has unwittingly retained its 'alternative' status in the otherwise 'shining' Delhi. The more we ignore history the more it leaps at us. In due course, I meet several Delhi residents who have never been to the dargah, let alone the ghetto known as Nizamuddin Basti.

NOTES

1. Mohammad Sadiq Dihalvi Kashmiri Hamdani, *Kalimat al Sadiqin*, A Hagiography of Sufis Buried at Delhi until AD 1614, New Delhi: Kitab Bhavan, 1990.
2. Bruce B. Lawrence, *Notes from a Distant Flute: The Extant Literature of Pre-Mughal Indian Sufism*, Lucknow: Great Eastern Book Co., 1985.
3. Amir Khusrau, *Qiran al Sa'dayn*, Lucknow: Nawal Kishore Press, 1875. This work is also known as the 'Conjunction of Two Planets'. It reads as a number of descriptive poems joined into one by means of ghazals expressing the poet's feelings upon the various episodes in the story that he has been describing.
4. Amir Khusrau, *Nuh Sipihr*. The *Nuh Siphir* is a panegyric of the court, peoples, languages and the flora and fauna of Hindustan. E. Sreedharan, *A Textbook of Historiography, 500 BC to AD 2000*, New Delhi: Orient Blackswan, 2004, p. 163.
5. *Three Mughal Poets: Mir, Sauda, Mir Hasan*, New Delhi: OUP (first published 1969), 1994, p. 259.
6. Dotting GT Road, away from the hustle and bustle of Chandigarh and somewhere between Ludhiana and Ambala, lies the dusty town of Sirhind. Sirhind is mostly known among Muslims through Sheikh Ahmed Sirhindi, the famous Sufi of the Naqshbandi order, who was conferred the title of 'Mujaddid Alif-sani', the renewer of the second millennium (of the Islamic calendar).

2

Realm of the Sufis

The Holy Quran states: 'He loveth them and they love Him' (5.59). This verse encapsulates Islamic mysticism known as Sufism. A confluence of two spiritual streams—the ascetic and devotional—took birth in Sufi thought and practice. By the twelfth century, multiple Sufi orders had emerged in the Islamic world. Between the twelfth and fifteenth centuries, coinciding with the expansion of Muslim rule, five great Sufi orders migrated from Central Asia and Persia into north India. The Chishti, Suharwardi, Naqshbandi, Qadri and Firdausi schools flourished in what we now know as Indo-Pakistan.

The Chishti school of Sufism was immensely influential in northern India and dominated Delhi. Using the Quran and teachings of Prophet Mohammad as the guiding light, a small number of mystic manuals such as the *Kashf-ul-Mahjoob* (The Unveiling of the Veiled) by Sheikh Ali Hujwari, formed the ideological basis of Sufi practice. Hujwari, one of the early Sufis, travelled to Lahore during Mohammad Ghazni's time and settled there. Through his teachings we learn about the intimate personal experience of mystical elation. Sufism is about achieving an intensely personal relationship with the Divine based on realizing God's attributes within oneself. It focuses on loving God through the service of mankind and establishing harmony with all of creation. Known as *tasawwuf* in Arabic[1] Sufism, it teaches ways of achieving tazkiya (purification of the mind, body and soul).

Countless Sufi establishments or khanqahs dotting the Indian spiritual landscape with deeply entrenched pilgrimage networks were the major means that brought the masses into the fold of Islam. These khanqahs blended local tradition with Islamic values and provided a caste-less, monotheistic version of spirituality where the charisma and wisdom of the pir or his descendants served as powerful elements to attract the local population. Indeed, the formal rites at these locations were backed by the inner journeys[2] of the Sufis that constitute the ultimate mystical experience. At the popular level, the pir was the face of spirituality and for the 'initiated', the gateway to inner peace.

In medieval India, the evolution of Sufism was not an isolated occurrence. Sufism in its diverse manifestations became the locus of potential religious syncretism. India was a fertile ground for the evolution of mystic practices, given that the people of India were already oriented towards mysticism. The Vedas and the Upanishads contained tenets for spiritual practices. For instance, the Rig Veda stated that divine reality was one and that poets had assigned different names to it. The Sufis sat under the same pipal trees that were already resonating to the chants from the *Chhandogya Upanishad* that claimed that 'variations' were only issues of words and names.

The innate unity of all beings as expounded by the Advaita philosophy was re-scripted in another context by the Arab philosopher, Ibn-ul-Arabi. In India, following the Persian variant, this was to be known as *hama-oost.* As the Mughal prince, Dara Shikoh, and many others were to document much later, *Aham Brahmasmi* of Advaita Vedanta and the *Wahdatul Wajud*—the inspiration for Chishti saints in particular—had much in common.

For centuries, these postulations have continued to bedevil and challenge extremists and purists on both sides.

Sheikh Hamid-ud-din Nagauri, a distinguished disciple of Khwaja Moinuddin Chishti of Ajmer, did not permit his disciples to use the categories of kafir and momin as the basis of any social discrimination. For instance, Sheikh Abdul Quddus of Gangoh, a renowned Chishti saint of the sixteenth century, thus admonished his disciples in a letter:

> Why this meaningless talk about the believer,
> the kafir, the obedient, the sinner,
> the rightly guided, the misdirected, the Muslim,
> the pious, the infidel, the fire worshipper?
> All are like beads in a rosary.[3]

In this melting, rich milieu of medieval India, the bhakti movement was to grow and spread as the religion of the people, away from the confines of narrow rituals and institutionalized obligations to God. The Sufis of medieval India explored Hindu thought processes and its 'peculiar' beliefs such as self-negation that had survived centuries. Several Sufis and their followers concluded that Ram, Krishna and the Buddha were, in all probability, prophets who preached monotheism, for in the Quran, God assures that there was never a time when He did not send prophets to people of different nations. A south Indian bhakti folk song thus echoes feelings of universal peace and brotherhood:

> Into the bosom of the one great sea
> Flow streams that come from hills on every side.
> Their names are various as their springs,
> And thus in every land do men bow down
> To one great God, though known by many names.[4]

Chaitanya, Kabir and Guru Nanak were aware of Sufi thought and this dynamic cross-fertilization of spirituality led to the evolution of regional languages, cults and syncretic creeds.

Eminent Indian historian, Romila Thapar, who has painstakingly researched on this issue, explores how Sufi and bhakti thought and practice coalesced at different points of history. Both strands propagated the primal belief of uniting with God, and love was articulated as the basis of such a relationship with the Creator. Similarly, during the initial stages on the mystical path, both Sufi and bhakti movements advocated the acceptance of a guru or a pir.

However, it has always been the intervention of the ruling classes that splintered common concerns and peoples' faith in coexistence, turning tradition into a limiting device. Today, we are faced with militant and politicized forms of the reinvented tradition in public domains across South Asia. The communal vision is inward-looking and exclusive and defeats the breadth of both Sufi and bhakti traditions. Interestingly, Sufi practice interacted as well as challenged the sociology of Hinduism as it had evolved over the centuries. However, adherence to the Islamic creed was a personal, regional and local process and did not stem from a central control or strategy.

Sufis were often castigated by Muslim orthodoxy and their traditions like using music to achieve mystical states were branded as heresy.

As Romila Thapar writes:

> India, with its earlier experience of asceticism, the philosophy of the *Upanishads* and the devotional cults, provided a sympathetic atmosphere for the Sufis. The Sufis in India dissociated themselves from the established centres of orthodoxy, often as a protest against what they believed to be a misinterpretation of the *Quran* by the Ulema. They believed that the Ulema, by combining religious with political policy and cooperating with the Sultanate, were deviating from the original democratic and egalitarian principles of the *Quran*. The Ulema denounced the Sufis for their liberal ideas and the Sufis accused the Ulema of having succumbed to temporal temptations. Sufis were never

deeply committed to the idea of rebellion since they were both, in theory and practice, isolated from those conditions which they opposed. The existence of recluses living apart from their fellows was familiar in India and Sufis were thus part of an established tradition.[5] It is not surprising then that Sufi pirs were as much revered by the Hindus as were Hindu gurus and ascetics, all of them being regarded by Hindus as being of the same mould.

Around 1221, Khwaja Qutubuddin Bakhtiyar Kaki established one of the early khanqahs in Delhi. Kaki had been sent to Delhi by Khwaja Moinuddin Chishti or Gharib Nawaz of Ajmer. Gharib Nawaz taught that the highest form of devotion to God was, 'to develop a river-like generosity, sun-like bounty and earth-like hospitality'. Sultan Iltutmish's Qutub Minar perpetuates his memory.

Khwaja Bakhtiyar Kaki's chief disciple was Baba Farid, the primal Sufi poet of Punjab, whose shrine is in Pakpattan (Pakistan). Baba Farid's khalifa was Hazrat Nizamuddin Auliya, who witnessed three dynasties of seven Delhi sultans rise and fall. He remained an anti-establishment figure by being detached from the court and holding a parallel people's assembly each day at his khanqah. Hazrat Nizamuddin preached that 'bringing happiness to the human heart was the essence of religion' and often said, 'on the day of resurrection amongst those who will be favoured most by God are the ones who have tended to a broken heart'. His successor, Hazrat Nasiruddin Mahmood, who came to be known as Chiragh Dilli, furthered the teachings of the Chishti Sufi order.

The Chishti Sufis of Delhi were generally anti-establishment and had a troubled relationship with the sultanate. Delhi Sufis were non-conformist, people's leaders and rarely met the sultans even though the official court always sought their allegiance for legitimacy. It was not just the urban population that was getting inspired by Sufism. In fact, the message of equality of all humans also brought them into contact with the rural masses. Thus, the Sufis became more effective religious leaders for peasants than the distant ulema. In addition to its obvious attraction for the non-conformist elements in society, Sufi thought also inspired rationalist forces, since it differed from standard religious escapism. For instance, Hazrat Nizamuddin Auliya dabbled in an investigation on the 'laws of movement' in one of his texts that follows an uncanny line of empirical thought. But Sufis were not the pioneers of this trend. They were mere extensions of the deeper philosophical Indian traditions that had blossomed over the centuries.

'The Sufis of Delhi,' Sadia Dehlvi reminds me, 'had a significant role in the religious and cultural history of South Asia. In the light of the hadith,[6] "God is Beautiful and loves Beauty", they encouraged beauty in religious expression and became patrons of art, literature, architecture, music and language. They considered local dialects as immediate and intimate modes of communication with the Divine and a way of nurturing love and amity amongst people. Delhi has been traditionally known as *Bais khwaja ki chaukhat* or the threshold of twenty-two Sufis although the important dargahs of the city far exceed this number.'

A healthy exchange of ideas between Sufi practitioners and Hindu yogis included the borrowing of concentration and meditation techniques from the latter. Sufi culture in Delhi embodied the religious tolerance for which Indian society strives even today. Sadia's mother loves to say, 'Sufi dargahs stand witness to our multicultural identity with people from various faiths continuing to seek solace and blessings at the threshold of these exalted Divines. Everyone who comes is blessed, no one goes khaali haath.'

Yet, at the khanqahs, a subtle pressure towards 'Islamizing' was also ever-present. The ulema and the orthodoxy, tied as they were to the sultanate and Mughal courts, were also shaping a discourse from the top. Over time, the Sufi movement was to absorb some elements of such conservatism. For example, to be fully acceptable in Muslim society, a Hindu convert had to shed his Hindu identity and cultural moorings. But this was difficult and has remained unachievable. An intense cultural amalgamation was at the core of society, and separateness was impossible.

There was, of course, the economic compulsion as well. Conversion to Islam opened up newer avenues of employment and economic advancement under the Muslim state, as well as relief from severe taxes.

Thus currents and cross-currents of politics, sociology and economics resulted in substantial numbers of Indians changing their religious identity. There was continuity at one level of the Vedic ethos, yet discontinuity with socio-religious hierarchies. History was never to be the same again. A permanent shift was taking place—irreversibly plural and factious in character and relentless in its interaction with what was imagined to be the 'local' India. Sufi khanqahs played a major role in promoting the message of equality and tolerance and later the Muslim state provided incentives of sorts.

There are few urban neighbourhoods that can match the magic of Nizamuddin East. Located opposite the Nizamuddin Basti and sandwiched between the ethereal Humayun's Tomb at one end and the noisy Nizamuddin railway station on the other, it is a better surviving metaphor for a Delhi that was. One morning, when I took a walk, I was completely spellbound by the atmosphere. It was not the colonial elegance of the Raj homes of Lahore or the modern opulence of contemporary cities. Here tombs appear from nowhere. So, an entry through the gates of the neighbourhood gives one a full view of the tomb of Abd-al-

Rahim Khan-i-Khanan (1626), a renowned general under Akbar and Jehangir. It is said that Abd-al-Rahim commissioned the translation of ancient Hindu texts into Persian and thereby laid the foundation for an inclusive court. A large-domed structure erected on a square garden, the tomb has the usual red sandstone and white marble trimming. It seems to be a lesser version of Humayun's Tomb. The garden is now just a flat tended lawn with attractive palm trees. It is said that the marble from this lonely tomb was ripped off and used to adorn a Mughal noble and prime minister Safdarjung's tombs (1754).

Facing the abandoned tomb of Abd-al-Rahim, the numbered gates of this colony lead you into tree-lined narrow lanes with a housing stock that is about to explode. But the overpopulation is well concealed by the shade and the criss-crossing of small parks where old couples stroll and kids run around. There are neem trees, old and stocky, with layers of mythical shade that led to enlightenment and self-knowledge in bygone eras. The amaltas trees burnt yellow that morning as I looked for Sadia's house. Pipal, pilkhan, palm and ashoka trees define the horizon.

I spot a gardener and ask him for directions. Taking advantage of this unplanned encounter, I ask him to name the trees. Most of them turn out to have the same names that they have in Pakistan. I chide myself for my silly assumption that somehow trees would change their names if they were to move out of Lahore. He mentions neem, aam, sagwan, sheesham, mursari and so on. And there are chandni hedges at the roundabouts, randomly grafted but well kept after a fashion.

I am not sure what pilkhan means but I see this huge tree just before the enclave where Sadia lives. Pilkhan's botanical name is *Ficus rumphii*, as I find out later. Having seen it in Dhaka and Karachi it was familiar to me. By the time I get to Sadia's residence, I have walked under an interesting jungle jalebi, a rogue kabuli keekar, clusters of gulmohars, papris and, of course, the jamuns that are empty of fruits which have been plucked this monsoon. There are little champaks everywhere with blooming flowers and their characteristic fragrance. Nankuram, the gardener at Khan-i-Khanan's tomb has been very kind. I return the favour with a small tip that makes him smile.

Nizamuddin East is imbued with a somewhat medieval air despite its new structures that include some sleek apartments defined by long rows of flashy cars on the small streets. Some of India's best-known editors, journalists, artists and authors live in Nizamuddin East. This is my own miniature vision of Delhi which refuses to go away even as I explore the rest of the city. It is simply amazing to buy a phone card while standing next to Humayun's Tomb or to pick up flowers in front of Khan-i-Khanan's tomb.

With little ado and Nankuram's guidance I reach the destination. Sadia Dehlvi, as her name suggests, indeed personifies Delhi in all its dimensions—the old, the contemporary, evanescent and permanent. 'I am a true Dilli-wali,' she says, 'one who lives and breathes Delhi, relishing every moment of it. I cannot be anywhere else but Delhi, I hope to die here as well and be buried in one of the graveyards in Hazrat Nizamuddin. A good neighbourhood is important both in this world and the hereafter.' Sadia shot to fame in the 1980s—a young, gorgeous, media person whose spitfire writings on women and minority issues won her the Best Journalism Award in 1989. In those days, few Muslim women were visible on the capital scene and perhaps this made Sadia something of a novelty.

Sadia is a scion of the Dehlvi khandaan, publishers of *Shama*, an Urdu literary and film monthly that achieved great popularity even in Pakistan. Her grand plans of preserving the Urdu language and its culture are temporarily on the backburner as her energies are now devoted to presenting an alternative narrative of Islam. During my years of travelling in Delhi, Sadia's book evolved and I am proud to have been her muse. She laments that one of the prices of Partition paid by Indian Muslims was the decline of Urdu as soon as Pakistan adopted it as its official language. However, she ensures it is the language spoken at home and has a tutor come home to teach her son Urdu. She constantly lectures her son about how Urdu is essentially about the refinement of one's sensibilities.

The much-bemoaned state of the Urdu language in India is no secret. By all accounts, its status is turning into somewhat of a relic with declining numbers of Urdu readers and speakers. For decades, Bollywood had kept it alive by employing lyricists and scriptwriters who shaped a mainstream Urdu-esque idiom for cinema. I found that the Hindustani now spoken and understood stands somewhere between classical Urdu and a 'pure' Hindi influenced by Sanskrit.

I agree with Sadia. Bollywood, possibly the last flag bearer of Urdu, now uses urban street lingo in its songs. It has jettisoned poetry and more and more lyricists use slang so that the songs can appeal to young people. I remind Sadia that this is the *'Dard-e-disco'* phenomenon. The days of *'Kabhi kabhie mere dil mein'*[7] are perhaps over.

'I am so Dilli-inspired, each nook and corner of the city has a story to tell,' Sadia always announces flatly. We stroll on the rooftop of her flat which overlooks Humayun's majestic tomb. As we discuss the myriad facets of Delhi, her profile, unaffected by age, merges into the skyline. She is also very Muslim, I discover. She begins her day with fajr and a half-hour recitation of the Quran. This is followed by a yoga routine including the head stand. 'I'm then equipped emotionally and physically to battle with the daily stress of city life,' she says. She is also a self-confessed diwani of the twenty-two khwajas who 'protect and bless my city. Little is known about some very important dargahs that lie here. Sufism is a message of love and peace, the answer to religious intolerance and extreme behaviour.' On Thursday evenings, this regular celebrity party face, once flashed frequently on Page 3 of city newspapers, is to be found lighting candles and listening to qawwali at Hazrat Nizamuddin Auliya's dargah. A hazri at the tombs of Qutub Sahab Bakhtiyar Kaki and Hazrat Shah Farhad is a weekend must. Sadia does not see any conflict in her eclectic lifestyle and seems comfortable with what most would perceive as a contradiction. We sit in her living room adorned by fabulous artworks that she has collected over time. Sadia is a fulsome woman with manic energy and charisma that is hard to miss. She was a femme fatale of yore, but it is a more sober version of Sadia that I meet in Delhi.

Sadia lived in Pakistan for a little over a year. 'The best gift from Pakistan is my son, Arman, who was born in 1992 at the Lady Dufferin Hospital in Karachi,' she says fondly. However, she says that Islamabad 'is pretty oppressive and limited for one used to living in buzzing metros where so much is happening all the time. I made many friends and possibly even some enemies! I have loads of family and friends with whom I am in touch all the time.' Sadia liked Karachi though, for she found a number of 'independent women' there and liked its relatively non-judgemental atmosphere.

Arman was born, as Sadia believes, through a mannat at Khwaja Moinuddin Chishti's dargah in Ajmer. His date of birth coincides with the great saint's urs on the sixth of Rajab[8] and Sadia firmly believes that Arman's extraordinary musical talent is a gift from this Sufi saint. Starting his training from the age of three, Arman is quite the little maestro at the tabla, harmonium and electric guitar. He is a student of the Dilli Gharana style of classical singing. Over twenty now, Arman already has many concerts to his credit. Like his mother, he is as comfortable singing verses from Khusrau and Ghalib as he is with heavy metal and rock. Later, Arman renders a few verses from Ghalib's poem 'Hazaron khwahishain aisee'. He gets Urdu and Quran lessons at home and has become a great favourite at Delhi's *milad mehfils* for *naatkhwani* and *qirat*.

Dinner consists of mouth-watering food from Al-Kausar owned by Sadia's family. Not content with contributions to the cultural landscape of Delhi, Sadia is equally passionate about Delhi's dastarkhwan or spread of food. She says, 'There are few *real* Dilli-walas left in Delhi, which has now become a multicultural city.' With 'fusion' food taking over, special efforts have to be made to keep the culinary traditions of our city alive. Thirty years ago, Sadia created the first kabab eatery kiosk on the streets of New Delhi. Earlier, authentic Delhi cuisine was only available in the gulleys of the old city. Al-Kausar's menu includes classic Delhi barbecues and Dilli ki biryani and qorma. For over three decades it has been the Delhi elite's favourite little dhaba.

In one of her irreverent moments, of which there are many in one day, she confesses, 'Other than sharing emotions and a similar culture, living in India and Pakistan is very different. In Pakistan, I never really found the space to exist freely as one does in India. Pakistan is about conformity and I have always been a non-conformist. I'm used to a diverse culture. Every time I landed in Delhi, I used to feel comforted at the sight of turbaned Sikhs at the airport. Thank God, my grandparents chose to remain in Delhi!' Minority status and the baggage of Partition have created a fragile environment for Indian Muslims but they continue to make their mark in every field.

An old friend and disciple of the iconic Indian writer Khushwant Singh, Sadia appears frequently in his writings. Singh's book, *Not a Nice Man to Know*, a compilation of some of his most well-known works, carries the dedication, 'To Sadia Dehlvi, who gave me more affection and notoriety than I deserve.' Sadia also appears on the cover of Singh's infamous *Women and Men in my Life*.

As I discover, Sadia is a key figure in Khushwant Singh's salon. She says, 'I have learnt many things from him. He is humble, lives simply, is accepting of everyone, a living example of peaceful coexistence.' She is always amazed at his 'accessibility and openness of mind and the ability to write at the age of ninety-eight. There are more people wanting to spend time with him than he has time for … what a wonderful way to grow old! He is truly a national treasure.' I remind her of an article where KS declared that Sadia was his best friend and the only one who would moan and cry at his death. She continues, 'I haven't known anyone else who works so hard and is so disciplined every day of his life. She describes the launch of his book, the *Illustrated History of the Sikhs*, where the Indian prime minister was the chief guest. During the evening, KS made a tongue-in-cheek comment that his words of praise for the prime minister should not go to his head! Only he, at his venerable age, could take liberties like that. On Sadia's marriage to Karachi-based Reza Pervaiz, the veteran Sikh wrote a piece describing how he 'gave away' Sadia or performed the kanya daan 'with cake, champagne and tears'. An intriguing relationship indeed! Singh proudly considers Arman to be his grandson and insists the lad call him 'nana'.

The story about the decline of the Dehlvi family is both interesting and sad. Over time, the fortunes of the family shrank and, though it is still considered one of the more affluent Muslim families, its fame as a pre-eminent family of yore is now a mere episode in the tale of the social historian of contemporary Delhi. Her family mansion at Sardar Patel Marg was sold to none other than Mayawati's Bahujan Samaj Party. Ironically, this was once a house that was a symbol of the high opulent culture of the Muslims of Delhi. Now, quite poignantly, it houses the offices of the largest Dalit party that is supposed to represent the 'lower' classes and is thus diametrically different from the cultural extravagance that Delhi's Muslim elites were famous for. Sadia makes an interesting comment, 'Mayawati shifting to an elite neighbourhood and Muslims shifting to other lesser localities symbolize what is happening to Muslims in India. The Dalits, because reservation politics have moved them forward, while development statistics prove that Muslims have slipped below the dalits. Whatever must be shall be.'

However, Sadia and her inimitable mother, Zeenat Dehlvi, are not peeved. They have adjusted well to their spacious apartments in Nizamuddin East and West respectively. Most importantly, they are close to the dargah and accept that God has his own little scheme that 'His believers cannot always comprehend'.

In the mellow dusk of Delhi we are driving through tree-lined roads towards Khushwant Singh's house. Sadia is restless as usual and the endless numbers of important and frivolous telephone calls only add to it. Sadia considers Singh to be a part of her inner world. He has continuously mentored and influenced her. I have no clue where he lives ... I know only that he lives in Sujan Singh Park.

Built by Sardar Sobha Singh during the Second World War, flanked by the charming Lodi Gardens half a mile away and Khan Market next door, Sujan Singh Park is one of the numerous hearts of Delhi. The Britishness of its layout and architecture is obvious. This, after all, is Lutyens's Delhi. The chief architect, Walter George, a disciple of Lutyens, has several other structures to his credit including the Scindia Park. During the Great War, younger military officers lived in Sujan Singh Park. This was also the period when the havelis and bungalows of Delhi were being morphed into the strange world of apartments. George designed the place so that each block of the four-storey building stands facing a small square park.

As we enter the apartment block known as Sobha Singh Mansion, where its prominent resident lords it over the rest of the metropolis, I find myself staring into the face of British India. I am a stranger here. But it is Sadia's space since she is a frequent visitor to this place. We enter the apartment from the rear entrance which is swarming with cats. Apparently, frequent visitors don't ring the bell; they just walk through this entrance.

The famous and illustrious son of Sardar Sobha Singh reclines on a chair that looks very comfortable with a footrest and except for a lone visitor, the durbar is not in full attendance. We are in a warm, intimate sort of room with books and artifacts casually placed, betraying a lack of meditated arrangement. What strikes me are two things—the wooden engraving of the Muslim kalima[9] on the wall and curtains with the imprint of asalam alaikum to which Singh points almost immediately after we have met.

Yet, this is not the house of a wannabe Muslim. Among several eclectic symbols, which make this post-Victorian apartment so un-British, there is also a gaunt Buddha sculpture reposing in one corner while a bust of Jesus stands in another. I am introduced to Singh and when he hears the words, 'Lahore' and 'Pakistan', his demeanour changes and his face lights up. Without any need to level with an imposed visitor who suddenly descended upon him, he points to a framed photograph at his side, asking me, 'Do you know this gentleman?' I make a dishonest guess (hmm ... this must be Pakistan's eminent jurist, Manzoor Qadir), and say, 'I believe this is Manzoor Qadir.' All those black-and-white photographs in old frames are the old world that Singh still lives in. Singh confesses that he can never turn away a visitor from Pakistan and they are always welcome in his home.

Qadir was his closest friend in Lahore and when Singh and his family had to move, it was Qadir who took charge of their property. They had to split permanently, irreversibly.

Singh's obituary for Qadir opens with these lines:

> My closest friend of many years lay dying; I could not go to his bedside. His wife and children were only an hour and a half's flight from me; I could not go to see them. I could not ring them up or write to them. And when he died, I was not there to comfort them. They are Pakistani, I am Indian. What kind of neighbours are we? What right have we to call ourselves civilised?

Singh's trauma is instructive. He does not belittle the existence of a separate Pakistan, nor does he call for a reunification. Like a pragmatic sage, he calls for a civilizational consciousness where acrimonies of the past can be overcome through grace.

As he sips on his precious drink of Scotch with soda, I look at him with a growing feeling of familiarity. I am not overawed by his larger-than-life persona nor does his Sikh turban unnerve my textbook conception of the 'non-Muslim'. His warmth is almost infectious, disproving his well-known lack of patience with visitors to his durbar. Well, I am with Sadia, so that helps. We speak in a special type of English littered with Punjabi phrases, Urdu couplets and Hindustani, all forming a peculiar semantics that is comprehensible to those present in the room.

Sadia and Khushwant flirt in a manner that reincarnates Electra in twenty-first-century Delhi. Just a while ago, Khushwant was half-teasing and half-complaining that I was her new young companion. While I blush away, Sadia ignores the comment, merely joking that I have the same name as her husband from Pakistan. The air never gets quite cleared. Singh draws up a flamboyant picture of Sadia; she keeps on explaining how she has evolved over the years—a new-age Sufi girl. Still half-laughing, Singh flicks through the manuscript of the translations of the great Urdu poets that he is undertaking, with, he confesses, much trepidation. While heaping innumerable praises upon Urdu and its poetry, he mourns the incomprehensibility of Ghalib's verse. Urdu poetry with its nuances, twists and the delicacy of expressing the banal and the metaphysical in the same breath has inspired him to devotion. He puts the manuscript in my hands and inquires whether he has translated the verse properly. I am part flattered, part nonplussed. As a result, I spend the next twenty minutes glancing through the script and then stop at these melodious lines from Mir, another of Delhi's 'grand people'. At Singh's request, I recite:

Mir ji zarad hote jaate hain
Kya kahin tum ne bhi kiya hai ishq?

Mir, you seem to be getting paler by the day,
Have you too fallen in love?

I break into heartfelt praise even though not all his translations are technically sound or capture the lyricism. This is the curse of the Urdu poetry of the ustads—the beauty begins to fade away the moment a translator commences his Procrustean task. The old wine does not go well with a new bottle. On the state of Urdu, Singh recites this couplet by Khurshid Afsar Bisrani:

Ab urdu kya hai, ek kothey ki tawaif hai
Mazaa har ek leta hai mohabbat kaun karta hai?

What is Urdu now but a prostitute in a brothel
Everyone has fun with her, but who really loves her?

That a ninety-eight-year-old man, despite ill health, is keeping the Urdu torch ablaze is enough to make any Urdu devotee extremely happy. Hopefully, these translations will serve to create a wider understanding of Urdu in India and abroad.

It is 8 p.m. and time for Khushwant Singh to retire. He is notorious for his discipline and for kicking out guests. Once, Prime Minister Rajiv Gandhi arrived late for a planned dinner. Singh said hello and went to bed. His baffled son was left to entertain India's PM. However, I do manage to squeeze in a little discussion on his book, *The End of India*, which I had read a year ago. It may not be the best book in his legacy but its timing was most opportune. When India was wounded from within after the ghastly Gujarat violence, this book reinforced the value of a non-negotiable creed which, for the lack of any better phrase, one calls 'secularism', the core of what India's founding fathers had stood for. Not the secularism of western Europe, but a home-grown desi compact, achieved and executed for more than a thousand years. He wrote:

> It is wrong and counterproductive to pretend that communalism is something that the Sangh Parivar invented in India. The Sangh's genius was in creating a monster out of existing prejudices. The Congress, especially under Indira Gandhi, played its own dirty role. The BJP is only more dangerous because of its brazenness ... everybody has blood on their hands. Every religious or ethnic group in India can and has been incited to kill and plunder ... Just about everyone killing everyone else.

I remind him of the term 'fundoo' that he used in the introduction. He explains, as does the introduction, that the term and its current explanation came from a novella written by Gita Hariharan. She defines the word: 'Fundoo: fundamentalist, fascist, obscurantist, terrorist. And the made-in-India brand, the communalist—a deceptively innocuous other-community hater.' Delhi is fortunate to be the home of a man with such uncompromising and unflinching faith in not just a secular India but in an India that is at peace within and without.

Another of Khushwant Singh's lasting contributions is his magnum opus, *The History of the Sikhs*, an erudite yet readable account, striking for its attempt to shed biases. One marvels at Singh's effort to rise above what he must have received as the 'real version of truth' from the annals of his community's written and oral accounts. If anything, his celebrated novel, *Train to Pakistan*, recounts the amity that existed between Sikhs and Muslims in Mano Majra, a village in Punjab, only to be upturned by the violence of Partition. I admire Singh's secularism and his iconoclastic status—neither high-brow nor laced with ideological pretensions. The well-known Singh slogan, 'Sex, scotch, and scholarship', also the title of one of his later books of essays, is the persona he uses to undermine the still-extant Victorian middle-class ethos. Both 'sex' and 'scotch' ironically, are not Singh's lifestyle symbols but a cover for his individualism which is famous for its unvarnished truth and the demolishing of religious claptrap.

I meet Singh a year later, and again the year after that. Each time I am fortunate to meet him with only a few people around him, thereby enabling an atmosphere where one could probe his memory a little deeper and the expanse of his spirit with ease. During our last meeting, his little Sony television flashed images of a victorious Narendra Modi who had won state elections in Gujarat in December 2007. The predictions of Indian media gurus did not come true once again and Modi's opposition was dejected.

Singh was evidently disturbed, even though he tried to crack joke upon joke about the 'imagined' defeat of Modi. But we, the attendees of his durbar, were under a mild spell of depression—Sadia Dehlvi, an enlightened Indian-Muslim woman, I, the non-Indian from a country that is supposed to have created Modis of a different kind, and another visitor, an Indian Christian, sharing the same anguish. Beneath the eye of time, identity is a house built on sand. In his book, *The End of India*, Khushwant Singh writes:

> Nehru was the first and probably only leader of the time who sensed that the challenge to India's democracy would come not from communism but from a resurgence of religious fanaticism ... what would become of predominantly Hindu India now that it was truly independent for the first time in centuries? ... when Dr Rajendra Prasad agreed to inaugurate the newly rebuilt temple at Somnath, Nehru sent a strong note protesting that the president of a secular state had no business to involve himself in religious matters.

The feeling that Hindus had been deprived of their legacy and humiliated by foreigners had deep roots. For eight centuries, Muslim dynasties had ruled the country and many Muslim rulers had destroyed Hindu temples. This was not peculiar to the Muslim rulers of India. In almost all ancient and medieval societies, this was the norm. Hindu rulers too, for instance, had persecuted Buddhists and Jains and destroyed their places of worship.

Further, Singh holds that '... the Rashtriya Swayamsevak Sangh (RSS) is anti-Muslim, anti-Christian and anti-Left. As long as it remained on the fringes of mainstream politics, it could be dismissed as a lunatic group. Not anymore.'

It was no longer just politics and propaganda which was escalating the cancer of extremism ailing both India and Pakistan at the societal and, more worrisome, personal levels. Poisonous textbooks, jingoism and twisted constructs of nation states had shaped a region which denied its own history and worse, obsessed with a vendetta that was coming to resemble a collective suicide arrangement. The year 1947 was a watershed, but to turn it into perpetual hostile militancy of two well-armed nations, and later, a third one in the form of Bangladesh, was a clear recipe for disaster.

Each meeting with Singh exalts my Delhi experience but each time it leaves more questions unanswered. There is, of course, his familiar exclamation, 'Ah, this boy is from my hometown!' What a strange sense of being locked in the middle of 'otherness'! Strange that it is true and odd that it is a mere memory that would soon be trampled by the 'relentless time-horse', to use a metaphor from Ghalib.

Time has that strange effect that makes us want to forget and yet relive the past. Khushwant Singh's narratives of Lahore and the Punjabi identity are replete with unshed tears and nostalgia. A cesspool of bitterness exists under the feet that walk on Delhi streets. Imagined boundaries constantly punctuate geographical borders. The ghost of Partition lives in every corner of Delhi in hidden tombs. Present-day immigration into larger Delhi is a continuum of what happened in that humid summer of 1947.

Independence, often indistinguishable from Partition, entailed a migration of people that defies mythology. It was nothing short of ethnic cleansing even though the term was not invented those days. Seven million Muslims and almost the same number of Hindus and Sikhs crossed the border on either side and found new homes, new countries. Millions lost their lives under the maladministration of the British Empire while hundreds of thousands of women were raped. It is said that in Punjab, nearly one hundred thousand people were never to be found. They were lost in the blurred victory of the new nation states. Missing? They are the invisible fodder of history.

On a hot summer afternoon, I read some personal accounts of those who had experienced Partition. Nothing has affected me more than these chilling lines by Alok Bhalla:

> My earliest memory is of a remote summer afternoon in Delhi in 1948. That day lies so far back in my biography that I sometimes wonder if what I remember ever really happened; if I haven't made some nightmarish image into a part of my being. Recently, however, my mother confirmed that the essential details of my remembrance were accurate enough. The day was like any other usual hot day in Delhi. The sun was harsh and indifferent; the dust was full of the dry buzz of flies and the smell of tar. The courtyard of our small house was surrounded by a high wall which was washed with white lime so that it could absorb the glare of the sun and resist the hot winds. The entrance to our house was through a small green door with a black chain lock on it. Three brick and cement steps led down from the door to the level of the road below and its burden of leaves outside. The details are important; their ordinariness is necessary both as evidence and as boundaries against the phantasmagoric. For without being sure that my memory is located in the real world, I cannot hope to make an ethical enquiry into the history of my age and place.
>
> I recall that as I unlocked the door to our house, I saw the body of a man stretched out on the steps below. He was lying face down. His bag had fallen near his feet; it was open and a few common household things had scattered out of it. His limbs were in disarray, his clothes were soaked in blood and the sun had begun to darken his skin. There was no one in the street, not even the usual garbage dog. My father had heard the sound of the chain on the door and had hurried out. Later, he told me that

> the man, marked with so many wounds, had earlier in the day sought shelter in our house. He was a Muslim trader who had been chased into our locality by violent men seeking revenge for blood spilled in Pakistan. We were Hindus and he had stayed with us in safety for a few hours. Towards noon, my father had gone out to see if the streets were safe. The man was obviously anxious to get back to his family. My father had looked about the street carefully and had thought that the man could negotiate his way back to his own neighbourhood without fear. Too late had my father realised that he had failed to notice one of the shadowy corners of the wall marking the grounds of old St Stephen's College in Kashmiri Gate. The man had turned back and had tried to reach our house again. My father had forgotten his name. There were too many who had been killed.[10]

Delhi was drained of 3.3 lakh Muslims and 5 lakh non-Muslims from the newly created 'Pakistan' rushed in. This was chaotic for the city—perhaps unmatched since the devastation wrought by the Mongols or what followed when the Mutiny of 1857 turned into a War of Independence. A city of empires turns into a vast refugee camp reeling in the pre-monsoon heat and humidity of Lahore and Delhi. That August brought the dark world of Hades out into the daylight. Blood fell with rain. Relief came to those lingering wounds destined not to heal. The agony was not peculiar to any religious community—it was personal, shared and universal.

Khushwant Singh is not alone. Another Lahore-wala who had to become a Delhi resident was Pran Nevile. A diplomat and patriot, Nevile has not let go of Lahore. His fine musings on Lahore and nostalgia for a lost identity are widely known.

The first time I met Pran Nevile was in Lahore. He was there to launch his republished book, *Lahore: A Sentimental Journey*, which documents his memories of Lahore, the city where he grew up. It was a monsoon evening, heavy and still, much like the weather when his family packed their bags for Delhi. Unusually fit and active for a man who has lived over seven decades, he appeared timeless. Sitting in Lahore, he traversed various paths and entire cities in his conversation. Having travelled the world as a foreign office star, Nevile could never ever forget his hometown of Lahore.

When I read Nevile's book, I knew what this criss-crossing was all about. The love of his city, so deep-rooted and honest, made the events of 1947 appear treacherous and evil. He transported his readers into the idyll that Lahore was. He unwrapped its composite culture with much nostalgia, 'I belong to a generation born and brought up in Lahore. Even after four decades, my emotional attachments to this great city are as deep as ever,' he admits. In another conversation, he declares, 'In a way ... I never left Lahore because it was always with me ... I am an un-reconstructed Lahoria, you can say, who never thought he would live anywhere else.'[11]

When riots shook Lahore in July 1947, Nevile's siblings moved to Delhi, but his parents were reluctant to migrate. Finally, persuaded by their Muslim friends, the parents also left with a fantastical certitude that they would return after the dust had settled. That has been the tragedy of Partition. Many, including Nevile's parents, who left in the flurry of events, were convinced that they would return to their homes, villages and cities. This was never to happen. The red lines merely grew thicker across the canvas of history. Nevile now leads a group of Lahore's former residents who meet regularly and share the memory of a city that yet lives with them. Perhaps my maternal aunt thought the same about her city, Amritsar, and her countless friends.

While driving on a busy Delhi road, I notice a small signboard that says 'Chirag Dilli', the area where the recluse saint lived and is now buried. Figures from an ancient and recent past still linger on Delhi's lanes. It is another matter that most of the residents of this overgrown metropolis have forgotten these tales.

Fables have furthered Sufi and bhakti thought and practice. Memory needs a playground, it seeks indulgence and reconciliation and it harks back to the unity now lost. Pran

Nevile and Khushwant Singh try to inject some order into the chaos of their ruptured memories.

But demons also need peace.

NOTES

1. Tasawwuf is the traditional Islamic science of spirituality (Sufism) focusing on one's relationship with Allah. In Arabic, the word for wool is *suf* and thus, those who wore it became known as Sufis.
2. There are three stations of peace in Sufism and the traveller on the spiritual path enters one of these three according to his spiritual state. The three stations comprise peace at the stage of islam (submission, abandonment to the divine will), peace at the stage of iman (the divine peace that enters the believer's heart) and peace at the stage of ihsan (the sanctifying virtue through which the sovereignty of evil comes to an end).
3. K.A. Nizami, 'The Contribution of Indian Sufis to Peace and Amity', in *Culture of Peace* by Baidyanath Saraswati (ed.), New Delhi: Indira Gandhi National Centre for the Arts, 1999.
4. Charles E. Gover, *The Folksongs of Southern India*, New Delhi: Rupa & Co., p. 165.
5. However, Muslim Sufis differed from Hindu ascetics in many ways, such as they were not celibate and did not impose a sparse or limited diet on themselves.
6. The term 'hadith' is used to denote a saying or an act or tacit approval or criticism ascribed either validly or invalidly to the Islamic prophet Mohammad.
7. A romantic song from a Bollywood film *Kabhi Kabhie.*
8. Rajab is the seventh month of the Islamic calendar. This month is regarded as one of the four sacred months in Islam in which battles are prohibited. The month is also a prelude to the month of Ramadan.
9. *La Illaha Ill Allah Muhammadur Rasool Allah.* This is the kalima or the testification of faith in Islam. A person cannot be considered to be a Muslim if he/she does not believe in the words of the kalima.
10. Alok Bhalla, *Stories about the Partition of India*, New Delhi: Manohar Publishers, 2011.
11. *The Friday Times* (Lahore), 3 January 2003.

3

Meeting Again

There cannot be a more haunting expression of shared tragedy than a poem, 'Lali akhiaan di payee dusdi aye' (The Bloodshot Eyes Bear Testimony of Many a Tear), written immediately after Partition by Ustad Daman (1911–84), a Lahore-based proletarian poet. It described what happened to Punjabis during those bloody months. It is a poem that was often-recited in Old Lahore's busy streets and baithaks. My father would read about these perfidious times to us:

> None of us may utter
> but you know and so do we
> a great deal have you lost
> and so have we;
> who was to foresee this struggle for freedom
> would tear things apart, destroy so heavily
> much pain much suffering have you borne
> and so have we;
> Yet there is hope
> regeneration and new life awaits us
> though many a death you died
> and so did we;
> Those who were awake and alert
> robbed, exploited, emasculated us

while for centuries you slept in stupor
and so did we:
These bloodshot eyes bear testimony
many a tear
you did shed
and so did we.[1]

Some years after Partition, this poem was recited at a mushaira in India. Prime Minister Jawaharlal Nehru was present at the occasion and he is reported to have cried when he heard this poem. Ustad Daman was asked twice to relocate to India but he did not. As he remarked to Ali Sardar Jafri, he feared that in Pakistan he would be killed by the mullahs while in India he would be eaten alive by the pundits.

Following the tradition of bhakti poets which entails living a simple life closer to ordinary folk, Daman was a tailor by profession and remained a wage earner all his life. In 1947, he lost his wife and child only to find and lose them again, this time to disease. The treatment was costly and his friends bore the burial expenses. Since he sympathized with the politics of Indian nationalism, the mobs burnt his house, his books and poetry. This was when he shifted to the outer part of the Badshahi Mosque where he lived for the rest of his life. An extraordinary life disrupted and fractured. A migrant in his home country, he did not have to go anywhere to suffer the pain but understood it well.

On the other side of the border, those who lived in Delhi never imagined that they would live anywhere else. Shaista Ikramullah wrote, 'For millions of people like me, to whom Delhi was synonymous with Muslim culture, a Pakistan without Delhi was a body without a heart.'[2] How could she ever have dreamt that she would have to leave the city that she adored? Many of the 3.3 lakh Muslims who left Delhi did not ever dream that either.

As in Lahore, the phantom of violence nurtured by the memory of Partition continues to haunt Delhi. Decades of progress and entrepreneurship may have dumped old skeletons inside closets. But the closets are shaky. Press the button of 'Lahore, Rawalpindi' in Delhi and the door flies open! Punjab's sense of identity was rooted in the village, mohallah or even the tree. All else came later. In Delhi, therefore, talking to Pakistanis is a catharsis of sorts.

Perhaps this is why the Punjabi poet, Amrita Pritam, did not wish to leave Lahore even when her community was attacked. The year 1947 rather unwittingly added the Lahori Amrita Pritam to Delhi's distinguished list of residents. Once in Delhi, she personified the lifelong anguish of one whose folk-apples of belonging were sliced through their cores by distant hands soiled by power.

Amrita Pritam lived and worked in Lahore at the All India Radio (AIR). Events took her away from her beloved Lahore when the family forced her to migrate. But she made a strange vow—if forced to leave Lahore, she would never visit the city again. And she lived by this vow even unto her last breath in 2005.

In Lahore, she played the sitar for the AIR, composed verses and published her first collection of poetry. Riding her horse-drawn buggy, she would frequent Lawrence Gardens. Her failed marriage with Pritam Singh happened in Lahore. And ironically, she also discovered her lifelong passion for the poet, Sahir Ludhianvi, in a Lahore literary gathering.

As she travelled from Lahore to Delhi amidst the horror, she composed her well- known incantation addressed to Waris Shah, author of the Punjabi epic of immortal love, *Heer Ranjha*. Her question, *Aaj aakhaan Waris Shah nu* (Today I say to Waris Shah), was a heart-wrenching poem that created a new sensibility on the subcontinental literary landscape. Stoking the anguish of millions, particularly Punjabi women who bore a disproportionate share of the tragedy, Amrita cried:

I say to Waris Shah today, speak from your grave
And add a new page to your book of love
Once one daughter of Punjab wept, and you wrote your long saga;
Today thousands weep, calling to you Waris Shah;
Arise, o friend of the afflicted; arise and see the state of Punjab,
Corpses strewn on fields and the Chenab flowing with much blood.
Someone filled the five rivers with poison,
And this same water now irrigates our soil.
Where was lost the flute, where the songs of love sounded?
And all Ranjha's brothers forgot to play the flute.
Blood has rained on the soil, graves are oozing with blood,
The princesses of love cry their hearts out in the graveyards.
Today all the Quaidos have become the thieves of love and beauty,
Where can we find another one like Waris Shah?[3]

It was not only Amrita Pritam who never wished to visit Lahore again. There were a number of prominent writers from Lahore who, after migration, never came back for a visit to the city of their past. These included Krishan Chandar, Rajinder Singh Bedi, Balwant Singh, Balwant Gargi and so on. They could not possibly face the change that was bound to occur in a post-Partition world.

Once in Delhi, Amrita did not push a claim for allotment of evacuee property there or elsewhere. She struggled at the Delhi station of the AIR as a scriptwriter and newscaster. Later, when her arranged marriage with a conventional man finally crumbled, she lived alone until Imroze moved in with her, heralding perhaps, the first publicly acknowledged live-in relationship of modern India. For forty years she lived in rented homes and only towards the end of her life did she build her own house in Hauz Khas. From Lahore to the new 'home' was a journey of forty years that nearly consumed her life.

Like Khushwant Singh, Amrita had an emotional connection with Pakistan. She encouraged many Pakistani Punjabi writers and published their work in *Nag Mani*, the magazine she edited. Her house was almost a family home, a familiar space, for several Pakistani writers. She would not even mind when some of the male writers would return and pen nasty profiles of her given that she was a bit of a bohemian and defied conventional lifestyles. Tender and embracing, Amrita lived with her Lahore–Delhi multicultural vision where forgiveness was a way of life.

Much as I tried to reach her, I could not meet her in Delhi. When I finally managed to connect with her, my trip had to be cancelled. She was in a semi-conscious state. In those months between my first and second sojourn to Delhi, Amrita Pritam died.

Perhaps I will meet her again in another realm as I think of a later poem that she wrote for her partner, Imroze:

> I will meet you again
> Where? How? I don't know
> Perhaps as a figure
> Of your imagination
> I will appear on your canvas
> Or perhaps on your canvas
> Appearing as a mysterious line
> Quietly
> I will keep staring at you.[4]

One of Amrita's best-known novels is *Pinjar* (Skeleton). A saga of the lives of kidnapped girls of rival communities, *Pinjar* relives the woes of the female victims of Partition. The story revolves around Paro, who, abducted by a Muslim man, Rashid, becomes the rejected property of a Hindu household when her family disowns her for having lived with a Muslim. Against her wishes, Paro therefore has no choice but to live with Rashid and becomes a mother to his son. Following 1947, haunted by her own plight, she rescues Hindu and Sikh girls and sends them to the camps. The other character, Lajo, reunites with her family but Paro stays back with her kidnapper turned saviour. Paro and Lajo represent thousands of Muslim, Hindu and Sikh women who were defiled by rioters and rejected by their families.

Amrita Pritam has immortalized the particular moment of Partition, a winding path of the past that continues to twist and meander into our present.

Ustad Daman wove elegies in Lahore. Amrita could not get Lahore out of her system. Khushwant reconciles with memory time and again. Prem Kirpal, a Lahori migrant to Delhi, wrote these lines to sum it all up:

> My beloved City of Lahore
> Still standing not far from Delhi
> Within quicker reach by air or train,
> Suddenly became a forbidden land
> Guarded by a sovereign state
> Of new ideologies, loves and hates.[5]

Kirpal's poem is befittingly entitled 'Spirit's Musings'. A spirit will break free of limits. These individuals, some, members of literary and other establishments, were not locating themselves in the politics of Partition per se. This was the personal that got submerged in the cruel and indifferent political.

The brutal political divisions in South Asia during the twentieth century have not been accorded due importance as a psychological phenomenon. Partition in India, Pakistan, and especially in Bangladesh have not undergone the much-needed healing process. Truth and reconciliation of the South African type still remains a vague dream perhaps never to be realized. Conversely, the post-colonial culture of closed-door secretive commissions exacerbates the grief and means nothing to people. In South Africa, politicians arrived at a resolution and only then could truth and reconciliation begin. In South Asia, there has been no political resolution.

Who will exorcise the ghosts of the past? It might be too late. The victims were also the perpetrators or at best, silent participants in the 1947 violence. What does it mean to inherit these ghosts and blood stains? They have so far, clouded rational judgements in the new states. The rewriting of history by victors is routine. In this case, there are no victors, yet the rewriting of history continues apace.

Centuries of coexistence was destroyed overnight by new definitions of 'we' the harmless and 'they' the harmful; hence 'they' should be attacked, raped and killed. Over time, violence lives on, sometimes in wars, at other times in the form of India's communalism and Pakistan's sectarian bloodbaths. The 'us' and 'them' shrink further and the circles of inclusion and exclusion diminish, assuring ultimate self-annihilation. Nations, like individuals, can become suicidal too.

Born well after Partition in Pakistani Punjab, the Partition's brutality still remains an enigma to me. How could violence emanate so suddenly? As a Pakistani, I believe that there were cogent reasons, economic and political, for Partition to have occurred. But for the communal particularism, where communal identity gained ascendancy over humanistic values to flow within rivers of blood, that remains a question never really answered.

My memory is scarred and my history garbled. Amrita Pritam felt the yearning and sense of suffocation as do all the children and grandchildren of Partition:

> Today I have erased the number of my house
> And removed the stain of identity on my street's forehead
> And I have wiped the direction on each road
> But if you really want to meet me
> Then knock at the doors of every country
> Every city, every street

And wherever a glimpse of a free spirit exists
That will be my home.[6]

Identities change but rarely vanish.

When another Delhi writer, Ajeet Caur, visited Lahore in 2004, she was taken to Fleming Road. As her fellow writers from Lahore related, she was walking in a trance. She broke down when she identified her house—the house that was hers and not hers. The city was once hers and now she had a different address, a different city and even a different country. Before her visit, writing about the room she was born in and lived in until she had to leave Lahore, she wrote, 'Some are born in gypsy families and others become gypsies through a conspiracy of circumstances.' Her poignant conclusion was, 'Poets are free to make the elements—the earth, the air and the sky—as romantic as they like, but I assure you that these elements are not only deaf and dumb, they are also blind.'[7]

Elements are indifferent, sometimes deaf and dumb. Hearts are not.

I am not sure how I met Bunty. It was perhaps through a reference from the office during one of my early work-related visits. Bunty Singh, brother of Sunny Singh and Goldie Singh, became my guide and companion. Sunny and Bunty have set up a mini empire of rental cars through investments made by Goldie who lives in Germany and is married to a 'good' German girl. Bunty, a boisterous, Internet-savvy young Sardar, found me to be somewhat like him. We spoke in Punjabi, often using lines that would quite miss those outside the 'Punju' realm. And we both were equally fascinated by each other—the thirty-something grandchildren of Partition.

So after an hour of awkward client-service interaction, Bunty decided to befriend me. It was just the right thing to have happened, I guess. How else would I know a real Sardar? Most of my Sikh interactions took place as a student in the UK decades ago.

However, as soon as there was mention of Partition, there was a palpable unease. It was only after a day or two that he confided how half of his family was butchered at a railway station. To use Amrita's words:

> Who can guess
> How difficult it is
> To nurse barbarity in one's belly
> To consume the body and burn the bones?
> I am the fruit of that season
> When the berries of Independence came into blossom.[8]

Bunty was a classic mixture of family oral histories and textbooks. The textbook narratives were humanized by real accounts of coexistence. But the confusion remained. For instance, when the familiarity increased, he would talk of 'Muslims' who cut up Sikhs and Hindus near Aimanabad, now in Pakistan. Yet these tensions were not enough for him to resent me as an individual. I too shared my narrative of Sikh brutality and also mentioned various characters and incidents from the Urdu stories of Manto. He was bewildered. The loss of humanity even in a fable can be unnerving. Bunty wants to hate me but cannot. He does not take money from me at the airport a few days later. Perhaps he finds in me the humanized phantom of the 'other'.

Bunty accompanies me to the Purana Quila that I have seen from the outside, time and again, as I pass by on the busy Mathura Road. It is exceptionally quiet, except for a few students with their books and an odd couple or two seeking intimacy in its not-so-dark corners. This is the landmark of ancient Delhi. The Mahabharata tells us that Indraprastha, Delhi's ancient name, meaning the 'abode of the king of the gods', was the great capital city which the five Pandava brothers created on the banks of the River Jamuna. The veracity of such a claim is disputed. Archaeological excavations show that there was indeed a township here but what sort of settlement it was is not known. Fifteenth-century BC, I tell Bunty, and he stares at me in disbelief.

I try to imagine King Yudhishthira but cannot conjure up a figure. All I know are the popular representations of gods, often aesthetically challenged, so I avoid those images. I resolve to find out more. But the horses and chariots do come before my mind for a split second and I smile at how history plays tricks with us—Aryans, Turkish chariots, Mughal caravans and now the bustle of urban Delhi, all jumbled here.

Quintessential to the Delhi experience, this site mixes time and memory. From 1450 BC to the present day, the monument tells various stories. The walls that stand today are most likely the work of the unfortunate emperor Humayun who chose this as his residence in Delhi and added many structures to the ruins. Proximity to the Jamuna must have played its part—in hot Hindustan, water and breeze were essential for survival.

The large fortified city of Purana Quila was symbolically named 'Din Panah' and, by 1538, much of the work was completed. However, the rise of Sher Shah Suri halted the process. Sher Shah Suri took over Delhi and ousted the feeble Humayun (known for his proclivity for opium and indecision). Sher Shah added a lot here—a stunning mosque and the octagonal Sher Mandal. Of course Din Panah became Dilli Sher Shahi. Sher Shah's reign, brief as it was and not of the Mughal ilk, has not been closely studied. The construction of the Grand Trunk Road that is shared by India and Pakistan is attributed to him. However, most notably, Sher Shah was a secular Pathan who was a true forerunner of Akbar in that he believed that religious freedom and a discrimination-free regime were essential for effective governance.

In 1555, Humayun regained control of Delhi and he returned to his Din Panah. In a year's time, he tumbled down the stairs of Sher Mandal with books in his hand, thereby ending his tumultuous life. Not far away from this place lies his magnificent tomb reflecting the grandeur of Gur-e-Amir of Tamarlane in Samarkand. He was succeeded by the greatest of emperors, Akbar. Little did Humayun know that three centuries later, his descendent, Bahadur Shah Zafar, would escape from the Red Fort to take a boat down the Jamuna and reach Purana Quila to go to Hazrat Nizamuddin's shrine. Also, Humayun would have never imagined as he was dying, that the last Mughal emperor would be captured by the British at his tomb.

Bunty tells me in chaste Punjabi, *'Aais jaga tay badi history haygee!'* ('Too much history in this place!') We walk around a huge well and cross the royal baths until we find a little tea stall. Bunty is amused at my ramblings. He is also interested in the Sikh shrines in Pakistan. These are well looked after, I reassure him and inquire why his family has not yet visited Pakistan.

The Mahabharata tells us that Delhi was founded on a jungle inhabited by ancient tribes. The Pandava brothers cleared the jungle and eliminated all its inhabitants to build Indraprastha. Thus, primordial Delhi set the pattern for violence—it has always marked the city's existence. Small wonder that all the Delhis that were to follow faced political upheaval involving a fair amount of violence. The first recorded war for the throne of Delhi—mythological as it might be—is narrated in the Mahabharata.

The events of 1947 added another life to this monument. Purana Quila was used as a vast refugee camp. Violence on the streets of Delhi had forced thousands of Muslim families to leave their homes and prepare for a long journey to Pakistan. The conditions of this refugee camp, where up to 100,000 people may have taken shelter, were appalling. Dr Zakir Hussain, later the president of India, bemoaned that those who had escaped sudden death came here to be 'buried in a living grave'.[9]

I am completely confused. Shall I appreciate the beauty of the ruins or the syncretic architecture of Sher Shah or its prehistoric significance? Or shall I look for traces of the blood of those who must have died here? Accidents of history can be deaf and dumb. Like Ajeet Caur's interpretation of the elements, history is alive yet indifferent to individual tales and personal suffering. I still have to probe into these difficult questions.

In September 1947, Mahatma Gandhi arrived in Delhi to take stock of the violence and ease communal tensions. A shaken, non-violent Gandhi visited Purana Quila to witness the conditions of dispossessed Muslim exiles—refugees in their own city. I can hear him making his appeal to Hindus by comparing the predicament of the Muslims to that of the five Pandava brothers who were exiles in their own kingdom for twelve years, 'It is said that in the Mahabharata period the Pandavas used to stay in this Purana Quila.' Thus Muslims 'are under your protection and under my protection'. Gandhi's tireless efforts in Delhi that included visits to the Jama Masjid, Old Delhi, as well as his rounds of fasting, brought a tenuous peace back to the city. But what a price he paid for attempting to clear the poison in the air!

Gandhi, in that season of Independence, stayed in Delhi and went from neighbourhood to neighbourhood to arrest the violence and bring about a truce between India and Pakistan and between Hindus and Muslims. Within months of his effective campaigning and fasting for these causes, he was assassinated. The greatest icon of modern Indian consciousness was an irritant in the dark world of Hindu fundamentalists. From 1934 to 1948, six attempts were made to kill him. The last one, by Nathuram Godse, was successful.

Delhi must have witnessed one of its coldest days on 30 January 1948. The country must have needed Gandhi's sacrifice to nurture its complex society and the new state. Over time, this gruesome murder of India's greatest leader has slipped into relative oblivion. The grievances of the assassins were that Gandhi supported the creation of Pakistan, he was fasting for the payment of dues worth Rs 55 crore to Pakistan and his 'appeasement' of Muslims were making Muslims more belligerent. Appeasement has become the bane of Indian politics. The major policy plank of the Bharatiya Janata Party (BJP) has been to end this policy of appeasement (of minorities) and Gujarat's chief minister Narendra Modi implemented a harrowing version of this political aim.

The same day we visit Gandhi's monument at Raj Ghat. We park the car under the keekar trees and walk. The monsoon breeze has cooled the air. There are a few flower sellers with heaps of marigolds. Bunty and I walk to the shrine and, passing through well-kept lawns, we reach the unostentatious marble platform. Not many visitors are around. This is a peaceful afternoon. As we return, I see an exquisite structure at some distance and find out that it is Zeenatul Masjid, the beauty of the mosques, built by Emperor Aurangzeb's daughter.

A Mughal mosque overlooks Gandhi's monument and the silent Jamuna flows, or rather trickles through most of the year, at a close distance. It is a shrunken river that has been filled with the blood and corpses of past sufferers but now it is choking with sewage and pollution. From Indraprastha to the sultanate and the Mughal takht of Dilli, the Jamuna has witnessed centuries of violence and has changed its course several times but has been faithful to Delhi.

I hold a mustard flower in my hand and put it inside the copy of Ahmed Ali's *Twilight in Delhi* that I have with me. In Delhi, time and again, I think of Ahmed Ali who could never return to the city he loved. *Twilight in Delhi* is a fine novel that portrays the decline and commercialization of Delhi during the colonial era. Delhi here is a Muslim character that lives in harmony with its non-Muslim residents but has to face modernity that is eating into its traditional character.

I know that the Hindi writer, Krishna Sobti, lives in Delhi. I want to meet her but somehow I cannot. Her stories, a few of which have been translated, have fascinating accounts of a composite culture that is fading worldwide. She was studying in Lahore in 1947 and had come to Delhi to spend her birthday. What a celebration it must have been! Momentous and life-changing, for she could never go back to Lahore. That evening of 15 August, when India was going to awaken to freedom, she and her brother celebrated the anticipated arrival of the long-hoped-for Independence. Sweets were prepared, speeches made and an impromptu exhibition of photographs of freedom fighters was arranged in their Delhi house.

The young Krishna Sobti and her brother invited everyone to congregate in the veranda of the house and started serving the sweets. But the visitors, rather than feeling happy, began to leave one by one. Was this independence or uprooting? Unknown to the Sobtis, this question was on the minds of millions of Indians that day.

Krishna's autobiography, *Zindaginamah,* plays with three languages—Punjabi, Persian/Urdu and Hindi—deliberately, thereby making a loud proclamation that there is nothing simplistic even in the anonymous villages of India. There are no linear histories, no simplistic solutions or causes. Life, time and events are all jumbled up and ordinary people, away from high politics, take this complexity in their stride. In this shared world there is no need to shed one's religious identities; coexistence between humans is not merely a possibility but a reality. And in today's world, there is no need to shed national identities for they are real. But coexistence is still the natural order of things, a kind of Darwinian impulse only sabotaged by suicidal maniacs.

Krishna's story is in so many ways reminiscent of what Fatima Jinnah, sister of Quaid-e-Azam and a politician in her own right, had to say in June 1947 to a visitor. When her Lahori friend, Kishwar Abid, visited her in Delhi and found that the floors of the house were being polished, she was shocked, wondering how this Delhi house would be retained in view of the imminent Independence and Partition looming on the horizon. We would come here for vacations, Fatima Jinnah had said. The great leader of Pakistan, Jinnah himself, had also intended to keep his Bombay house; he wanted to visit Bombay frequently and spend time there after his retirement. Jinnah's house in Bombay is still an unresolved issue—a plank for sloganeering and jingoism.

Bizarre, people would say. But no one could really imagine the extent of the carnage and bitterness and the suddenness of it all. Not even the steel frame of the colonial administration. What a traumatic summer and how unpredictable it was!

The schizophrenia of that summer and the preceding months was mind-boggling. The Muslims of India had multiple voices. Jinnah held that the 'problem in India is not of an inter-communal but manifestly of an international character, and must be treated as such ... it is a dream that Hindus and Muslims can evolve a common nationality, and this misconception of one Indian nation has gone far beyond the limits, and is the cause of most of our troubles, and will lead India to destruction, if we fail to revise our actions in time.'

Reversing his earlier 'Ambassador of Hindu-Muslim Unity' stand, his discourse, as articulated in his 1940 presidential address to the All India Muslim League was final:

> The Hindus and Muslims belong to two different religious philosophies, social customs and literature. They neither intermarry, nor inter-dine together, and indeed they belong to two different civilisations which are based mainly on conflicting ideas and conceptions. Their aspects on and of life are different.

However, concurrent to Jinnah's 1940 address, Maulana Abul Kalam Azad addressed the Congress as its president. He summarized the nationalist Muslim viewpoint thus:

> Eleven hundred years of common history [of Islam and Hinduism] have enriched India with our common achievements. Our languages, our poetry, our literature, our culture, our art, our dress, our manners and customs, the innumerable happenings of our daily life, everything bears the stamp of our joint endeavour ... These thousand years of our joint life [have] moulded us into a common nationality ... whether we like it or not, we have now become an Indian nation, united and indivisible. No fantasy or artificial scheming to separate and divide can break this unity.

Reconciliation efforts were initiated and there was dialogue. The last of the plans to save the unity of India was packaged under the Cabinet Mission proposals that ensured a weak centre and strong regional centres with provincial autonomy. In 1946, Jinnah agreed and Azad was biased in its favour too. However, the hard line represented by Patel and intellectualized by Nehru, rejected the Cabinet Mission Plan. Patel, like many Congress leaders, was opposed to confederal structure for post-Independence. The Congress eventually 'accepted' the Plan in June 1946. However, Nehru hinted at an infamous press conference in Bombay on 10 July 1946, as the incoming president of Congress, that his party, with its absolute majority in the House, did not consider itself bound by the scheme of the Cabinet Mission Plan.[10]

But this was no start of a clean, linear narration of history. How could the complex web of shared centuries be separated so easily? A bitter-sweet irony in post-Partition Pakistan was that Pakistan's first national anthem was composed by Jagannath Azad, a Lahore-based Hindu, upon Jinnah's request. The national anthem written by Azad was sent to Jinnah who approved it in a few hours. It was sung for the first time on Pakistan Radio, Karachi, then the capital of Pakistan. The opening lines were:

> Oh land of Pakistan, each particle of yours is being illuminated by stars.
> Even your dust has been brightened like a rainbow.[11]

Days before his death in 2005, Jagannath Azad recalled the circumstances under which he was asked by Jinnah to write Pakistan's national anthem,

> In August 1947, when mayhem had struck the whole Indian subcontinent, I was in Lahore working for a literary newspaper. All my relatives had left for India and for me to think of leaving Lahore was painful. I decided to take a chance and stay on for some time. My Muslim friends requested me to stay on and took responsibility for my safety. On the morning of August 9, 1947, there was a message from Pakistan's first Governor General, Mohammad Ali Jinnah. It was through a friend working in Radio Lahore who called me to his office. He told me, 'Quaid-e-Azam wants you to write a national anthem for Pakistan.' I told them it would be difficult to pen it in five days and my friend pleaded that as the request has come from the tallest leader of Pakistan, I should consider his request. On much persistence, I agreed.

Azad further related that Jinnah wanted the anthem to be written by an Urdu-knowing Hindu, 'Through this, I believe Jinnah Sahib wanted to sow the roots of secularism in a Pakistan where intolerance had no place.' Jinnah had already made his intentions clear in his inaugural speech as the governor general of Pakistan on 11 August 1947. In that speech he declared, 'You will find that in course of time, Hindus will cease to be Hindus and Muslims will cease to be Muslims, not in the religious sense because that is the personal faith of each individual, but in the political sense as citizens of the state.'

Azad moved to India later. The Partition project was accomplished as the new states of India and Pakistan moved towards selective positions of nationalism.

And on the other side, the song, '*Sare jahan se achchha, Hindustan hamara*,' composed by Mohammad Iqbal, poet of the east, is still the most popular patriotic Indian song. We were fed with the version that one fine day, Iqbal had seen a dream for Pakistan and Jinnah implemented it despite the evil designs of the Hindus and the British. But then, why was *'Sare jahan se achchha'* sung in *India*, I used to wonder as a child. Only with the passing of years did I find out that the mishmash of history, fascinating as it was, was pretty tough to unravel and make sense of.

Bunty is keen that I should visit Gurdwara Bangla Sahib with him. We first drive to Connaught Place (CP), not far from the gurdwara, for an errand. Built by the British in the nineteenth century, CP represents Raj nostalgia. The white-colonnaded shopping area encircles a park in the somewhat Raj attempt to create an English aesthetics driven by homesickness where the streets of London were recreated to provide sahibs and memsahibs with a piece of home. Today, Connaught Place is fully independent and fully Indianized, complete with beggars and hawkers and Hindi film music.

United Coffee House, a highlight of CP, was a venue for intellectual and literary discussions until it was razed for the construction of a larger market. But the Standard Restaurant from the Raj still stands. However, the Raj menu has been replaced with globalized food. Kake Da Dhaba and Kwality, serving Punjabi food, are more popular in CP than was the case earlier. Wengers, however, still serves savouries, cakes and sandwiches reminiscent of the Raj. I liked CP. It was home again for me—the Raj Mall Road in Lahore and the feel of Murree Mall with quaint shops and colonial architecture. But CP is a grander version, given that Delhi was the resplendent jewel in the Empire's crown.

The Gurdwara Bangla Sahib used to be the bungalow of Raja Jai Singh Amber, a noble at the court of Emperor Aurangzeb. The eighth Sikh guru, Shri Harkishan, stayed here for a few months as a guest of the raja. Over centuries, this place has been a pilgrimage site for both Hindus and Sikhs. Bangla Sahib has been upgraded and spruced up. Modern interventions in its architecture are obvious. There is a well which offers holy water to pilgrims; Bunty insists that I drink the amrit and I do.

The Sikh guards looked splendid in their turbans and swords. Devotees bathed in the beautiful pond while several pilgrims slept in various corners of the gurdwara compound. The soothing strains of shabad kirtan lent the ambience an elevation and calm. The Guru Granth Sahib, the sacred book of the Sikhs, was lovingly protected and cherished by priests who swirled pankhas over it. Outside, the place was thronging with sardars and women dressed in flower-patterned shalwar-kameezes.

We ate the sacred and delicious halwa prasad. I guess Bunty was eager to show me *his* bit of heritage after our treks to various parts of Delhi.

The gurdwara also runs social service organizations in its vicinity. The local Sikh community runs a hospital in the basement of the gurdwara and also manages the Khalsa Girls School in the adjacent building. I then force Bunty to go with me to the art gallery downstairs. The Sikh general, Sardar Bhagel Singh, had overseen the erection of nine Sikh shrines in Delhi in 1783 during the time of Shah Alam II. Today, the art gallery remembers him daily since it has been named after the good general.

I have one question though—did Raja Jai Singh Amber know that his patron was to, as popular history goes, order the execution of Guru Tegh Bahadur?[12] Whilst Aurangzeb was a short-sighted man with clear propensity for puritanism, singling him out may not be appropriate as many historians have pointed to the inclusive nature of his court and the army. I want to recite this verse by B.D. Pandey to Bunty, but refrain. I recite it later to others as I just cannot control the urge to do so:

Hazaaron saal ki yeh daastan;
Aur yaad hai unko sirf itna;
Kay Aalamgir zaalim thaa,
Hindukush thaa, sitamgur tha.

> All they remember of a long thousand years' tale
> [Is] that Aurangzeb was tyrannical, a cruel Hindu-killer.

Violence is embedded in the histories of South Asia and seems widely accepted as if it was inevitable. No violence can ever be inevitable.

The trauma of 1947, barely healed or forgotten, was to take a new shape in 1984. The murder of Prime Minister Indira Gandhi, daughter of Independence and Partition, by two Sikh guards, led to an unending spate of killings and persecution of the Sikh minority. Mongols, Turks, mutineers, English soldiers and the mobs of 1947—all came together to create a new nightmare for Delhi that has neither healed nor been forgotten. Bunty was too young but he remembers hiding somewhere for days with no food. His father repeated the horror saga to make him relive and remember what should not be forgotten:

> In Delhi, the names of Sikhs were taken out from ration card lists by area ration shop owners. The neighbourhood we lived in went through premeditated attacks. The cinema, owned partly by a Sikh, was burnt down, a chemist shop that belonged to a Sikh met the same fate, a Sikh grocery store owner could hardly find anything in his store as everything was looted and burnt. All the houses in my locality owned by Sikhs were set on fire. But today we see the same businesses back up and running by Wahe Guru's mehers (blessings). Lots of my friends were surprised to see me and my family alive when we returned. I had no hard feelings for Hindus earlier, but the way my friends reacted, made me think twice about the trust I could put in them. Everyone was blaming the whole situation on politicians and goonda elements but I believe it was more than that. Or else why would school-going kids feel surprised (not in a good way) upon the return of their (Sikh) classmates after such a bloodbath in the city? Obviously, at their homes, their parents and elders must have been talking against Sikhs. Anyway, we do not hate Hindus. How can we? Our best friends and relatives are Hindus, but a string once broken will always have a knot in the middle.

Bunty and I remain silent for many awkward moments. I don't fancy hearing this narration any more.

My blog acquaintance, a lady—such relationships are now possible—was also in Delhi. Her life changed on that autumnal day of judgement in 1984. Her journals—intimate, public and haunting—are her way of coping:

> My husband, son, two brothers, two cousins and my two unborn daughters were killed. Suni, my cousin sister, her not-yet-born daughter and I survived.
>
> I was badly beaten and was in a coma for several weeks. When I woke up, I started keeping this journal ... For me, the journal is as natural as for me to breathe; it has been a part of my life from the time I first learned to write. The language and some of the sentiments expressed, especially toward Hindus, are pretty rough. I apologise for neither. Although I rarely use such language and I long ago stopped blaming the Hindus for what happened, given the time and circumstances, I think both are entirely appropriate.

But Delhi is not daunted. Its expanse and spirit copes with tremors well. The surface fault lines are real but so is the world underneath. The phoenix has no choice but to rise again and again.

Our history teacher, Major T, was a big, round man with a wry sense of humour. By sheer accident of circumstances he ended up at the high school after a career in the army's Education Corps and later the Foreign Service of Pakistan. Wherever he worked, he was critical, sharp and fiercely independent in his views. His stint at the Foreign Office was cut short by the then prime minister of Pakistan, Zulfiqar Ali Bhutto, who wrote adverse remarks in his personal file that plainly declared him to be a threat of sorts to the Pakistani establishment.

The reason was simple. Major T challenged official history and the touted 'ideology of Pakistan'. He was not alone in this contested terrain. Many Pakistani scholars have argued, with the help of historical records, that the term, 'Ideology of Pakistan' is a construction that was non-existent at the time of Pakistan's creation. Justice Munir has very clearly identified the first time when this phrase was coined. In his monograph, *From Jinnah to Zia*, he writes:

> The Quaid-e-Azam never used the words, 'Ideology of Pakistan' ... For fifteen years after the establishment of Pakistan, the 'Ideology of Pakistan' was not known to anybody until in 1962, a solitary member of the Jama'at-i-Islami used the words for the first time when the Political Parties Bill was being discussed. On this, Chaudhry Fazal Elahi, who recently retired as President of Pakistan, rose from his seat and objected that the 'Ideology of Pakistan' shall have to be defined. The member who had proposed the original amendment replied that the 'Ideology of Pakistan' was Islam.[13]

Major T was extremely well read and would jokingly term his love for books as 'lust' for books. In those years of my life, I found his discourse most fascinating and radical as it was at variance, sometimes completely, with the official version of history. Not that I agreed with him in entirety. He nevertheless opened my inner eye to the complex vastness of Indian history and helped me to discover how difficult it was to accept *any* version of history, even of the present, as the final one.

Hailing from the Khyber Pakhtunkhwa Province of Pakistan, members of Major T's family had been supporters of Bachha Khan (Khan Abdul Ghaffar Khan) and his Khudai Khidmatgaar movement. By extension, this meant that he was predisposed to the Indian nationalist view of history. How odd that he was to live in a country which his ancestors believed should not even exist.

He would often quote Azad, Nehru and Gandhi and was unreserved in his views on the Muslim League and its somersaults in the first half of the twentieth century. Over time, his views evolved and, like some other historians, he viewed Partition as the collective endeavour of powerful interests and groups within Muslims who wanted to perpetuate their dominant position—the *salariat* classes of the United and Central Provinces, bureaucrats, Muslim entrepreneurs of Sindh and Bombay and, of course, the pirs and feudals who thought that Pakistan was the best vehicle for safeguarding their class interests.

Indeed, for me, this struck a dissonant chord at an impressionable age. On the one hand, I had grown up with the inevitability of Partition, and, on the other, I was confronted with a semi-Marxist discourse on Independence and Partition. Over time, Ayesha Jalal, the eminent Pakistani historian, helped answer my questions by putting things in a more accurate perspective. The central thesis of her widely acclaimed book, *The Sole Spokesman*, was that Jinnah, as the spokesman for Muslims, used Partition as a bargaining chip within the United India context, and it was the pressure from the Indian regional movements, such as those of Bengal and Punjab, and the intransigence of the Congress leadership, that led to the creation of a separate country for Muslims. The irony is that Jinnah stood for a united India and wanted maximum rights for the Muslim-majority provinces. The Cabinet Mission Plan was the last opportunity for India to remain undivided but Congress scuttled this opportunity. The regional interests in Punjab and Bengal were capitalized by the Muslim League in opposing an all-powerful Centre. The 'two nations' argument of the Muslim League resonated with the Muslims in the Muslim-majority provinces in the north-eastern and north-western ends of India.

The Indian Parsi author, H.M. Seervai, whose brilliant monograph is attached to the book, *A Constitutional History of India*, argues along the same lines. He is direct and unsparing in his attack on Gandhi, Nehru and Patel for their reluctance to accept the Cabinet Mission Plan, thereby pushing Jinnah and his followers towards Partition. The mission proposed a three-tiered federal structure for a united India within which the constitution-making process could be effected. In this federal model, the Centre's authority would be limited to communications, defence and external affairs. The three sub-federations A, B and C were able to bind the provinces within them not to abandon their respective sub-federation or 'group' until after the constitution-making process had been completed and elections were held. Jinnah was comfortable with this proposal but its rejection by the Congress, as Seervai explains, made Partition inevitable.

The divide and rule policy of the British, as epitomized by Lord Linlithgow's famous line, 'For the Hindoo-Mohameddan communal amity is a dangerous threat to our interest in the Indian subcontinent', is well known. Yet, this is simply inadequate to explain all that happened. Suffice it to say that history has no postulates and now Pakistan is a country on its own and has survived, and rather well too, given all the problems it faced internally and regionally. However, stereotypes are difficult to shed. They raise their little heads time and again, and fervour for textual orthodoxy fostered by nation states does not help at all.

For many years, until a revision was attempted under General Musharraf's rule, textbooks had defined the existence of Pakistan *only* in relation to Hindus, and hence Hindus had to be demonized as much as possible. It was mostly after the separation of East Pakistan in 1971 and during the era of General Zia-ul-Haq when I was growing up, that the Hindu rhetoric became intense.

The 'pre-Ideology' textbooks did not profess hatred. Even in newly born Pakistan, created through a bloody Partition, early textbooks were free of the pathological hate that later crept into the narratives. For instance, early history books contained chapters not only on the oldest civilizations of Mohenjo-Daro and Harappa, but also on early Hindu mythologies such as the Ramayana and Mahabharata. They covered too, rather extensively, the Hindu kingdoms of the Mauryas and the Guptas. Gandhi was also respected and Congress intransigence was a popular line instead of 'Hindu machinations'.

It was under Zia-ul-Haq that Pakistani history suddenly began with the Arab conquest of Sindh and swiftly jumped to the Muslim conquerors from Central Asia, wallowing in the glories of Shah Walliullah, Iqbal's dream and then Jinnah. An entire history got rewritten.

In these refashioned versions, Pakistan wanted to appear as a truly Islamic state. The ulema,[14] who had once bitterly opposed the creation of Pakistan, were converted into heroes of the Pakistan movement. Not to mention that the Quaid-e-Azam, Mr Jinnah, was also described as a pious, practising Muslim.

Thus the Hindu–Muslim 'differences in culture' led to India's 'evil' designs against Pakistan (the three wars with India). I remember reading that in December 1885, an Englishman, Allan Octavian Hume, established a political party named the Indian National Congress to politically organize the Hindus of India. And that Hindu nationalism was imposed upon Muslims and their 'culture' and that the All India Congress turned into a purely Hindu organization.

Mercifully, Major T's teaching disproved many of these myths for me. But many among my generation have not learnt anything other than what was taught at schools through a careful recreation of history.

Another historian of the Zia era, K.K. Aziz, whom I happened to know in person, was a strong voice, albeit a lone one, when he published his famous book called *The Murder of History in Pakistani Textbooks.* Aziz highlighted countless inaccuracies, distortions and prejudices in each officially prepared and prescribed textbook. He undertook a brutal yet incisive post-mortem of sixty-six textbooks, making a list of distortions. For instance, he quoted the following statement from a textbook:

> After the partition of the sub-continent, Hindus and Sikhs started a properly planned campaign of exploiting Muslims generally in the whole of Bharat and particularly in East Punjab, as a result of which, Hindus and Sikhs, enemies of mankind,

killed and dishonoured thousands, nay hundreds of thousands, of women, children, the old and the young with extreme cruelty and heartlessness.

To which Aziz replied, 'Hindus and Sikhs were not the only aggressors in the riots of 1947; Muslims also killed, raped and looted wherever they had the opportunity.'[15] He had a personal reason for saying this. He had migrated from his beloved Batala in East Punjab and was unable to return until his old age. His beloved town and ancestral home had changed altogether. He could not stop crying for days.

In the words of Dr Tariq Rahman, eminent linguist and historian, the mutilation of history was to sound the nation state with loud martial aims:

> First, the non-Muslim part of Pakistan is ignored. Second, the borrowing from Hindu culture is either ignored or condemned. Third, the Pakistan movement is portrayed mostly in terms of the perfidy of Hindus and the British and the righteousness of the Muslims. After the Partition, in which Hindus are reported to have massacred Muslims while Muslims are not shown to have treated the Hindus in the same manner, India is portrayed as the enemy, which is waiting to dismember Pakistan. The separation of Bangladesh in 1971 is portrayed as proof of this Indian policy rather than the result of the domination of West Pakistan over East Bengal. Above all, the 1948, 1965 and 1971 wars are blamed entirely on India, and Pakistan is shown to have won the 1965 war. The armed forces are not only glorified but treated as if they were sacrosanct and above criticism. All eminent personalities associated with the Pakistan movement, especially M.A. Jinnah and Iqbal, are presented as orthodox Muslims and any aspect of their thoughts and behaviour which does not conform to this image is suppressed. Indeed, the overall effect of the ideological lesson is to make Islam reinforce and legitimise both Pakistani nationalism and militarisation.[16]

It is not surprising that while the Hindu extremists lamented the negative role of (Muslim) invaders, Pakistani textbook authors inserted this stuff:

> ... during the 11th century, the Ghaznavid Empire comprised what is now Pakistan and Afghanistan. During the 12th century, the Ghaznavids lost Afghanistan, and their rule came to be confined to Pakistan ... By the 13th century, Pakistan had spread to include the whole of Northern India and Bengal ... Under the Khiljis, Pakistan moved further southward to include a greater part of Central India and the Deccan ... Many Mongols accepted Islam. As such, Pakistan remained safe for Islam ... During the 16th century, 'Hindustan' disappeared and was completely absorbed in 'Pakistan' ... Under Aurangzeb, the Pakistan spirit gathered in strength. This evoked the opposition of the Hindus ... After the death of Aurangzeb in 1707, the process of the disintegration of Mughal Rule set in, and weakened the Pakistan spirit ... The shape of Pakistan in the 18th century was thus more or less the same as it was under the Ghaznavids in the 11th century.

But this stereotyping was not taking place in isolation. The parallel tweaking of textbooks was also taking place in India. Since 2005, the Congress government has been trying to scrap thousands of textbooks through the National Council of Educational Research and Training (NCERT), the Central government body that sets the national curriculum. Thus, over time, India has also been subjected to the 'saffronization' of history where India's Muslim rulers have been portrayed as barbarous invaders and the medieval period set as the dark age of Islamic colonial rule which erased the glories of the Hindu empires that preceded it.

One textbook held that the Taj Mahal, the Qutub Minar and the Red Fort, three stars of Islamic architecture, were designed and commissioned by Hindus. The illustrious historian, Romila Thapar has been attacked for identifying the 'Aryans' (venerated by the saffron brigade as the founders of the Indus Valley civilization) as nomadic tribes who actually came from Central Asia or the Middle East. Thapar was therefore asked to leave the Indian Council for Historical Research immediately after the Hindu nationalist Bharatiya Janata party (BJP) assumed office in 1999.

Under this saffronization, references to the caste system, or the ancient practice of beef-eating were either downplayed or simply eliminated from historical narratives. Hindu nationalists and revivalists have clamoured to emphasize the separateness of Hinduism and its resilience in the face of 'foreign' invasions. A pro-BJP writer exclaimed, 'If highlighting only Muslim rule in India as a gift to humanity and dismissing the pre-Muslim period as a dark age amounts to history, we are against that sort of history.' Most poignantly, the deletion of Gandhi's assassination by a Hindu extremist in 1948 was a huge travesty.

In Delhi, I discover how more than 23,000 Vidya Bharati schools operated by the Hindutva movement[17] across India, teach that Jesus Christ, through his travels in the Himalayas, drew his inspiration from Hinduism. That a Hindu named Samudragupta built the Qutub Minar originally known as Vishnu Stambha, and the Taj Mahal was actually a Hindu temple known as Tejo Mahalaya (Shiva's Palace). Most interesting was the Red Fort which I discovered was a Brahmin palace that the Hindu-hater, Shah Jahan, took over and converted into his royal residence. And the most critical one—that the biggest holocaust, that is, the Partition, was in effect unleashed by the Muslims against Hindus in India.

In 2002, the NCERT undertook to rewrite Indian history texts. Its director, J.S. Rajput, remarked in an interview, 'Every country should write its history from its own point of view. Our history books have been written from a Euro-centric view because we were a colony for so long. History books should instil a sense of pride in the young mind and should be rooted in our culture.' Perhaps the difference between Pakistan and India is that, while in the former, only a handful of individuals have been raising their voices, in India, organized groups and the media actively condemned this sort of intellectual vandalism. The Indian History Congress, a large association of academic historians, in its 2002 conference, vowed to show vigilance in view of such brazen attempts to communalize textbooks and saffronize history.

P.N. Oak, head of the Institute for Rewriting Indian History, has also emerged as a revisionist icon. Oak argues in his books, *Some Blunders of Indian Historical Research* and the *Islamic Havoc in Indian History*, that contemporary Indian history is nothing but myths circulated by British historians and followed by secular Marxist and pro-Muslim Indians. Similarly, another icon for the Hindutva brigade is Francois Gautier, who with his pseudo sense of history, has reinforced that 'Hindu-bashing' has been a popular pastime among secular historians.

In 1998, a BJP minister, Murli Manohar Joshi appointed Hindutva sympathizers into the Indian Council of Historical Research. Some of them were representatives of the World Hindu Council's panel which insisted that there was a historically verifiable temple at the site of the Babri Mosque.

Another boost in revisionism was the work of Koenraad Elst titled *Negationism in India: Concealing the Record of Islam* only to be supported by Francois Gautier's book *Rewriting Indian History*. These books depict Muslims to have contributed nothing to India other than 'death, destruction and subjugation'. Gautier's words are just the inverse of those of the Pakistani right:

> Let it be said right away: the massacres perpetrated by Muslims in India are unparalleled in history, bigger than the holocaust of the Jews by the Nazis or the massacre of Armenians by the Turks, more extensive even than the slaughter of the South American native populations by the invading Spanish and Portuguese.

Gautier also provides legitimacy to the inhuman propaganda against Gandhi: 'Gandhi did enormous harm to India … for ultimately, no one contributed more to the Partition of India, by his obsession to always give in to the Muslims; by his indulgence of Jinnah, going as far as proposing to make him the Prime Minister of India.' Another poor attempt to justify the heinous stab right into the heart of post-Independence India by the fanatic Nathuram Godse.

Thus this reinvention of the past is a shared attribute. In Bangladesh, the Pakistani past has also been erased from textbooks and historical records. The leading Pakistani poet, the inimitable Fehmida Riaz, who is a favourite of mine, was disappointed during her stay in India with the growing trends of exclusion—an anathema to the plurality of India. I thought of her poem 'Naya Bharat' (New India):

> You turned out to be just like us;
> Similarly stupid, wallowing in the past,
> You've reached the same doorstep at last.
>
> Your demon [of] religion dances like a clown,
> Whatever you do will be upside down.
> You too will sit deep in thought,
> Who is Hindu, who is not.
> Keep repeating the mantra like a parrot,
> Bharat was like the land of the brave …[18]

In 1967, the Bombay High Court issued a landmark judgment on historiography and historicity that could very well be made popular across South Asia: 'History is not to serve as a handmaid of a particular school of thought. History must be impartial and objective. To rewrite history according to the views which are popular or which are necessary for bolstering up nationalistic egoism or jingoism, is perversion of history.'[19]

Irfan S. Habib, another eminent historian who would be considered a Muslim apologist, has undertaken an incisive study on the errors and half-truths in Indian textbooks.[20] Some examples are: Mughal emperor Babar deliberately chose a site for a mosque in a place where the 'tenth and last avatar of Vishnu was to appear at the end of the yuga.' Similarly, he questions: the English East India Company established in 1600 in India? India, 'a land of free looters'? Lenin leading merely a coup in Russia in 1917?[21]

Numerous such errors of commission and omission were detected by Habib and his associates. For instance, some of the textbooks have erased accounts of Akbar's social policies such as prohibition of the slave trade, disapproval of sati and prohibition of involuntary sati. Serious exclusions in dealing with the histories of kingdoms lead to an association being made between violence, cruelty and Muslims, rather than showing these as generic trends common to all medieval ruling classes.

I came across a candid personal account by India's eminent playwright, Vijay Tendulkar, wherein he recounted his experiences of studying in a school where Muslim children were stereotyped as 'butchers' and killers 'of cows and animals'.[22] Tendulkar's words were chilling:

> The bias which had been intentionally and unintentionally sown in our minds when we were children now grew into confirmed opinion. Muslims were an aggressive, rowdy, savage, rabid minority ... dogs with a cut tail. Their leaders used them for their gains and like fools, secular Hindu leaders were playing into their hands at the cost of the interests of us Hindus who were a majority but suffered at the hands of a mere minority. As a growing boy in my teens, I too held this view though not with the fanatic rage of the typical white-collared Hindu of that time.

In states where the BJP is the ruling party, college libraries have been directed to stock titles such as *Why Hindu Rashtra? Hum Mandir Wahin Banayenge* (That is where we will build the temple), *Shilanyas se Shikhar ki Ore* (From laying the foundation stone to attaining the peak), among other gems. In Gujarat, after the pogrom, the state government still pursues a relentless agenda of exclusion and demonizing the other.

However, sections of the media, vigorous citizen's groups and professional historians keep on challenging these poisonous trends. And a Dalit politician recently led the largest state of northern India, Uttar Pradesh, so all is not yet lost. How could Nehru and Gandhi disappear from the innards of contemporary India so soon?

This is why, in my 2008 visit, I noticed in the newspapers, that only a small gathering was present at the ceremony to bequeath Gandhi's ashes to the Ganga.[23] The man who taught India to be simple, self-sufficient and non-consumerist does not fit into the Delhi malls.

Perhaps, this is why I am sometimes pensive while walking around in Delhi.

NOTES

1. Translated by Mubashar Hasan.
2. S. Ikramullah, *Huseyn Shaheed Suhrawardy: A Biography*, OUP, p. 51.
3. Translation by Darshan Singh Maini in *Studies in Punjabi Poetry*, New Delhi: Vikas, 1979.
4. Translated by Panini Anand, *Outlook India*, web version, 31 October 2005.
5. Quoted in Pran Nevile's *Lahore – A Sentimental Journey*, New Delhi: Allied Publishers, 1993, p. 18.
6. Translated by the author.
7. Ajeet Caur, *Pebbles in a Tin Drum: An Autobiography*, New Delhi: HarperCollins, 1998.
8. Translated by Harbans Singh.
9. Cited in Abul Kalam Azad, *India Wins Freedom*, New Delhi: Orient Blackswan, 2000.
10. Azad has also criticized this in the following words, 'Jinnah may have raised the flag of Partition, now the real flagbearer was Patel.' *India Wins Freedom*, 1988 edition, p. 201.

11. Translation found at: http:21thecurrentaffairs.com/what-unsungminorities-have-done-for-Pakistan.html
12. Guru Tegh Bahadur was the youngest of the five sons of Guru Har Gobind. He became the ninth guru of the Sikhs on 20 March 1665.
13. A.H. Nayyar and Ahmed Salim, *The Subtle Subversion: A Report on Curricula and Textbooks in Pakistan*, Sustainable Development Policy Institute, Islamabad, 2006.
14. The ulema refers to the educated class of Muslim legal scholars engaged in several fields of Islamic studies. They are best known as arbiters of the shariah law.
15. K.K. Aziz, *Murder of History in Pakistan*, Lahore: Vanguard Books, 1993.
16. Tariq Rahman, *Language-Teaching and World View in Urdu Medium Schools*, Research Papers Series, SDPI, 1995.
17. Comprising the Bharatiya Janata Party (BJP), the Rashtriya Swayamsevak Sanstha (RSS), Vishwa Hindu Parishad (VHP), Shiv Sena and the Bajrang Dal (brigade of devout Hindus who worship the monkey god).
18. Translated by Khushwant Singh.
19. *Anant Janardan* vs *State*.
20. Irfan Habib, Suvira Jaiswal and Aditya Mukherjee, *History in the New NCERT Textbooks: A Report and an Index of Errors*, Indian History Congress, Kolkata, 2003, p. 129.
21. Parvathi Menon, 'Books of Bias and Errors', *Frontline*, Vol. 20, No. 18, 2003.
22. Tendulkar, 'Muslims and I', available at http:21www.geocities.com/indiafas/India/the_prejudice.htm
23. Nilamben Parikh, Gandhi's great-granddaughter, dispersed his ashes at Mumbai's Chowpatty beach in January 2008. Parikh is the granddaughter of Gandhi's estranged eldest son, Harilal, who did not perform his father's last rites at the burning pyre due to his differences with the Mahatma.

4

The Sultanate's Ruins

On each Thursday of my Delhi sojourn, Zeenat Aunty, Sadia's mother, would take us to Mehrauli, a township now considered part of suburban Delhi. Devotees of the Chishti shrines have to present themselves at the dargah of Khwaja Qutubuddin Bakhtiyar Kaki, whether it is the initiation of a pilgrimage to Ajmer or a culmination of prayers at Hazrat Nizamuddin's shrine. Quite appropriately, the dargah is close to the Qutub Minar in the quintessentially medieval Mehrauli.

Khwaja Kaki is the 'Qutub-ul-Aqtaab' or Qutub of all Qutubs. In Sufi parlance, a 'Qutub' is the perfect guide for a heart; literally it means a hub or axis.[1] A leading disciple of Khwaja Moinuddin Chishti, Khwaja Qutub Kaki mentored both Baba Fariduddin Ganjshakar of Pakpattan and Hazrat Nizamuddin Auliya and therefore has a central status in the Chishtiya line of Sufism. Khwaja Qutubuddin Bakhtiyar Kaki was born in 1173 in a town called Aush or Awash in Transoxania.[2] His original name was 'Bakhtiyar' and the addition to his name 'Kaki' was attributed to him because of the legendary miracle that he performed. 'Kak' was a kind of bread popular in medieval times (perhaps a precursor of the bakhar khani still sold in old Delhi), and the saint, as oral and written accounts record, created this bread for hungry visitors and devotees.

Khwaja's dargah is more sombre than Hazrat Nizamuddin with an ambience that transports the visitor back to medieval times. The unchanged architectural character is a rare treat—the alleys, tombs and arches are all reminiscent of the sultanate or early Mughal style. The mazar compound has four banyan trees at each corner of the square, and a canopy, resting on marble pillars, protects it.

It is also more formal than Hazrat Nizamuddin which has a more populist feel. Timings here are strict and I have to wear a topi before entering. Women are not allowed inside the courtyard, thanks to the patriarchal clergy. So there is a melee of women, old and young, burqa-clad and burqa-less, who stand by the screens and pray from a distance.

Just before sunset, the *dua e roshnai* commences. A local attendant comes in with offerings of flowers, incense and chadars for the grave and recites in mellifluous Persian laced with Hindustani words—'He is the leader of saints and servant of the poor.' I find this secular devotional mode quite astounding. In Pakistan the secular khuda hafiz has been thrown out by Zia-ul-Haq's Arab-centric Islamization, leading to a sort of cultural purge in the dear homeland. While life and linguistics have also changed in India, there are still little enclaves where the old world exists. Invisible to many in Delhi this is a forlorn, quirky old world.

Luckily, the tomb is not crowded and we have moments of peace. I sit in a corner outside as the doors are closed for the sunset prayer. There are endearing old men here, who must have sat here for decades. Next to Qutubuddin's tomb is the resting place of his famous disciple, Qazi Hamid Nagauri, who is remembered for his continuation of the inclusive ethos of the Chishti saints. Qutubuddin's wife, a pious woman who renounced the world along with her husband, is also buried in the vicinity adjacent to the grave of Khwaja's wet nurse. They lie in an enclosure where men are not allowed.

Zeenat Aunty, our twenty-first century follower, has adopted a *hujra* that she has restored. It was once the meditation room of Sheikh Hafiz Jafar, who served at Khwaja Qutub's dargah for over fifty years as an Imam of the mosque and happens to be the father of one of her family's spiritual mentors. Passing through the sultanate archways, little entrances and simple pavilions we reach the hujra. It is a little room with a hexagonal ceiling and the walls have little alcoves where candles or lamps must have been lit each evening.

Zeenat Aunty, Sadia and I sit there for some time in the medieval ambience. A little later, local residents of the dargah, who know aunty well, bring in the langar or communal meal, comprising a well-brewed spicy yellow dal cooked on slow heat, and rotis.

A qawwali begins as we are leaving the tomb. Legend has it that Khwaja Qutub was extremely fond of the Sama[3] and was in a trance for four days before his death or 'reunion' with Allah. The qawwal enacts this tradition with his two young sons. The qawwal children of Delhi, waiting for small tips, have contributed to centuries of Indian music and have no connection with the hi-tech urban studios of the metropolis.

As we walk back, we encounter beggars, mystics and lost souls and finally find our shoes. The same path is now dark because there are no street lights or amenities, only sewage spilling out from open drains. We see dimly lit carrom-board clubs full of Muslim boys. It is a ghetto, charming for its medieval ambience but pretty dismal otherwise.

As we are driving back, Sadia shows me the posh outlets of Delhi designers and haunts of artists who have bought properties in the area. A popular chic Italian restaurant is also located here where we plan to go on my next visit.

My next visit to the dargah is in broad daylight. I discover an old mosque, Moti Masjid or the Pearl Mosque. Sadia tells me that this mosque was built by Emperor Shah Alam in 1709. The little hidden gem is closed but we manage to see a portion of it. And, of course, we walk over to the Zafar Mahal. The abandoned empty summer palace of the last Mughal emperor is covered with graffiti. A few goats have also found a home there.

On another visit I enter the calm little mosque. Next to it is a cluster of graves screened off by a carved filigree screen of white marble. These are relatives of Zafar and there is one striking empty space—this is where Zafar wished to be buried. But events after the Mutiny of 1857 took him to Burma where he died in oblivion. An oft-quoted verse in Urdu that I grew up with emerges on the horizon like a forgotten season:

> What an unfortunate man Zafar is, for his burial
> He could not find two yards in his beloved land.

Zafar Mahal displays the later Mughal aesthetic. There is a huge gate built by Zafar known as the Haathi (Elephant) Gate. Zafar Mahal was used by the royals during the festival Phoolwalon ki sair, a multicultural event that involved Hindus, Muslims, mullahs and pundits all in one go. The wide ramp leads to the main palace, a series of structures made of marble, red sandstone and thin lakhori bricks, a speciality of the Mughal era. Few things are intact and most of the splendour has vanished.

Close to the palace are the ruins of Jahaz Mahal and the still functioning Hauz-i-Shamsi. The hauz was made on the orders of the second king of the Slave Dynasty, Sultan Iltumish, in AD 1230. We saw some residents washing clothes in it, though the original hauz was considered sacred. It was a key marker in the historical Phoolwalon ki sair festival that still takes place. This colourful procession of flowers, faithfully followed by the later Mughals, was a multi-religious event, which invited public participation and became an aesthetically charged, slow-paced marathon of medieval times. Starting from Chandni Chowk, Delhi's elite ministers and court officials would pass by various landmarks of the city, offering flowers at Hindu temples and Muslim shrines and then would end up at a grand cultural event at the Lodhi-era Jahaz Mahal. The Mahal is surrounded by a narrow moat and must have served as a royal pleasure resort in the summers. Although one of its walls has collapsed completely, it still is an elegant feature in the crowded heart of Mehrauli.

A plastered dome near the gate dates back to the fifteenth century with additions from later centuries. There are features inspired by European designs, such as a fireplace, in one of the walls. The staircase to the balcony is wide with low steps, surely modern in concept. A far cry from the slippery ancient stairs of Purana Quila where Zafar's great-grandfather Humayun fell and lost his life.

The procession of flowers, made more festive with music, would then march towards the dargah of Khwaja Qutubuddin Bakhtiyar Kaki and the Yogmaya Temple next to it. For two centuries, from the time of Akbar Shah II to Bahadur Shah Zafar until the British stopped it in 1857, every king of Delhi went to the tomb of Khwaja Bakhtiyar and also to the Yogmaya Mandir. Ghalib described it well in one of his letters:

> In this city is a festival called the 'flower men's festival'. Everyone, from nobles to artisans, goes off to the Qutub Minar. All the shops in the city of Muslims and Hindus alike stay closed throughout this time.

I was told that this procession was restarted by the government of India in the 1960s though it may have lost its earlier symbolism and mass participation. I have still not managed to attend one.

No place in Delhi displays as much historical and cultural ambiguity as Mehrauli. Signs of ancient habitation have been found here but the recorded history of the area begins from the ninth and tenth centuries when the Hindu kingdoms of the

Tomars and, later, the Chauhans made this their seat of power. The legendary Prithviraj Chauhan of Ajmer also ruled Delhi from Mehrauli. There were about twenty-seven temples as some historians have recorded.

Around the first century, Ptolemy of Alexandria recorded the existence of a city he called 'Daidala', also referred to as 'Dilli', a small town perhaps until the Tomar Rajputs adopted it as their capital in the eighth century. The Tomars built a number of monuments, including the fort of Lal Kot. The Chauhans expanded Lal Kot and rechristened it Quila Rai Pithora.

However, things were to change as numerous warring kingdoms and the absence of a central power made India an easy target for Turkish soldiers of fortune. The most infamous was, of course, Mahmud of Ghazni who supposedly 'invaded' India seventeen times, though twelve seems to be a more verifiable figure. Mahmud, filled with the zeal of his new faith, Islam, had little empathy for the ancient religious practices of India, and thus, his looting of temples, most notably the Somnath Temple in Gujarat, has become the fulcrum for historical revisionism. He was neither interested in consolidating domestic power nor in establishing an empire; rather, the wealth that he took from India was enough to glorify him back home. He did end up creating governorships in Lahore and Multan that were always vulnerable to local insurgencies. Thus he returned again and again to maintain his hold.

As historians have shown, the looting of temple wealth was not a Muslim practice per se. Local rulers also indulged in this. Power and control are not always derived through religion or compulsion of faith. However, legitimacy of power in those times was, almost always, bestowed by an eager and ever-ready clergy. The divine right to rule, govern and, if needed, plunder has always been the comfortable refuge of ambitious men and, sometimes, women.

At the end of the twelfth century, it was Mohammad of

Ghaur who finally established Turkish rule in Delhi by defeating Prithviraj Chauhan and thus became the pioneer of a tale that was to unfold and swirl over a millennium of Muslim rule, with numerous eccentric characters seeking and sustaining power. The Turks, their slaves of Central Asian descent and later the direct descendants of Tamerlane, better known as the 'Mughals', were primarily politicians, generals and rulers; their faith was almost always incidental barring a few examples such as Emperor Aurangzeb and his efforts to impose the shariah.

Qutubuddin Aibak, appointed commander by the Turkish ruler, Mohammad Ghori, captured Delhi and became its ruler in 1192. However, he did not live long. Ghori also did not live long. Though construction of many of the Mehrauli landmarks such as the Qutub Minar and water reservoirs were initiated by Aibak, for strategic reasons his main interest was Lahore where he had to contain the Mongol threat. Aibak's favourite pastime, playing polo, took his life way too soon and power fell into the hands of another 'slave', Iltutmish.

Under Iltutmish, Delhi received much importance. The ultimate sanction by Baghdad for the establishment of a sultanate in Delhi meant that the Islamicate had been established there. But he also did not live long and a war of succession led to his famed daughter, Razia, becoming the first female Muslim ruler of Delhi. She was killed shortly afterward by court intriguers and powerful nobles (courtiers who exercised tremendous influence and authority). Razia is ostensibly buried close to the dargah of Shah Turkman, a thirteenth-century Sufi of the Suharwardi order.

The line of slave rulers continued and Delhi underwent transformations and expansions with each of the sultans. During the late thirteenth century, another Delhi was created by Kaiqubad (he of the watery death), the son of Balban who ruled in relative peace and stability despite the constant fear of Mongol invasion. Kaiqubad was not the best of rulers, but he built a fort-palace, along with a surrounding township and called it Kilugarhi. The name has since been corrupted to Kilokri, a village near Maharani Bagh.

Another Delhi emerged in the early fourteenth century, when Alauddin Khilji chose Siri as the site for a fortress. Timur, the legendary Mongol, reported in his memoirs after he invaded Delhi that Siri was a fairly well-developed and populated medieval town. Today, Siri is just another large ruin with the fairy-tale fort walls disappearing piece by piece.

The Tughlaqs who ruled Delhi created Tughlaqabad. Ghiyasuddin Tughlaq (whose unusually fortified tomb stands opposite the Tughlaqabad Fort), created this city in over four years. However, he died shortly after Tughlaqabad was settled. Ghiyasuddin was a competent administrator and a builder with a keen eye for aesthetics. He was succeeded by his whimsical son, Mohammad-bin-Tughlaq, who, not content with his father's urban expansion, ordered the creation of another city to be named Jahanpanah. This was a grand urban complex which encompassed bits and pieces of the older fortifications, such as Dilli, Siri and Tughlaqabad.

History was to repeat itself as a predictable script when the third Tughlaq, Feroze Shah Tughlaq, designed and built Ferozabad in 1354. This was at the site where the present Feroze Shah Kotla exists north of the Red Fort. There is not much there either except the ruins and some clear marks of an urban centre.

Until 1533, little was added by the later sultans to the urban landscape of Delhi. The main reason was that Delhi remained a constant attraction for Mongol forces. The later sultanate dynasties—the Saiyyads and the Lodhis—were therefore more concerned with saving what they had inherited. However, under the Lodhis, several architectural innovations took place.

It was under the Mughals that Delhi was yet again reinvented, first by Humayun, who chose the ancient site of Indraprastha to settle the capital and, then, a little more than a century later, by Shah Jahan who built a city after his name that survives as a Muslim ghetto today—Old Delhi. The succeeding occupants of Delhi, the British, ventured to create the 'New Delhi' of today. Since the end of British rule, there continues till date, the migration of job seekers from other parts of India in a new invasion of Delhi.[4] Old constructs of Delhi remain layered in Mehrauli while the new Delhis are being assembled elsewhere.

It is not surprising that Mehrauli and its surrounding areas are littered with the tombs of kings, queens, princes, princesses, generals, saints and poets. It became a statement of continuity, in the political sense, to create a tomb, as well as for a personal quest for immortality that a striking building ensured. Sometimes the mausoleums were erected and adorned even before death embraced the elites.

Many tombs are not clearly marked and this perhaps helped to augment oral histories. The takhti and the kalam shapes of the graves tell us if the person buried is a male or female—the kalam, a longitudinal shape, indicates that the person buried below is male, while the takhti, a flat, rectangular shape, signifies female.

In Mehrauli, I find the tombs of Iltutmish, Balban and Alauddin Khilji. However, Razia's neglected grave is far away from Mehrauli and located in a cul-de-sac in the narrow streets of Old Delhi. Much of this heritage lies by the wayside, crumbling, neglected, at the mercy of a whimsical conservator, the Archaeological Survey of India (ASI).

Delhi's monsoon sun constantly flirts with the polluted horizons as it does in Lahore. But as I get to the Qutub Minar the air becomes most enchanting. Qutub Minar has signs and numbers of all kinds. Believed to be created through the materials of several temples, the adjoining Quwwat-ul-Islam Mosque, the later addition of Alai Darwaza and some other smaller monuments defining the edges of the Qutub Complex are eerie and intriguing. If on the one hand they tell a long story, on the other, they also narrate a tale of tragic neglect. Even though the ASI has taken several steps, the maintenance of the monuments is far from satisfactory.

The *Delhi Gazetteer* provides intricate details of the Qutub, measuring it at 238 feet and one inch, with 179 steps leading to the top. In 1803, an earthquake damaged the cupola that adorned the top of the minar. It was replaced with a Mughal pavilion by Major Robert Smith but that was found to be so out of character with the rest of the monument that Lord Hardinge ordered it to be replaced with the iron railing that one finds there today.

Architecturally, it is an oddball. It is a mosque on the platform of a temple. Animal shapes pop out with Islamic calligraphy while a sacred temple iron pillar stands in front of the mosque entrance. It is simply wondrous and a subject for detailed study. Each addition to the complex made from the time of Aibak to the Khiljis reflects the evolution of Indo-Islamic architecture. I could well understand, even as I stood there wonderstruck, how the songs of the bhakti poets resonated with this fusion. The place epitomizes the synthesis of faiths and beliefs, thus creating a newer version of composite India and adding further diversity to the land.

It is clear that the area was not abandoned until the early Mughal era. I move on after staring at the minar for some time and then find Adam Khan's tomb. This lonely structure, dating back to 1562, represents a twilight zone between the noisy outer market of Mehrauli and the ghostlike calm of the Delhi Ridge. Like several Mughal monuments, it is peaceful and more centred in its design, showing that the Muslims had established themselves and were no longer daunted by the richness of indigenous traditions. The enormous dome and heavy walls are simple and less decorated than what the Mughals were to create later.

This monument is also referred to as 'Bhool Bhulaiyan', a labyrinth. The thick walls hide secret passages that are closed to ordinary mortals like me. Adam Khan was the son of Maham Anga, one of Emperor Akbar's powerful wet nurses. When Adam murdered Atagah Khan, husband of Akbar's other wet nurse, Ji Ji Anga, Akbar had Adam killed. A devastated Maham Anga also died later and the grief-struck (and perhaps, a little guilty too) Akbar raised this octagonal tomb for his foster-mother and her unfortunate son. Atagah Khan, the lucky one, found a place in the Hazrat Nizamuddin complex and is buried close to the saint.

The rocky and undulating hill spurs, covered with keekar and beri bushes, were also documented by the *Delhi Gazetteer* of 1874. It described how the soil sparkled with mica. One can still see, amid the smog, the 'hills of Delhi' 'which, though not attractive in themselves, give a pleasant view across the Jamuna and, in clear weather, allows, it is said, even a glimpse of the Himalayas. The horizon is not as clear as suggested by British chroniclers. The wildlife of the region was also something to write home about— pigs, foxes, hares, partridges, ducks, snipes, muggers, deer, blackbucks, snakes and crocodiles were plenty along the banks of the Jamuna; even leopards were seen at Tughlaqabad.

The labyrinths of history make Mehrauli spectacularly haunting and prod me to explore more. I would need a lifetime. So I return to the monuments on a subsequent visit. Not alone this second time but with my permanent guide, Sadia Dehlvi, who is an accredited walking tour leader or a 'heritage specialist' as they say these days.

Since 2000, the Indian National Trust for Art and Cultural Heritage (INTACH) has done a remarkable job of enclosing and creating the Mehrauli Archaeological Park, and a unique park it is. There are numerous tombs, mosques and step wells that are sometimes difficult to follow. We trace the path from the main entrance. This is a peaceful walkway dotted with keekar trees and babool shrubs that meander along the snaking track. There are large signs posted, appropriately enough, on red sandstone posts.

Many families are here on this lazy Sunday morning, readying to picnic, almost unaware of where they are. Perhaps they will gobble up all the parathas and snacks in their lunch boxes first and then head towards the ruins, I joke with Sadia, who tells me off for being rude.

We first come to the tomb of Ghiyasuddin Balban, the sultan who ruled Delhi from 1265 to 1287. Getting to the tomb is a little arduous with all the bushes and rubble. But it is such a charming place with exquisite yet simple arches. 'Sunil loves Geeta' proclaimed a graffiti and then a little sketch showing a copulating couple. Ruins are an easy canvas to document sexual fantasies.

Balban's tomb, or whatever is left of it, was the resting place of the last slave sultan. Further, architecturally, this tomb displays the authentic Islamic arch—a first in India. Prior to this tomb, most buildings, including the screens around the Qutub Minar, had used corbelled arches. Corbelled arches were an indigenous form which was in vogue and were different from those of the Muslim world that had developed the art of radiating arches.

Sadia shows me the *gumti* as we reach the path again. We reach a stream that flows into the undergrowth and bushes of oblivion. The path crosses the stream and leads you to one of the most impressive structures in the park, the sixteenth-century step well known as the Rajaon ki Baoli. One can see the adjacent mosque and tomb in the shimmering light of the afternoon. This rather grand step well was built in 1506 during the reign of Sikandar Lodhi (1489–1517). The baoli was built for the masons who worked on the monuments. Adequate water supply, living quarters and a mosque ensured that this was a fitting rest house for the highly talented workers. The magnificent step well is five storeys deep with exquisitely pillared galleries on both sides and wide steps leading downwards.

Another halt for us is the twelfth-century Gandhak Baoli (sulfurous reservoir), which is the source of the stream we had passed by earlier. It is easy to miss this five-tiered baoli from the path as it rests below ground level. The narrow, sculpted pillars hold five galleries above the well and uncannily resemble the temple-like pillars of the Quwwat-ul-Islam Mosque.

Sadia is most keen for me to see the summer palace used by Delhi's fabled British resident, Thomas Metcalfe. The latter had renovated old structures to create a boathouse and a dovecote in that sprawling grandiose space. There was a time when a man-made lake nestled here, but now the emptiness of thc place, despite the enchanting ruins, is rather sad.

We find the renovated tomb of Quli Khan. The octagonal building must have been stunning when it was constructed and adorned. Little wonder that Metcalfe made it into his summer palace which he called Dilkhush. Its architecture bears the imprint of the early Mughal style. But inside the tomb, which has lovely views on all sides, there is only graffiti vandalism. There is an attempt to erase it once in a while but the visitors are unsparing. Why should they care? After all, aren't these only relics of those barbaric invaders who forced many of the natives to convert? I realize I am bitter in my reaction to the vandalism, so I look for other explanations. Perhaps they have no clue. Or maybe it is just that the present is far more important than a past buried in countervailing interpretations of history.

Metcalfe's house in the ASI Park known as Dilkhush, or Heart's Delight, underwent some interesting innovations. The sarcophagus was replaced by a billiard table and the Mughal style was fused with Georgian gateways and adorned with follies. Not just that, as an English response to the nearby Zafar Mahal, Dilkhush had a lighthouse, a small fort, a pigeon house and a boating pond!

I am completely astounded by the background of this structure. Sadia, the heritage diva, narrates the story to me in a piecemeal manner which is just the way I like it. The cacophony of trailing tour guides can be irritating sometimes. I have been told how upset Zeenat Aunty is with Sadia's new-found passion. As an old Dilli-wali, reared in grandeur, she is appalled at her daughter becoming an ordinary 'guide'. Sadia's various attempts to enlighten her on the heritage industry have had little impact.

We stand in the billiard room like ghosts and then we pass through the guest rooms and the kitchen area. His daughter Emily's book, and the letters written by Sir Thomas indicate how delightful Dilkhush was to the eccentric sahib.

Another of Metcalfe's vital contributions to Delhi is the collage of sketches and images of monuments[5] that he commissioned to an artist called Mazhar Khan. The collection with notes was presented to Emily. What a remarkable gift from a father that must have been!

Before Sir Thomas, his elder brother, Charles Metcalfe, lived in Delhi when he started his assignment as assistant to the British ambassador, Sir David Ochterlony, in 1806. Like his boss who adopted Indian ways, Charles Metcalfe created a house in the Shalimar Gardens in north Delhi and also found a native partner, a lady called Sikh Bibi whom he had met in Lahore. A pavilion and the bungalow which the senior Metcalfe had built still exist in the otherwise forlorn Shalimar Gardens.

However, it was the younger Metcalfe who imbibed India to an unprecedented degree. Sir Thomas reached Delhi around 1812. While he remained very much a sahib and, unlike his elder brother, did not indulge in a harem-fest, he was to leave a lasting legacy of Raj life. Metcalfe smoked a silver hookah, built houses that displayed his deep aesthetic appreciation of Delhi's architectural treasure trove and, perhaps unwittingly, became the precursor of modern conservation strategies. Other than the Mehrauli house, he also built a residence called Jahan Numa (World Compass) along the River Jamuna. There were English-style gardens, a library with 25,000 books and a formidable art collection.

However, the events of 1857 pressed the more intolerant and arrogant British buttons making them more and more aggressive. Thus, the firangis changed their attitude towards India, Indians and Delhi. The Empire was formally extended and the natives had to be taught many lessons.

The early years of post-1857 British rule were ruthless. Sir Thomas's son, a magistrate then, indulged in butchery and was eventually removed from his assignment.

The older Metcalfes and the youngest were all fashioned by their times and beliefs. Each one's individual attitude represented the way the Raj officials traversed within the strange and exotic India, sometimes altering their initial mercenary and extractive world views. By the late nineteenth century, however, the predictable 'white-man's-burden' belief was to assume a central position in the imperial discourse. Belittling 'Mohammedans' and their legacies, including their monuments, became a matter of paramount importance. The destruction of Shahjahanabad and Mehrauli after 1857 bears testimony to this fact.

The sixteenth-century mosque and tomb of Jamali Kamali are the glory of the ASI Park in Mehrauli. The mosque with its central arch square is soulful and is a perfect place to spend one's afternoon in seclusion. The fairly well-preserved tomb is perhaps the hidden jewel within the meandering folds of the ASI Park. The intricate patterns on its ceiling, painted in bright colours of blue and ochre, reflect the intimacy of the twin graves. The burly, smiling caretaker lets us in. His polite manner, given that he is an underpaid state employee in what appears to be a boring job, is a surprise. The twin graves, Jamali and Kamali, friends and muses, are located next to each other.

The construction of this monument began during the reign

of Babar, the first Mughal emperor. The sultanate features are apparent in its design; however, the arch also heralds the advent of Persian influence via the new ruling class.

Jamali was the nom de plume of the saint poet, Shaikh Fazlullah who lived through the reigns of Sikandar Lodhi, Babar, Sher Shah and Humayun. Kamali's antecedents are blurred. Some say he was the beloved mentor of Jamali, but whatever be the case, the intimacy between the two is beyond the blurred lines of doubt. That they rest in peace under a magnificently painted ceiling with Indic, Turkic and Persian motifs implies that they were meant to be together even in death.

The master–disciple closeness in Sufism or other mystical orders cannot be fully understood from the 'outside'. Rumi and Shams, Hazrat Nizamuddin and Khusrau, Sarmad and Abhay Chand, Jamali and Kamali, would appear as avant-garde men of their times (as society did not take to them very kindly) for they expressed a particular same-sex intimacy, which may convey homo-erotic undertones in contemporary studies of their relationships. However, be that as it may (or may not), it was also about arriving at the 'common goal of divine love' rather than just a pursuit of desires of the flesh. Today, these powerful, spiritual relationships are considered 'hip' and celebrated in various festivals.

Sadia and I sit silently outside Jamali Kamali for several minutes and imbibe the peace. Nearby, a small group of female labourers are carrying, rearranging and chiselling stones. Wearing tattered saris, they are quite oblivious to what the place is all about. They are from Madhya Pradesh and have come for work under the government's employment generation scheme and earn one hundred rupees a day. For a flash, the state of the ruins and the priorities of modern India make sense.

Accidents in one's mundane life can be dramatic. One such event was my getting to know the singer, Vidya Rao. Initially, this acquaintanceship was through the Internet as she became a regular reader of my claptrap blogs. But in due course we crossed cyber lines to become real friends. And where does Vidya live? In Mehrauli with her adorably lazy and attention-hungry cat, Sufi. The white Sufi was found by Vidya at the Hazrat Nizamuddin dargah. As I discover, Vidya is also aware of the fondness of Prophet Mohammad for cats.

Within months, I received books that she was editing for a publishing house as well as illustrations and CDs of her music. Another Delhi connection constructed with such joyous unpredictability and musicality.

Vidya Rao is a performer of the delicate style of thumri-dadra. Endowed with a voice like that of a nightingale, she has been a disciple of the celebrated singer, the late Naina Devi. As I find out, Vidya later studied with Shanti Hiranand and the eminent Girja Devi. Her initial training in the more strictly classical khayal style was under the late Professor B.N. Datta and thereafter under Pandit Mani Prasad. Thus, Vidya's musical journey criss-crosses Delhi, for khayal's great-grand ancestors were the Sufi singers at Delhi shrines.

Vidya also sings folk styles such as Kajri, Chaiti and Hori and dabbles in the Urdu ghazal. Not content with this endless list, she sings the devotional poetry of medieval bhakti and Sufi saints, splashing her talents on to the elegiac Islamic terrains of Soz, Marsiya and Noha (performative styles that lament the martyrdom of Prophet Mohammad's grandson and his family at Karbala), and praise-forms such as Naat (Urdu or Persian poetic eulogies for Prophet Mohammad). Ostensibly, these are 'Muslim' forms as one would note in the contested climes of our world, but Vidya's vision and talents cross these lines. A renaissance woman, Vidya collaborates with other musicians as well as artistes from other disciplines such as painters, writers and theatre persons, to create innovative works.

It is from Vidya that I learnt about the indigenous eulogies for

Prophet Mohammad, once popular in Uttar Pradesh and which are delightfully syncretic and earthy—'*Tore gumbad ki hariyali ho, to pyaas bujhe in nainan ki*' (The greenness of your tomb, O Prophet, will quench the thirst of my eyes). Today in Medina, Muslims are forbidden to touch and celebrate their proximity to Mohammad's tomb as it is considered to be irreligious according to the tenet of Wahabi Islam. South Asian Muslims remain a different creed despite the growing influence of Wahabi ideology through petro dollars and the Pakistani state's strategic alliances with Saudi Arabia.

When we meet in her cosy Mehrauli apartment, with the view of the Qutub Complex almost like a painting in her living room, Vidya tells me, 'Poets, artists, singers, dancers, mystics, ordinary men and women have, over the centuries, filled in the stitches of this beautiful fabric of my culture. Like Kabir, I take it in my hands and sing how the tapestry created over centuries, torn as it may be, defines me and protects me.'

Vidya and I sit there and talk about her recent work with a team that is producing short films on Kabir's poetry and music while Sufi the cat, feeling neglected, snoozes on a large red cushion. She also tells me that, in addition to Sufism, Buddhism appeals to her. Each year, Vidya spends several days in a monastery hidden somewhere in the Himalayas. Her music is the vehicle of her inner search and her spirituality her strength.

In those memorable conversations that took place in Delhi's freezing December or crispy spring, Vidya inspired me with her 'belongingness' and pride in an inclusive culture. She wrote to me once:

> There is an extraordinary good fortune that is mine, to be born here—woman, singer, Indian, to be heir to this shimmering tapestry that is my history and my culture. Where else but here, how else but being born who I am, could I claim as my birthright the songs of the Qawwals of the dargah of Hazrat Moinuddin Chishti and Hazrat Nizammudin Aulia, the chanting of hymns

> at Kashi Vishvanath, the silence of Sarnath, the heat of the rocks on Arunachala Hill, the icy cold of Himalayan snow, the blue of the western sea and the sentinel boulders of the Deccan?

Intrigued as a Pakistani by a Hindu woman singing Muslim devotional poetry and songs, Vidya further surprised me:

> Where else could I claim the right to speak in a hundred languages, all mine, all deeply loved? Where else worship in a thousand different ways, where thrill to the touch of the charming Kanha, where lose myself in the complex metaphysics of Nalanda, where weep and mourn the martyrs of Karbala? Where else could I rejoice to see the flames of the blooming tesu and semal, and the lace of kachnar blossoms, where fill my lungs with the scent of re-born rain-washed earth?

After our first meeting, at Sadia's dinner party, Vidya transformed everyone's mood with her thumris, including the one by the late Begum Akhtar in a concert in Pakistan, lamenting her separation from her beloved and then reconciling with it by finding meaning in it. Vidya's repertoire is vast and intense and I dare say, a bit eccentric. What a sensation she would be if she were to visit Pakistan and sing in Lahore and Karachi, that is, if the visa regime was not so tragically myopic. In Delhi we make fanciful plans only to forget them soon.

Over the years, Vidya has also started to contribute to my blog, to comment on various posts, bringing a capacious depth marked with music and philosophy, silence and meditation, to my musings in cyberspace. So keeping in touch is now an effortless game.

One day, at the Café Turtle in Khan Market, Vidya also introduced me to Shubha Mudgal, another well-known musician. Shubha is a cheerful and friendly person devoid of the self-important nonsense that stars are usually known for. Her collaboration with Pakistani artist, Salman Ahmed of the band Junoon, was a hit a few years ago. Based on the ancient

Sufi rhythm of ghoom tana, symbolizing the divine wheel that weaves life, it was a celebration of the borderless-ness of music and the inseparable-ness of the musical heritage of India and Pakistan. This explains why, despite official and state posturing, Bollywood music is such a rage in both Pakistan and Bangladesh, not to mention classical music.

NOTES

1. Meanings for the word 'Qutub' include pivot, pole, axis and celebrity.
2. Also Transoxiana (Latin), literally meaning 'across the Oxus River', it is the ancient name used for the portion of Central Asia corresponding approximately with modern Uzbekistan, Tajikistan and south-west Kazakhstan. The region was one of the satrapies of the Achaemenid dynasty of Persia under the name 'Sogdiana'. (Wikipedia<http://en.wikipedia.org/wiki/Transoxiana>).
3. 'Sama' is a Sufi ceremony. These rituals often include singing, playing instruments, dancing, recitation of poetry and prayers and wearing symbolic attire. It is a particularly popular form of worship in the Chishti order of the Indian subcontinent.
4. The 2001 census survey revealed that the total population of Delhi at 13.8 million comprised 8.2 million people from within Delhi and 5.3 million migrated population from other states of India. The local migrant identities have also blurred now. The *Economic Survey of Delhi* 2007–08 records that the influx of population from other states has been estimated at 203,000 whereas growth due to natural increase in Delhi was comparatively less at 224,000 in 2006. Independence and the population movements led to migrants creating many Delhis defined by ethnicity and class.
5. *The Delhi Book* is now in the possession of the British Library as discovered by William Dalrymple.

5

Earth's Music

Raj Kumar Hardev, a prince of Deogarh, a principality located in the Deccan in southern India, was an eccentric character. He came to meet Hazrat Nizamuddin Auliya, and ended up staying at his khanqah for years, eventually converting to Islam. He rose to occupy the powerful position of prime minister under Mohammad Shah Tughlaq, whose daughter he had married during his stay in Delhi. He lost his life in the labyrinths of intrigue that characterized Delhi courts in those days. But his legacy for succeeding generations is his memoir, *Chahal Roza*.[1]

Allaudin Khilji had sent one of his commanders, Khwaja Hasan Sanjri, to Deogarh to secure the allegiance of the southern kingdom to the Delhi Sultanate. Hardev met Sanjri at the latter's military camp and heard of the famous saint, Hazrat Nizamuddin Auliya, in Delhi. Sanjri narrated how the pir's teachings inspired the negation of worldly pursuits. Hardev inquired what sort of healer the master was. Sanjri declared that Hazrat Nizamuddin cured the malaise of the heart. 'He is a Sayyad,[2] his name is Sayyad Mohammad and people call him the sultan of sheikhs,' Sanjri added. The description of the pir charmed Hardev immensely, and a few days later, he left the Deccan for Delhi to meet Sanjri's pir.

In the days to come, Hardev lived at the khanqah and entered the inner circle of companions of Hazrat Nizamuddin Auliya. Such was the inclusive environment at the khanqah that Hardev converted to Islam. It is through his journal, *Chahal Roza*, that we get an authentic, first-hand account of Hazrat Nizamuddin's life and views and also his extraordinary relationship with Amir Khusrau.

Over seven centuries ago, Hardev wrote on the genesis of the Urdu language:

> In a special majlis tonight, Hazrat sent for me along with Sanjri, Amir Khusrau, Khwaja Sayyad Mohammad and my relatives, Sumbul Dev, Seetal Dev and Jeetal Dev. When we were all present, Hazrat instructed us saying, 'You all must get together and prepare a language that the Hindu residents of India and the Muslims who have entered India can both use easily to communicate in dealing with one another.' Then addressing Amir Khusrau and Khwaja Sayyad Mohammad he said, 'I mentioned this to you both before also.' Amir Khusrau informed him that he was already working on a children's reader for which he had chosen the title *Ikhlaq-e-Bari*; he then recited some verses from *Ikhlaq-e-Bari*. Hazrat liked the verses very much. He went on to say, 'This too is a very useful work but write such verses in the Hindi language which people can understand.'[3]

Centuries later when my children hold an Urdu Qaeda,[4] I cannot help but remember this conversation that must have taken place in the magical kingdom that was Hazrat Nizamuddin's khanqah.

Hardev also relates how Hazrat Nizamuddin instructed Muslim and Hindu musicians to prepare songs in Hindavi, which later blossomed into Urdu or Hindustani. He is reported to have said:

> Nowadays, many Hindi words have been mixed with our Persian language and Khusrau's Turkish language and people

> have begun to use these Hindi words in gatherings and in their homes. But there are others who do not want the mixture of Hindi words in Arabic, Persian and Turkish languages. They must be made to understand that it is advantageous to them ... this can only come about when they stop being stubborn and help the spread of Hindi languages.

Musing in the derelict Urdu bookshops in Nizamuddin Basti, I wonder if the RSS, post-Independence Pakistani jingoists for that matter, have ever bothered to read this testament. Regardless of the way politics changed things, Khusrau's songs are sung across South Asia.

The arrival of spring and the harvest season has been celebrated ever since man discovered land tilling as a means of sustenance. The Basant (spring) festival is also celebrated with much fanfare in my hometown, Lahore. Over time, this festival has fallen victim to corporate distastefulness on the one hand, and religious bigotry on the other. Oblivious to both trends, Lahoris have continued to celebrate it.

And in Delhi, nothing is more spectacular than the fusion of colour, music, chaos and serenity during the Basant celebrations at Hazrat Nizamuddin's dargah.

> Rejoice, my love, rejoice,
> It's spring here, rejoice!
> Bring out your lotions and toiletries
> And decorate your long hair.
> Oh, you're still enjoying your sleep, wake up.
> Even your destiny has woken up,
> It's spring here, rejoice!
> You snobbish lady with arrogant looks,
> The King Amir is here to see you.
> Let your eyes meet his,
> Oh my love, rejoice!
> It's spring here again!

Hardev's shadow walks with me on my daily visits to the

tombs of Amir Khusrau and Hazrat Nizamuddin. The shadow whispers in my ears. The street is noisy, yet I hear him clearly:

> I heard that today is the early spring festival of the fifth of the lunar month, and I see crowds of people, hands full of mustard blossoms, heading for the mandir nearby which was supposed to be a shrine to Kalkaji Devi … I was standing outside with these thoughts when I saw Amir Khusrau coming from the direction of the khanqah of Hazrat and I ran towards him … I was surprised to see that he too was carrying mustard blossoms in his hands and I asked, 'are you going to the spring festival with the Hindus too?'[5]

Both Amir Khusrau and Hardev then walk in search of Hazrat Nizamuddin. They find him in a melancholic state as he has lost a close member of the family. Amir Khusrau cheers him by placing the yellow blossoms (mustard flowers) at his feet and, speaking in Hindavi, informs him, 'My Arab friend, I'm celebrating your Basant.' That day, the Hindus were going to place the yellow flowers of Basant at their deities' feet. And he was following this by adulating his pir and strewing flowers at his feet:

> People say that I am indulging in idol worship
> Yes yes, I do it! People have nothing to do with it …

And then Khusrau sings this verse, for the day of Basant:

> Shed tears of joy at the coming of spring and clouds
> O cupbearer, bring out wine and strew flowers …

Hardev sees it all. The moment Amir Khusrau, sings the verse in his melodious voice, he is joined in the song by Hazrat Nizamuddin's other companions. Hazrat Nizamuddin himself is in tears and he stands up and begins to whirl. Khusrau and the other two companions present recite Hindavi and Persian verses while singing. Hazrat Nizamuddin continues to whirl in an ecstatic state. When the initial torrent of emotion subsides, Hazrat Nizamuddin picks up the mustard flowers and takes them to the grave of his relative and says, '*Ashq rayz ameedan abro bahar*' (Shed tears of joy at the coming of spring and the clouds).

On that electric afternoon, Hazrat Nizamuddin asks Khusrau if he was coming back to the khanqah with him. Khusrau answers with more poetry:

> Many a night has poor Khusrau not slept in the desire
> that he may sleep with eyes resting under the blessed feet
> of Hazrat Nizamuddin.

This was not unrequited devotion, and Hazrat Nizamuddin quickly retorted:

> Even if a saw is placed upon my brow to part me from my
> Turk (Khusrau),
> Even then I will not give up my Turk ...

This master–disciple relationship went beyond known Sufi associations. Their common understanding of society, politics and cultural nuances also informed this celebrated relationship. Hardev states that Hazrat Nizamuddin also recited the famous 'Man tu shudam' (I have become you):

> I have become you, you have become me
> I am the spirit, you are the body ...

At this, Khusrau, overwhelmed, clung to Hazrat Nizamuddin's feet and sang:

> So that no one can say after this that you are another and I
> am another ...

The birds must have dotted the clear, crisp spring sky on that auspicious day, and the fragrance of the season must have mixed with the intoxication of this love. In this spell, the master utters these words about his loving disciple:

> Get up Khusrau. On the Day of Judgment, when everyone will
> come before their Lord with their Book of Deeds and my Lord,

after seeing my Book of Deeds, will inquire from me, 'Nizam what have you brought me from the world, I will answer, I have brought you the gift of the devotion of Khusrau's heart.'[6]

Many centuries ago, Hardev must have stood where I stand today, in complete awe. These monotheists, of the same faith as the invaders, were singing strange tunes and whirling. Who were they, and what madness had overtaken them? Look at the Turk Khusrau circling around the master whom he also calls the beloved. What a beatific state of frenzy this is! Tears welled up in the corners of his two bright Turkish eyes as he sang the verse:

> The pilgrims at Mecca search for the House
> But I search for the Master of the House.

Thus the celebration of Basant became an annual festival at the khanqah, and, now, at the tomb of Hazrat Nizamuddin Auliya. Other khanqahs of the Chishti order followed suit. The local shrine keepers tell me about the whole process: 'The qawwals from the dargah collect mustard flowers each Basant and then start offering them to the mazars of the various Chishti saints. After that they return to the Hazrat Nizamuddin dargah.' Around the dargah in the basti, there are several signs of the Basant day, such as the dyeing of the clothes in yellow or the basanti colour. Basanti caps and scarves are worn, and qawwalis are sung after offering fatiha[7] at the tombs and graves in the vicinity. Today, the Basant festival has become a ritual which lacks the original spirit. But colourful and festive it is.

Maheshwar Dayal, in his book, *Alam Mein Intekhab: Dilli*, describes one such Basant Festival in Delhi during the time of Bahadur Shah Zafar (1837–57) in the following words:

> ... the chill was on the decline. Spring had arrived. Dilli wallahs were setting up fairs for the spring as usual. Many were offering flowers and ittar on the Qadm Sharif.[8] It was a Thursday. There

> was such a crowd that not a hair's breadth of space was empty on either the Red Fort maidan or the shores of the Jamuna. The curtains of houses, the chadars of women, the turbans of men, and the clothes of children—everything was dyed basanti—even the candles hanging from the rampart were basanti. It was as if mustard was growing in every nook and corner. Indoors and outdoors, people danced the whole night. Thousands of giant balloons made of mustard-coloured paper with candles lit inside were being flown in the air. By four o'clock in the morning, the whole sky became basanti. It seemed as if the mustard was flowering in the eyes of the sky.

Amir Khusrau's passionate devotion to Hazrat Nizamuddin is legendary. Khusrau, of Turkish parentage, was taken by his family to Hazrat Nizamuddin when he was a young boy. From that first encounter till the moment of the latter's death, they were close to each other. Khusrau was a friend, a disciple, a khanqah poet and a musician; in short, the life of Hazrat Nizamuddin's era in Delhi. Khusrau did not live for long after the death of Hazrat Nizamuddin. In fact, the latter had once expressed that had it been allowed by Islamic law, he would have wished to be buried in the same grave as Khusrau.

While Khusrau was a noble at the Delhi court and served under several sultans, his heart lay elsewhere. He was a poet of outstanding merit, an innovator and pioneer of the Hindustani idiom. In addition, he was a Sufi disciple and learnt of 'love' through an experiential process rather than through conventional instruction.

The urs rituals[9]—the death anniversaries of Hazrat Nizamuddin and Amir Khusrau—are two other events that are celebrated with much fanfare. For the Sufi, death is not an occasion to mourn since the departure from the temporal world is but the ultimate destination for a mystic reunion with the Creator, the cosmic beloved. Satrahvin Sharif (Blessed Seventeenth) after Eid-ul-Fitr is the death anniversary of Hazrat Amir Khusrau.

As luck would have it, I was in Delhi when the annual urs rituals were taking place not far from Sadia's house. I was in town on business and managed to visit the dargah only in the evening. The ecstatic qawwalis and music enchanted me. The charaghan or lighting of the lamps had transformed the dargah compound into a magical space. The tradition of Sufi qawwali is attributed to Khusrau as he introduced Arab and Turkish musical instruments and enriched the traditions of Indian classical music. Khusrau's poems and odes are still sung today.

The feminine voice in Sufi devotion invokes the divine feminine principle and likens their love to a man–woman relationship. Khusrau's sensuous odes to his murshid[10] enshrine the poetry and music of devotion. There is also the incorporation of native Indian traditions and popular beliefs borrowed from the vocabulary of sacrifice, self-abnegation of women for their husband-gods, and their families:

> Beholding your appearance, oh Nijaam[11]
> I offer myself in sacrifice.
> Amongst all the girls, my scarf is the most soiled,
> Look, the girls are laughing at me.
> This spring, please dye my scarf for me,
> Oh Nijaam, protect my honour.
> In the name of Ganj-e Shakar[12]
> Protect my honour, oh beloved Nijaam.
> Qutab and Farid have come in the wedding procession
> And Khusrau is the loving bride, oh Nijaam.
> Some have to fight with the mother-in-law,
> While some with sisters-in-law,
> But I have you for support, oh Nijaam.

Another popular legend surrounding the festival of Basant at the Chishti khanqahs is that Khusrau had dressed up as a woman in yellow with mustard flowers on Basant day.

In the subcontinent, the use of the feminine voice has been a common tradition. Bulleh Shah and Waris Shah, two prominent

Punjabi poets, also used the female voice as the ideal form of love-devotion. The poet-disciple presents himself as a woman while the Creator or the murshid is depicted as male:

> Hey, I've just had an affair with my darling,
> Don't care what the neighbourhood girls say;
> Just had an affair with my darling.
> Oh, his beautiful face, charming like an idol,
> I've just made a place in the bottom of his heart.
> I, Khusrau, give my life to Nizamuddin in sacrifice,
> I've just had him call me his most favourite disciple.
> Don't care what the neighbourhood girls say,
> Just had an affair with my darling[13]

In the north Indian tradition, prevalent in Pakistan, India as well as Bangladesh, the Sufi imagines himself to be a bride, where the babul ka ghar or the father's home is a metaphor for the temporal world, while the *piya* or beloved, with his home and in-laws, is the final destination symbolizing the culmination of a journey. Little wonder that what is sung at the dargahs is rendered tearfully:

> ... dear Khusrau, you have to go to your in-laws' alone;
> no friends will accompany you now.

I slip into a reverie as Arman, Sadia's son, sings for us. An ustad from Old Delhi comes twice a week to train him. Arman, admittedly a small exception to the general rule of forgetting, keeps up the tradition of musicality in the Nizamuddin area. For this was the very place where Hindustani music found newer dimensions, adopting many streams from the Islamic world to become what it is today.

The curious melange of musical fusion in north India started with Arab and Mongol incursions into India. However, it was the arrival of the Sufis and their accompanying musicians that served as a catalyst to the emergence of contemporary Hindustani classical music as we know it today. The engagement began with the bhakti movement's yogic ideas, initiating a process of inclusive sociability at the core of which was the ability of Hindavi, and later the Urdu language to express metaphysical thought; and it was this that found an immediate audience.

The famous music composer A.R. Rahman's devotion to the Chishti saints and the naming of his music conservatory in southern India after Khwaja Moinuddin of Ajmer, is a continuation of this vibrant, ongoing and, very possibly, endless process.

It is widely believed that Amir Khusrau founded the popular Hindustani musical tradition. His training with Nayak Gopal, a Hindu musical guru of the fourteenth century, is symbolic of the interfaith musical dialogue which took place in medieval Delhi. Khusrau's two shaagirds—Samat and Nigar—had been given into his tutelage by Hazrat Nizamuddin Auliya in order to enhance their spirituality and give their devotion a musical expression and purpose.

These two exceptionally gifted disciples are said to have created the line of Qawwal Bachche.[14] This eclectic lineage became the musical manifestation of the Chishti khanqahs and dargahs, leading to the evolution of the classical khayal in the nineteenth century. The Hazrat Nizamuddin dargah thus became a site that facilitated musical experimentation through the centuries and also inspired other musicians and singers in the Chishti centres of Ajmer, Multan, Ajodhan and Delhi. Music then became a focal point for literary and cultural exchanges.

The Pakistani qawwal Nusrat Fateh Ali Khan and his ancestors also belonged to this network of Chishti-inspired musicians. He is said to have been blessed by the dargahs of Hazrat Nizamuddin and Ajmer prior to his appearance on the world stage.

Qawwali was not the only innovation conjured up by the enigmatic Khusrau. He pioneered musical forms such as the qaul, ghazal, tarana, naqsh-o-gul and khayal, and improvised existing percussion forms into the tables, as the legend goes. Khusrau somehow connected the musical experimentation taking place from Spain to the borders of China as he incorporated musical traditions from Persia, Spain, Turkey and Arabia, and synthesized them in the Indian context.

Little wonder that today, qawwals often communicate effortlessly with global audiences despite singing in an alien language. However, the key to this dynamic is the reliance on a certain musical style and rhythm to create an ambience, reach a trance-like state and generate ecstasy for listeners and performers alike. The appeal of qawwali outside South Asia is therefore its uncanny universal strength in awakening the consciousness of listeners. Qawwals hold that the experience of the transportation of the soul, or reaching the divine, also known as 'ma'rifat', requires little textual aid. Thus, the possibility of a direct mystical experience is inherent in the qawwali form.

Khusrau's contribution to musical culture as a synthesis of local and foreign devotional traditions established a base for the Mughals to further nourish this sensibility. Dialogue with indigenous and folk traditions continued, and fusion deepened. Even today, while walking around Chandni Chowk, I can hear these fused and merged tunes blaring out of a BJP political camp. Such are the ironies of history.

A few hundred yards away, Sadia's talented son, Arman Ali, has been playing the tabla since the age of seven, and intends to master the intricacies of his instrument and the musical tradition of the Dilli gharana. Arman, in his twenties, has mastered a centuries-old tradition, which is threatening to die out. Once, Delhi's musicians played for the Mughal emperors. Today, a minuscule group of classical musicians lives in a neighbourhood of Old Delhi, struggling to keep themselves and the gharana alive. The seventeenth-century neighbourhood of the walled city still houses many descendants of the musical geniuses of the past.

Arman's ustad, Mustafa Husain, hails from Daryaganj in Old Delhi and complains: 'People are ignoring classical music and pop music, is the order of the day.' He adds, 'We have to rediscover our traditions.' The families now survive on individual patrons such as Arman's family. Classical music is not easy to learn, and requires patience and a lifetime of dedication. It needs patronage to survive as a continuously evolving art form. Corporate groups now support classical music concerts in various parts of Delhi as well as outside. But still, many musicians resort to doing 'popular' concerts at weddings and elite parties to make a living.

Daryaganj and its alleyways are choked with foodstalls, autorickshaws and motorbikes. I wanted to visit the area since I had heard such legendary tales about this locality. However, walking there amidst the dense housing and layouts was a struggle. There are people everywhere, but this area of Shahjahanabad, or Old Delhi, is as forlorn as the musicians who live there. It is clear that no one really cares about the value and symbolism of this place.

Musicians have lived here for centuries. There is a sense of rootedness and bonding which keeps these families here. As I stroll through the musicians' lane I hear sweet music and, the frenetic pace of the street notwithstanding, these are moments of sheer magic. One shopkeeper tells me that there is a continuous sound of singing or instruments being played wafting from a window. Despite the abysmal conditions, it is impressive that they manage to keep Delhi's fading traditional music alive.

In Nizamuddin Basti too, traditional qawwals flourish against all odds. Ustad Meraj Ahmed, a direct descendant of Ustad Tanras Khan, who was a royal singer at the court of the Mughal emperor Bahadur Shah Zafar, is perhaps the greatest qawwal living here. His troupe was asked by Deepa Mehta to sing a qawwali for her film, *Fire.* They were paid well but were shocked when they finally saw the film—they just had a two-minute appearance and the film was about a homosexual relationship between two women! Tauba tauba! It is interesting to note here that these qawwals also sing bhajans for Hindu festivities like Devi jagarans (singing all night and keeping vigil in honour of the mother goddess) and are also hired to sing at cocktail parties.

The advent of Islam gradually influenced ancient ragas and talas, and generated newer musical genres and instruments.[15] For instance, since the nineteenth century, Indian classical music has seen the flourishing of the khayal genre, which embodies the culmination of this syncretic process that has existed for nearly seven centuries.[16] Khayal entails a repertoire of short bandishey where the vocalist employs a few lines of poetry as a means of impromptu yet rule-based improvisation. The singing is accompanied by the tabla and often a harmonium, sarangi, violin or dilruba. Khayal's basic components are rooted in the religious, folk and theatrical music of India, but its present-day form has its roots in the musical renditions at Persian courts and Sufi khanqahs in India.

Linear versions of history hold that Indian music, a monolith since Vedic times, was interrupted by Muslim influences on the shuddha 'Marga' tradition. However, this is too simplistic an analysis as the complex bundle of traditions, collectively known as 'Indian classical music', evolved through different ages and accepted several influences such as the developments of the Gupta period and then of Buddhism. However, musicologists note that from the twelfth century onwards, Islamic elements started merging into the diverse streams of existing north Indian music, making it a rich mosaic of multiple traditions. It should be clarified that the classical music of peninsular India, Carnatic music, remains largely uninfluenced by Muslim traditions. Khusrau was a pioneer of this merger, and created the 'Hindustani' (north Indian) musical tradition which was a fusion of Indo-Islamic elements, both musical and linguistic. This tradition came to inform the devotional and court-centred cultural developments in medieval India.

During the later sultanate period, from the fourteenth to sixteenth centuries, classical music was patronized by and shaped in regional kingdoms such as Jaunpur, Gwalior and Bijapur, reaching its pinnacle in the succeeding Mughal courts.[17] Akbar's court, for example, saw the ascendancy of dhrupad. Originating as devotional singing at Hindu temples, dhrupad's ancestry can be traced back to the Vedas. The name is derived from dhruva-pada or refrain, and refers to both a poetic form and a musical style. Unlike its successor, the khayal, dhrupad is more austere without too many minute embellishments. However, like the khayal, it is modal, employing a single melodic line in one particular raga or formalized framework of melodic rules.

The maturity of Indian classical music during Akbar's reign coincided with the increased use of regional dialects, which was a legacy of bhakti poetry and songs. Myriad forms entered Mughal music, which included the Arab, Persian and Khurasani musical styles; it also included the various qawwali styles and ghazals. Devotional Hindu temple music and regional influences—all converged into the hybrid known as 'Hindustani classical music'.

As music evolved during the medieval era, hierarchies emerged among masters and disciples. At the top were the kalawants and baykars;[18] qawwals and dhadhis fell into the second category. These hierarchies were not fixed, but shifted constantly as and when they attained mastery over certain forms. Qawwali was popular as was dhrupad. However, by the eighteenth century, khayal assumed the status of high culture.

A chance meeting with musicologist Lakshmi Subramanian in a restaurant on the India International Centre's rooftop was enlightening. She and her co-author, Jon Barlow, write:

> In instrumental music, as in vocal music, the advent of the Muslims brought about profound and far-reaching changes. Muslim musicians brought with them Persian and Khurasani instruments; the chang, a harp/zither, the rabab and barbat, respectively skin-covered and wooden topped lutes, the tambur or the long-necked lute with a wooden sound-board that would later be hybridised with the been to become the Indian tanpura. They had various forms of fiddles including a bowed rabab, a prototype of the early sarangi.[19]

As I dug deeper into this musical kaleidoscope thanks to Lakshmi's enduring research, and the anecdotes I had picked up from my father and a music-obsessed friend in Pakistan, the little pieces started to connect. Attending concerts in Delhi and listening to the music teacher at Sadia's house, I was amazed at how these ancient and medieval musical notes had pervaded centuries of conflict and confluence and generations of coexistence.

Tansen, that most well known of Mughal maestros, taught his disciples a dhrupad-inspired method of playing the rabab. His talented son-in-law, Naubat Khan, revolutionized Indian instrumental music by experimenting with string instruments and introducing complex, innovative melodies that were also assimilative of different local traditions. Within the span of a few centuries, the simple melodies of the Nizamuddin Basti had evolved into a high art form at the splendid Mughal court. However, with the decline of the sultans and the Mughal preference for Agra and Lahore, it was not until the reign of Shah Jahan that Delhi once again became the musical capital of northern India.

After Shah Jahan, music in Delhi again witnessed a decline during Aurangzeb's rule, but regional kingdoms made up for it. But, for most of the eighteenth and early nineteenth centuries, Delhi was the crucible of experimentation, expanding the contours of artistic and cultural endeavours. After the city was ravaged in the late eighteenth century and with the decline of the power and resources of the Mughal court, patronage was shared by regional and local nobles and other influential people. But until the time of Bahadur Shah Zafar, classical music, qawwali and other forms continued to evolve in Delhi.

Historical accounts suggest that Aurangzeb wanted to bury music deep under the earth so that no echo of it would rise again. Following this stern diktat, his withdrawal of patronage of music in 1667[20] lasted almost thirty years. A crisis was triggered that forced the high musicians to look for alternative patronage. During this time, the kalawant musicians or leading artists, started to imbibe the stylistic features of the qawwals.[21]

For a long time, Delhi remained unaffected by the decline of the Mughal Empire as its rich trader-merchant class and nobles continued to patronize the arts. The mystical spaces of Delhi, such as dargahs and khanqahs, contributed to the augmentation and sustenance of music. During the eighteenth century, the Chishti Sufi school underwent a revival under Shaikh Kalim Ullah (1650–1729) and his successors, notably Shah Fakhruddin, who converted Delhi once again to be the focal point for Chishti Sufi practices including Sema (the ceremony of the whirling dance) and qawwali. The Naqshbandi[22] order also was undergoing a shift under scholars such as Shah Waliullah (1703-63), and the Delhi-based Sufi, Mazhar Jan-e-Janaan. Celebrations of Sufi saints in Delhi increased during this time[23] and eyewitness accounts bear testimony to this trend.[24] Delhi's musical culture was complex; the wealthy displayed extravagance in musical practices while the shrines and khanqahs promoted music with simplicity and austerity.

But it was under Mohammad Shah Rangeela (1719-48), buried in the Hazrat Nizamuddin dargah complex, that Delhi became the epicentre of musical experimentation and the refinement of the khayal. During this time, Niamat Khan, the celebrated kalawant, improvised on original compositions of the khayal and took conventional dhrupad to new heights. Working under the nom de plume 'Sadarang' (ever colourful), Niamat's compositions found wide appeal in Delhi. Noting this person's genius, Mohammad Shah Rangeela, who had expelled him earlier, had to recall him to the court and accept his creativity which exalted his *beenkari* to the status of the singing of dhrupad.[25] As learned musicologists have noted, 'It also marked the entry of khayal, albeit via the zenana (through the mad-hatter queen, Lal Kunwar, wife of one of Aurangzeb's grandsons), into the domain of court music, an important step on its route to becoming the dominant secular form.'[26]

Dhrupad became the core and the been, 'ang', a vital component of Niamat Khan's rendition of the khayal and of his innovation, the bara khayal, which was a slower and more intense version of the fast-tempo original.

Niamat Khan 'Sadarang' and his disciples added many rich layers to vocal music and endowed a high stature to instruments such as the sitar, sarod, surbahar, sarangi and tabla. Music historians also attribute the expanded range and greater tonal variety of instruments to him. Feroze Khan, the talented nephew of Niamat, was a sitar maestro and improvised on new ways of playing it.[27] All these elements also led to the evolution of the alaap—'the deep sustained resonance that could convey the calm, reflective dignity of the dhrupad ang.'[28] Since then, the solo alaap form emerged as a major musical form in India.[29] Alaap—an integral component of khayal rendition—also found its way into mainstream Indian and later Pakistani film music with Lata Mangeshkar, Mohammad Rafi and Noor Jehan rendering its populist versions.

By the time the Mughal glory had dwindled, the khayal was so well-formed and developed that it survived and transformed through the creativity of Niamat Sadarang[30] to rise as the major musical tradition of north India, inspired by Sema and later enriching musical activity at the Sufi centres of Delhi. It was to flourish for many centuries to come. Delhi was acknowledged as the fountainhead of innovations.

These intimate little tributaries flowing from the river of the Hazrat Nizamuddin dargah and basti watered the music of Delhi. The unearthing of the music of Delhi remains one of the most fascinating discoveries of my inner eye.

However, Delhi's tragedy was not just the decay of the government of the day but also the city's fabled wealth and splendour which made it a ripe victim for the foreign invasions of Nadir Shah and Abdali. Towards the end of the eighteenth century, artists, poets and musicians left the city one by one and found homes elsewhere in the regional centres of power and patronage. Lucknow, the capital of the independent kingdom of Awadh, was a favourite destination. Under Asaf-ud-Daula's rule, which ended in 1797, Lucknow emerged as the cultural hub of India. Earlier, Nawab Shuja-ud-Daula (1754–75) had also promoted famous Delhi artists such as the khayal gurus, Jani, Ghulam Rasul, Chajju Khan and Jivan Khan, who were leading dhrupad singers and players of the rabab. By the nineteenth century, the music of Delhi had found safety and financial security at the court of Lucknow.[31]

Other venues for migration from Delhi were Jaipur, Gwalior (that was later to become a khayal planet), Benares, Bettiah, Rewa, Darbhanga and Banda. Music was an exalted symbol of the court and the stature of a kingdom, and Delhi provided that extra bit of glory by exporting its individuals and musical streams. This search for glory and grandeur partly explains why Nawab Wajid Ali Shah of Lucknow patronized music and poetry during his rule in the mid-nineteenth century. Music was not just a pastime but a symbol of public aesthetics of the court and its nobility.

The emptying out of Delhi in these fractured times did not mean that music disappeared from the streets and havelis of Shahjahanabad. The qawwals at the dargahs continued to embrace new artists and followers, including India-inspired

Europeans such as Antoine Polier[32] who provided employment to qawwals as teachers. Delhi earned the reputation of being the leading centre for the sitar. Masit Khan,[33] in the early nineteenth century, was the most well-known sitar player in Delhi and took the instrument to new dimensions. At the same time, the tabla was also undergoing a metamorphosis, and acquired an elevated status as an integral accompaniment to khayal singing.

Tanras Khan was a celebrated khayal expert who was central to the court of Bahadur Shah Zafar up to the year 1857. Ghalib was a frequent visitor to regional patrons such as the nawab of Rampur. Mir too had taken shelter in the regional courts.

Mughal Delhi's formal death in 1857 was transformational for the empire as well as for classical Hindustani music. The central court had already become impoverished and the most talented artists had left the city. However, after the British took over, they completely withdrew official patronage to the tradition and, within decades, the world of music and musicians had shrunk into the streets of Daryaganj.

One of the reactions to this changing environment, especially after the disruption and dislocation caused in 1857, was the desperate endeavour of musicians to organize themselves into music gharanas or family-based schools, which allowed their survival and continuity in uncertain times. Towards the end of the nineteenth century, Hindustani music culture moved even farther from Delhi and its surroundings to wealthy urban centres such as Lahore, Calcutta and Bombay.

The gharanas were integrated with the Qawwal Bachche gharana and the inheritors of the Sadarang style of music rendition and singing. For instance, the Patiala gharana, a substantial part of which moved to Pakistan after Partition, was historically under the tutelage of Tanras Khan (Qawwal Bachche) of Delhi and other disciples from Gwalior. Qawwal Bachche gharana remained the source of musical lineage, textual documentation and innovation through the centuries.

All the families known to have been singing the khayal were at one point initiated into music through the Qawwal Bachche ancestry.

The 'nautch' as a form of entertainment found an audience and patrons in kothas. Nautch performances were devoid of its spatial connection with the court, the spiritual intersection with the dargah and, of course, the financial patronage of the Mughal Empire. The degenerate Mughal nobility and princes such as Mirza Jahangir, son of Emperor Akbar II (1806–37), became notorious patrons of nautch into which was packaged paid sex. Similar trends were brewing in regional centres, most notably Lucknow, which gave rise to the famous and somewhat tragic tale of Umrao Jan Ada. Nevertheless, courtesans played a huge role in keeping Indian classical music, particularly thumris, a lighter classical form, alive.

The post-Mutiny years ushered in modernity and this had a far-reaching effect on the music of Delhi. From having to face the politics of empires, it now had to contend with forces of modernity—'new' sensibilities and cosmopolitanism. The elites were learning English and adopting different ways; this spelt inevitable doom for the tradition of classical music. Social and economic shifts after 1857 brought in a different milieu for entertainment and a new definition of 'performance' and 'concert'. In this changed milieu of the late nineteenth and early twentieth centuries, Muslim musicians struggled with an 'orientalized' nationalism that emphasized a reinvented (and glorious) Hindu past, and the new emphasis on 'formal' education as opposed to the guru–disciple traditions of transmitting music.

A millennia had been ruptured, never to recover and only to flow into another phase of India that began with a westernized, English-speaking elite which embraced modernity, democracy, and the 'futility' of the Muslim past; perhaps not in that order.

NOTES

1. Here I have relied on an English translation of the Urdu version published as *Nizai Bansari* by Khwaja Hasan Nizami Dehlvi and *A Diary of a Disciple of Nizamuddin Auliya*, translated by H. Sajun, Lahore: Talifat-e-Shahidi, 2001.
2. Used as an honorary title for a descendant of the family of Prophet Mohammad.
3. Ibid., p. 97.
4. Qaeda refers to the basic textbook used in early years in education to teach Urdu and/or Arabic.
5. Ibid., p. 111.
6. *A Diary of a Disciple of Nizamuddin Auliya*, translated by H. Sajun, Lahore: Talifat-e-Shahidi, 2001.
7. The 'Sura Al-Fatiha' or 'The Opening' is the first chapter of the Quran. Its seven verses are a prayer for God's guidance. This chapter has an essential role in daily prayers. Muslims recite the 'Sura Al-Fatiha' at the start of each unit of prayer.
8. A sacred space in the Jama Masjid in Old Delhi.
9. Derived from the Arabic word 'Uroos', literally a wedding.
10. Meanings for the word include, 'spiritual guide, advisor, leader', often used to describe the Creator.
11. In the Poorbi/Hindustani style, Nijaam is an appellation for Nizam.
12. Hazrat Nizamuddin Auliya's pir.
13. 'Some Qawalis and Folk Songs of the Khusrau Tradition', available at <http:21www.angelfire.com/sd/urdumedia/lyrics.html>
14. Allyn Miner, *Sitar and Sarod in the 18th and 19th Centuries*, New Delhi: Motilal Banarsidass, p. 84. Also see Birendra Kishore Roy, 'Indian Music and Mian Tansen' cited in Miner's paper.
15. Swami Prajnananda, *A Historical Study of Indian Music*, New Delhi: Munshiram Manoharlal Publishers, pp. 117–27. Also, M.R. Gautam, *The Musical Heritage of India*, New Delhi: Munshiram Manoharlal Publishers.
16. I am heavily indebted to the excellent study of this theme undertaken by Jon Barlow and Lakshmi Subramanian, in 'Music and Society in North India: From the Mughals to the Mutiny', *Economic and Political Weekly*, Vol. 42, No. 19, 2007.

17. Bonnie C. Wade, *Imaging Sound—An Ethnomusicological Study of Music, Art and Culture in Mughal India*, Chicago: University of Chicago Press, pp. 160–83.
18. Jon Barlow and Lakshmi Subramanian, 'Music and Society in North India: From the Mughals to the Mutiny', *Economic and Political Weekly*, Vol. 42, No. 19, 2007.
19. Ibid.
20. Katherine Butler Brown, 'Did Aurangzeb Ban Music? Questions for the Historiography of his Reign,' *Modern Asian Studies*, Vol. 41, No. 1, 2007, pp. 1–44.
21. It is believed that many kalawants converted to Islam during the Mughal era and were inspired by the Chishti Sufis. They also performed at the Sufi dargahs. See Barlow and Subramanian, 'Music and Society ...'.
22. Naqshbandi is one of the major tasawwuf spiritual orders of Sufi Islam. It is nearly 1,400 years old. Tasawwuf is the traditional Islamic science of spirituality focusing on one's relationship with Allah.
23. Satish Chandra, 'Cultural and Political role of Delhi, 1675-1725', in R.E. Frykenberg (ed.), *Delhi Through the Ages, Essays in Indian History, Culture and Society*, New York: OUP, pp. 210–11.
24. Darqah Quli Khan, *Muraqqa E Dehli, The Mughal Capital in Muhammad Shah's Time*, Foreword by Nurul Hasan (English translation with an introduction and notes by Chander Sekhar and Shama Mitra Chenoy), Deputy Publications. Also see Shama Mitra Chenoy, *Shahjahanabad, A City of Delhi, 1638-1857*, New Delhi: Munshiram Manoharlal Publishers, pp. 173–74.
25. Jaideva Singh Thakur, *Indian Music*, Prem Lata Sharma (ed.), Sangeet Research Academy, Calcutta, 1995, pp. 231–32. Also see Allyn Miner, *Sitar and Sarod in the 18th and 19th Centuries*, p. 87.
26. Jon Barlow and Lakshmi Subramanian, 'Music and Society in North India: From the Mughals to the Mutiny', 2007.
27. Ibid., pp. 76–77.
28. Jon Barlow and Lakshmi Subramanian, 'Music and Society in North India: From the Mughals to the Mutiny', 2007.
29. Allyn Miner, *Sitar and Sarod in the 18th and 19th Centuries*. See also Adrian Mcneil, *Inventing the Sarod: a Cultural History*, Kolkata: Seagull, 2004.

30. Sadarang has been so central to the notion of khayal that he is commonly credited with having invented it despite its having been in existence long before him.
31. Allyn Miner, *Sitar and Sarod in the 18th and 19th Centuries*, p. 97, cited in Barlow and Subramanian.
32. Ibid., pp. 93–94.
33 Allyn Miner, *Sitar and Sarod in the 18th and 19th Centuries*, p. 93. The *gat toda* is explained in detail by Miner. Masit Khan is credited for adopting actual dhrupad compositions for melodies to use in his gats.

6

Lover's Heart

Delhi was once a paradise,
Where love held sway and reigned;
But its charm lies ravished now
And only ruins remain.

No tears were shed when shroudless, they
Were laid in common graves;
No prayers were read for the noble dead,
Unmarked remain their graves.

But things cannot remain, O Zafar,
Thus, for who can tell?
Through God's great mercy and the Prophet
All may yet be well.

Bahadur Shah Zafar[1]

Shahjahanabad, or Old Delhi, was built by Emperor Shah Jahan. The work started in 1639. Seventeen years of labour and design resulted in a city without parallel. In terms of architectural grandeur and significance, Shah Jahan's court was rivalled only by that of the Ming emperors, and Shahjahanabad, as the capital city, had to be a suitable setting for this jewel. The court, a locus of splendour, existed around the majestic

Lal Quila, the Red Fort complex. This royal inner sanctum, with multiple pavilions, palaces, gardens and halls of audience, remained the Mughal seat of power until 1857, when the last Mughal emperor, Bahadur Shah Zafar, was deposed following the tumultuous events of the Mutiny and its aftermath. This was the end of Delhi's status as the capital city, at least for the next fifty-four years, as the seat of government had shifted to modern, thriving Calcutta in the east. The British took control of India and, in the early twentieth century, built New Delhi by moving the capital once again to this historical power saddle. Delhi was only to regain its position as the fulcrum of power when the British shifted the capital from Calcutta in 1911. Since then, Delhi has remained the capital of India. The Red Fort, quite befittingly, became the symbol of independent India after 1947.

We are with a small group of tourists. The old city is disappearing brick by brick. This is callous, inevitable destruction. I wonder what must have prompted Shah Jahan to leave Agra and return to this imperially jinxed city. Was it his passion for architecture? It must have been in 1639 when the orders were issued for the construction of the Red Fort. Within nine years, Emperor Shah Jahan and his son, Prince Dara Shikoh, held their inaugural court at Diwan-e-Aam.

It is believed that several decapitated bodies of ordinary mortals working on the site are buried under the foundations of Shahjahanabad. Perhaps it was Delhi's resplendent fate to rise once again from amidst the corpses. The 3.8 mile-long[2] city wall took four years to be erected; it had fourteen gates, the names of which represented the ethos of the time—Lahori, Turkman, Kashmiri—among others. Names for these gates were chosen for a variety of reasons—as satraps of the vast empire as well as for the directions which some of these gates indicated, showing a particular province or 'suba'. An old canal was revived for water supply and one of its branches crossed Chandni Chowk, the city's commercial centre, underlying the dominant urban aesthetic laid out by Shah Jahan's daughter, Princess Jahanara. Another canal flowed through the Red Fort. The length, style, utility, route and aesthetic of this canal was inspired by the literal and metaphorical glory of a Mughal garden aimed at recreating; the Islamic 'paradise' reserved for the afterlife, but glimpsed on the temporal earth through a ruling dynasty's sovereignty.

Around 100,000 to 150,000 people lived here between 1800 and 1857—the last and defining period of Mughal India. It was definitely smaller than the other cultural haven, Lucknow. However, the small population made Shahjahanabad more manageable. It also facilitated the preservation of cultural integrity and communal harmony in Delhi, where a multi-class culture influenced by the Sufi tariqa flourished. In the words of C.F. Edwards, who was scripting accounts of old Delhi:

> The intimate residence together, side by side, in the same city of Musalmans and Hindus, had brought about a noticeable amalgamation of customs and usages among common peoples ... I have had more convincing and corroborative evidence of especially friendly relationships between Hindus and Muslims in old Delhi than I have had concerning any other factor.

The medium of Urdu and the commonly shared Delhi aadaab were the vehicles for articulating this bonding and understanding. By the 1850s, Khusrau's project of creating a new language that was a blend of the local and the foreign, the ruler and the ruled, had fully penetrated the cultural ethos of Delhi. The Delhi College[3], now known as Zakir Hussain College, was a fine seat of Indo-oriental learning, and represented this peculiar and delightful cultural nuance where scientific learning mingled with a wider cultural learning. It imparted an education of a comprehensive, old-world variety where manners mixed with reason and the spirit of inquiry, harmonized with traditional respect for teachers.

Cultural and recreational activities were also shared by all communities regardless of their religion and creed. The sandy slopes on the banks of the serene Jamuna near Delhi Gate, Mahabat Khan ki Reti, were used for kite flying and other matches. Pigeon flying was another popular sport and a swimming gala was an annual event. Wrestling clubs also flourished and Dastangohs[4] spun stories on the steps of the Jama Masjid.

In the last days of Shahjahanabad, the city's spirit was personified by Bahadur Shah Zafar. Zafar was a poet-musician, a keen builder, a regular chess player and kite flyer. He was the 'Jahan Panah' (protector of the world) in the eyes of the people of Shahjahanabad. But there was a deep decline in this introverted city which harboured an almost unreal sense of complacency. The British were everywhere in north India and, very soon, events would lead them to this decaying world to destroy and rebuild it in order to suit imperial purposes.

I imagined the bustle of Chandni Chowk from Lahori Gate to the Fatehpuri Mosque. The shade of green trees would reflect in the Nehr-i-Bahisht (river of paradise). About halfway through, it would pass through a circular pool to reflect moonlight. The section from Lahori Gate to Dariba was known as Urdu Bazaar, catering to needs such as uniforms and items of everyday use of the imperial staff. Towards the Kotwali was a market for flower sellers. Adjoining bazaars would sell gold, jewellery and the finest of merchandise.

The Chandni Chowk of today is still a commercial centre, but quite uninspiring and run-down. The canal and the pool have dried up and disappeared, but all the names remain. Unrelenting noise is a constant irritant and the area is nothing but a trader-merchant slum now. The moonlight struggles to find a corner through which it can shine down but cannot find it.

From Kotwali Chabutra,[5] a street known as Johari Bazaar or the jewellers market with saraafs and mahajans snaked towards Chandni Chowk. Further up, Chandni Chowk, the square where an octagonal pool measuring one hundred yards on each side reflected the moonlight, was Jahanara's own feat of architecture that emerged in 1650 with a garden, bath, caravansarai and shops on all its sides. Records say that there were 444 double-storey shops. Fed by the flowing canal water, a talaab or a pool was also improvised to reflect the moonlight. Towards the north, there was the Begum ki Sarai and in the south, a hamam or public bath; while at the end of Chandni Chowk, there was the Bazaar Kalan near the Fatehpuri Masjid. Pavilions with gardens attracted birds. A slice of Mughal splendour for the ordinary citizen indeed!

Sarais or inns, precursors of today's hotels, were located here. One such sarai, independent of ecclesiastical patronage, was Begum ki Sarai. Jahanara built this sarai between the Red Fort and the city. This double-storey inn was squarish in shape with arched private chambers adorned with contemporary paintings in the Indo-Persian style with great views on both sides. Wells were provided for. Bernier noted that this, the most imposing building in Delhi after the Jama Masjid, was a 'rendezvous for the rich and the great, Persian and Uzbeg and other foreign merchants who were ... accommodated ... with personal security'. Stephen P. Blake reports that the inn 'contained ninety rooms, each beautifully painted and appointed ... in the middle of the courtyard was a garden filled with watercourses, pools, trees and flowers'.[6]

Now the trees have disappeared and not even a bush stands there. The year 1857 was a turning point not just in the inner life and grandeur of the old city, but also for its gardens, parks and trees; the easiest preys of modernity. On the first day of 1867, a train steamed into Delhi station north of Chandni Chowk. The station gobbled up acres of land where once Jahanara's garden existed. In the twenty-first century, construction of the hi-tech underground metro has contributed to the large-scale uprooting of trees—a mere continuation of this merciless scheme of things.

At its zenith, Chandni Chowk was a fabled area frequented by local elites, Armenian and Turkish adventurers, Persian poets and Italian merchants. Just a little distance away, stood one of the world's richest courts. Rumour had it that it required fourteen full years to evaluate Shah Jahan's riches! There were bustling tree-lined boulevards with coffee houses for the rich, wafting aromas of the imported bean from Persia, and shops selling Chinese eyeglasses, jewellery, cheetahs and even eunuchs! Today, cheap Chinese consumer goods are sold here, bringing history to another kind of full circle.

Shahjahanabad boasted of high-end as well as the ordinary haveli as they tried to replicate the grandeur of the palace into their daily lives. Each of these havelis had a definite architectural style and contained gardens. Like havelis elsewhere, each one was a world within itself—quarters for women, guests and family, with carefully designed courtyards quietly breathing inside. The diwan khana and library were also necessary spaces. The inner sanctums—private studies, bedrooms and living spaces—overlooked fruit trees and fountains and enjoyed much light and openness. Verandas were another architectural feature, as were basements, particularly cherished as a refuge from the unsparing summer heat. High ceilings and terraces captured the purva or the eastern breeze that blew on summer nights; sleeping under the stars brought the skies closer to the edges of the beds in Shahjahanabad.

Through the centuries, these havelis existed as sites of cultural patronage, especially of music and the sama associated with the city's Sufi circles. A contemporary account of the later Mughal period mentions Zafar Khan Roshan-ud-Daula, whose house was like a mountain of gold, its walls and doors lavishly gilded and decorated with costly tapestry and hangings of gold and floors covered with carpets of the richest silk. Zafar Khan organized the celebrations of the Bara Wafat (the Prophet's birthday) and the urs of Khwaja Bakhtiyar Kaki on a grand scale. Once a week, Zafar Khan held a Majlis-i-Sama to which he invited mystics, saints, and eminent citizens of the city. Zafar would tear up his golden clothes while in a state of trance and distribute gold and silver pieces among the performers. At the end of the music party, the attendees were offered opulent meals served on gold and silver.

The gardens of these havelis have now been converted into more housing blocks as the population grew; the once spacious residences are cluttered with bricks and humans. Ghettos, already scripted by history, now burst with the forces of demography. The Delhi Metro is continuing the drama that began more than a century ago as it rips through trees and green chunks of land, reeling under expressways and other traffic decongestants. An underground highway plan, a few years ago, had threatened a foray into Sundar Nursery in Sundar Nagar, potentially uprooting a thousand trees of more than a hundred species that may have been written and wailed about. Mercifully, the plan was shelved, but one is not sure for how long.

Congested and filthy, with an occasional tree dotting the roads, Shahjahanabad is the epitome of rampant and ugly commercialization. The beautiful havelis and their fountains have reincarnated themselves into camera shops, mechanic shops, banks, clothes stalls, and even an out-of-place McDonald's outlet. Four centuries later, the eccentric Sadia Dehlvi went to Chandni Chowk to buy her cycle rickshaw as part of her activism to promote an environment-friendly mode of local transport. Many go there to look for spare parts for their smoke-emitting vehicles. Splendour is just so transient.

Shahjahanabad's architecture and cultural magnificence was not confined to this location. It extended beyond the immediate walled precincts of the city. Kuchas and *katras* multiplied over the years. Harbash Khan ka Phatak, Bangash ka Sarai, Haveli Haider Kuli, Qasim Jan ki Galli, Jarnail Bibi ki Haveli, Begum ka Bagh, Kucha Ghasi Ram, Namak Haram ki Haveli—these were some of the well-known structures mirroring the way of life that existed inside Shahjahanabad.

Mir Taqi Mir, the outstanding Shahjahanabad poet, distressed at the sacking of Delhi by the Afghan emperor, Ahmad Shah Abdali, wrote in 1748:

> *Dilli ke kuche na thay auraq-e-musavvir thay*
> *Jo shakl nazr aaye tasveer nazr aayee!*
>
> The lanes of Delhi were leaves of an art album
> Whichever face was seen, was a picture in itself

In the merciless heat of May 1857, three hundred mutinous sepoys—Punjabi and Pathan—entered Shahjahanabad and massacred every British resident they spotted and declared Emperor Bahadur Shah Zafar as their sovereign. Zafar, caught between the rising power of the British and the discontent of the local population, found himself trapped in the leadership role. He must have known that the mutiny was doomed to fail but he had no choice other than to be a reluctant symbol of the old regime. A month later, Shahjahanabad was attacked by the British and thus began a siege of Hindustan's Mecca that was to change its destiny forever.

During the following four months, the Mughal capital was besieged and destroyed by British artillery. The number that died was mind-boggling, and the suffering of the local population immense. Lack of water and food meant starvation for most of the city's inhabitants. The sordid tale ended on 14 September 1857, when the British invaded and captured Shahjahanabad, looting, plundering and killing as the Nadir Shahi and Abdalian forces had done before them.

In the days that followed the capture of Zafar and the British takeover of Shahjahanabad, the city's inner world splintered. Twenty-one princes were hanged in a single day. The emperor was humiliated, treated like a common criminal, and exiled. The Lahori and Delhi Gates were renamed after Victoria and

Alexandra. The Red Fort and Jama Masjid were used as barracks thereby trampling on centuries of culture; the palace rooms, so exquisite, were broken down or partitioned to create insipid, ugly-looking structures. Worst of all, the Fatehpuri Masjid was sold as private property to a trader, Lala Chunna Mal, and Zeenatul Masjid became a bakery of the Raj. Khas Bazaar and Khanum Bazaar were reduced to rubble, and a number of streets were erased from the face of Shahjahanabad.

Unfortunately, such brazen destruction of a culture and history has not been the subject of academic inquiry. There are accounts—secular and Muslim, nationalist and partial—but there are also political agendas between the spaces and full stops. Many years after the destruction of Shahjahanabad, when another monument, the Babri Masjid, was attacked and razed to the ground by Hindus in 1992, V.S. Naipaul, a Nobel laureate and a wannabe white man, described the tragedy as 'an expression of creative passion'! The white man's burden remains alive to this day, resulting in, among other things, the periodical emergence of troubled 'natives' such as Naipaul.

There are many in Delhi today who advocate the preservation of havelis and the renewal of the old city and its character. But the world has moved on. The lovingly lived and planned Shahjahanabad has even lost its name. The makers of 'New' Delhi have named it 'Old' Delhi. Its ambience has been consumed and twisted by market forces. The lingering shadows of Partition have also bolstered the alien 'otherness' of this large ghetto, which is forgotten as India searches for its new confident sense of self and nationhood. If the historical dross has to be removed so that the present can shine, so be it. It is a small price after all; a few hundred monuments here and there, and a few centuries of culture.

If Princess Jahanara was to come back to life and visit Old Delhi, she would definitely refuse to own up to Chandni Chowk.

Much of Delhi's past is defined by men. In fact, the annals of the sultanate and Mughal history, barring a few exceptions, are largely tales of powerful and quarrelsome men vying for power and patronage. The patriarchal societies of the day, influenced by Central Asian Islam, ensured the invisibility of women. Other than the ill-fated rulers Razia Sultan and Queen Noorjahan, who gave up purdah and participated in the brutal politics of men, a woman rarely rose to a position of authority or influence. Noorjahan was more successful, but her example was not the norm since she was Persian. She did not belong to the local Indo-Mughal aristocracy and her family had been favoured by Akbar. She was considered to be a wily player of power politics herself, much like South Asian female politicians of today who derive power from male relatives. As Emperor Jahangir battled opium and alcohol addiction throughout his reign, Noorjahan became the real power behind the throne and ruled with an iron fist.

After nearly half a century of faceless women, Princess Jahanara (1614–81) broke the taboo and became a major power centre within the complex dynamics of the Mughal court. Shahjahanabad and its residents were familiar with Princess Jahanara who was a confidante of her father, Emperor Shah Jahan, as well as of the latter's eccentric son Dara Shikoh. As the eldest daughter, she had a special role in the royal household as first lady—a position that fell within her control after the death of Mumtaz Mahal, the inspiration behind the Taj Mahal in Agra. Interestingly, it was the mystical path that provided a social and royal sanction for Jahanara's high-profile public role. For Princess Fatima Jahanara was initiated into the Sufi ways along with her younger brother, Dara Shikoh. These young royals were inspired by the Qadri Sufi, Mian Mir, in Lahore. Mian Mir's Sufi sister, Bibi Jamal Khatun, happened to be close to the Mughal siblings. Though Mian Mir was an adherent of the Qadri order, Jahanara was also a devotee of the Chishti saints, especially Hazrat Nizamuddin Auliya in Delhi and Khwaja Moinuddin Chishti in

Ajmer. The princess travelled to Ajmer after recuperating from severe burns caused by her perfume catching fire, and thanked the saint for saving her life.

This is perhaps why she authored the well-known biography of Khwaja Moinuddin Chishti, the *Munis-ul-Arwah.* We learn of her pilgrimage to Ajmer in 1643 and the mystical ecstasy that overcame her one evening while she was circumambulating the tomb. Jahanara ordered the construction of a multi-pillared marble pavilion in front of the tomb. Appropriately, this porch is today called the Begumi Dalan, a name derived from her title, Begum Sahiba. After her death in 1681, she was laid to rest in the courtyard around the serene tomb of Hazrat Nizamuddin Auliya.

As a patron of mystical literature, Princess Jahanara commissioned translations of several works of classical literature, as well as erudite commentaries on these. Like Empress Noorjahan, Jahanara promoted the arts as well. She was a poet in her own right and her name was linked to various prominent men of letters of the time.

Thus we have a female voice, personal and direct, from the seventeenth century, in *Risala-i-Sahibiya* (Madam's Treatise). Here Jahanara documents her journeys into mysticism with the help of Mullah Shah Badakhshi. This is an elegant document that is interspersed with Jahanara's verses and also highlights her political lineage originating from Timur. Sufism in Mughal Delhi during Shah Jahan's reign created a relatively genderless arena where Jahanara could nurture her spiritual inclination and identify herself as a Sufi disciple, and an artist and scholar in the literary and spiritual landscape of the seventeenth century. The patronage of Sufi rituals also enabled a diluted purdah regime and provided legitimacy to the public role of an unmarried princess as an active leader and contributor to the religious and cultural milieu of Delhi.

Jahanara remained loyal to her father and remained imprisoned with him until he died in 1666. She died sixteen years later and bequeathed all her property to Khwaja Moinuddin's dargah, but, under the pretext of Islamic law,[7] Aurangzeb permitted only one-third to be gifted for this purpose.

Each time I visit Hazrat Nizamuddin's dargah, I stop at Jahanara's small, serene tomb chamber with delicately carved latticework on white marble that has become pale and brownish with time but marks her beauty and soulfulness. The tomb has no ceiling and fuses with the open skies in deference to her wishes. The inscription says it all:

> Let naught but green grasses cover my grave,
> For mortals poor, it's a grave-cover brave.

Hindi cinema dwelt on Jahanara's unfulfilled love for her childhood companion, Mirza Yusuf Changezi, in Vinod Kumar's 1964 hit film, *Jahan Ara*. This was a doomed romance as the dying Mumtaz Mahal reportedly made Jahanara promise that she would never leave her father. A heartbroken Yusuf wandered the country sick with love as did Majnu from another Arabic tale. However, this may well have been fictionalized and not much can be said with certainty.

However, chroniclers have written extensively about the special bond between the emperor and Jahanara which, if true, was out of bounds in the Mughal-Islamic milieu of the day despite the secularism and hedonism of the ruling dynasty. Several European chroniclers suggested that Shah Jahan had an incestuous relationship with his daughter Jahanara. Joannes de Laet, Peter Mundy and Jean Baptiste Tavernier hinted at such allegations. Francois Bernier, a French physician and traveller, wrote:

> Begum Sahiba, the elder daughter of Shahjahan was very beautiful ... Rumour has it that his attachment reached a point which is difficult to believe, the justification of which he rested on the decision of the mullahs, or doctors of their Law. According to them, it would have been unjust to deny the king the privilege of gathering fruit from the tree he himself had planted.

Tales of Shah Jahan's promiscuity were also picked up by other travellers.[8] However, historian K.S. Lal pointed out that his son, Aurangzeb, may have been involved in 'magnifying a rumour into a full-fledged scandal', and that 'Aurangzeb had disobeyed Shah Jahan … he had him incarcerated for years, but if he really helped give a twist to Shah Jahan's paternal love for Jahanara by turning it into a scandal, it was the unkindest cut of all his unfilial acts'. He remarked that under 'these circumstances, it is not possible to say anything with finality'.

Nevertheless, this *was* a unique relationship as Jahanara spent the best years of her youth with her father, and also the miserable years at Agra Fort under imperial custody. This was also the place where Dara's head was sent to the royals as a present from Aurangzeb. Many of these anecdotes have been distorted over time through oral histories or the accounts of semi-reliable European travellers. As with so much else, it is difficult to determine their veracity.

But the Mughals were extraordinary in most respects—not only in their 'outer' life of buildings and symbols through which they aimed at immortality, but also in their unconventional personal lives.

As I wander through the old city, I look for any little sign of Jahanara's tasteful contributions to Shahjahanabad. Little is left of her sarai or the gardens gifted to her by the emperor or the haveli that she is reported to have commissioned. Even if they remain, time has changed their face making them unrecognizable.

Chandni Chowk is home to silversmiths, repair shops, clothiers, spicy street-food vendors and traditional sweet shops. We visit the silver market (Dariba Kalan), the wedding market (Kinari Bazaar) and the lane of parathas (Paranthewali Gali).

Preservation of heritage is not much emphasized in India, Pakistan and Bangladesh. Much of old Dhaka and Lahore also faces the same fate as Shahjahanabad. Erasure of memory seems necessary for the nation state's exclusivism.

Sadia escorts me through the colourful bazaars of Old Delhi. Yes, the jeweller's lane that still survives close to Chandni Chowk bears faint stamps of Jahanara, though she would be quite cross to see the open drains and untamed sewage not to mention the milling crowds—not quite royal! But then, Jahanara was also a Sufi, a people's princess, so she may have actually enjoyed the throngs of people. The lanes are still enchanting. Some of the streets have old construction; little crumbling bricks and stonework at the edges about to enter the drains. We take a turn and enter a lane exclusively selling Old Delhi snacks—baqar khanis and knick-knacks made out of myriad dals (lentils). Long before the advent of branding and intellectual property, Baqar Khan of Delhi had named the small bread after himself. These small flat cakes were a preserved form of bread used with meals. Now this is a tea-time snack.

A long morning walk has left us exhausted, so we stop for chai. We sit at a dhaba facing the Jama Masjid—a poetic vision blurred by a plethora of electric poles and hanging wires that put the intricacies of this cultural relic to shame. I am filled with a disconcerting and nagging feeling, and want to vent. Sadia is attentive like most times and grants me the chance to speak in neurotic frenzy. I shout, 'The tales of Mughal history are biased in favour of kings, courts and men and by narratives of power and war! What about the women?'

I want to draw her attention to the other 'invisible' princess of the Mughal era. Finding an audience, I begin with verses composed by Aurangzeb's exceptionally gifted daughter Zebunissa:

> No Muslim I,
> But an idolater,
> I bow before the image of my Love,
> And worship Her.[9]

Princess Zebunissa, the eldest daughter of Emperor Aurangzeb, was close to her father. Her remarkable story has been overshadowed by the political turmoil that led to Aurangzeb's capture of the Mughal throne and what ensued later. Zebunissa was a favourite of her father and received much exposure to the affairs of the court. Having received a sound education in the arts, languages, astronomy and sciences of the day, Zebunissa turned out to be a highly sensitive princess. She never married and kept herself occupied with her poetry and spiritual quest.

This is perhaps the greatest of ironies—Aurangzeb's daughter was an antithesis of her father's personality and politics. Zebunissa was a Sufi and a gifted poet. In 1724, after her death, her scattered writings were collected under the name, 'Diwan-i-Makhfi', a metaphor for her invisibility in her father's court and, at the cosmic level, the invisibility of God. Given her father's dislike of poetry she could only be makhfi or invisible. And, like all rebels, she was subversive as well. She attended and participated in the literary and cultural events of her age dressed in her veil and also had a string of lovers, admirers and protégés.

We have to leave, so our conversation is unfinished. Later in the evening, we sit in Sadia's Hazrat Nizamuddin apartment where her evening durbar has swelled with 'young friends', the literati of Delhi, the Urdu-walas and, of course, the visiting white people. So I continue with my stories; indeed, there cannot be a better audience. Luckily, there are others who add to what I know. Alas, in spite of all this, I have yet to find a single sign of Zebunissa in Delhi.

Zebunissa did not share her father's orthodox views on religion and society. Steeped in mystic thought, her ghazals sang of love, freedom and the inner experience:

Though I am Laila of Persian romance,
my heart loves like ferocious Majnun.
I want to go to the desert
but modesty is chains on my feet.
A nightingale came to the flower garden
because she was my pupil.
I am an expert in things of love.
Even the moth is my disciple!

No moth am I that in impetuous fashion
Fly to the flame and perish. Rather say
I am a candle that with inward passion
Slowly and silently consumes away.[10]

Zebunissa held a separate court, and was a patron of the arts and letters as well as of many poets of the era. One of her long-time companions was the émigré Iranian poet Ashraf. It is said that there was more than friendship in this literary association and there were several rumours of other indiscreet liaisons as well. However, there is a paucity of direct evidence on this subject. Zebunissa is also said to have been excessively fond of one particular *kaneez* or servant girl. This intimacy was also the subject of gossip. Perhaps it was the same Mian Bai who was gifted the beautiful Chauburji garden in Lahore.

Somehow, Zebunissa managed to retain her individuality and independence. She established many libraries and arranged for the translation of several classical Arabic and Sanskrit texts into Persian—a clear sign of the influence of her aunt, Jahanara, and uncle, Dara Shikoh. Anecdotal accounts also tell us how Aurangzeb tried to undermine Zebunissa's poetry and interest in astronomy.

Reading through Zebunissa's poetry, one can understand why Aurangzeb had reservations about her verse. Her inclusive vision ran against the puritanical state and society that Aurangzeb cherished. Look at these lines from a poem in Diwan-i-Makhfi called 'I Bow Before the Image of my Love':

No Brahmin I,
My sacred thread
I cast away, for round my neck I wear
Her plaited hair instead

Like most Mughal nobility, Zebunissa loved Lahore. The famous Chauburji was an entrance to a vast garden (that no longer exists). The Chauburji building had the Arabic *ayat-ul-kursi* (an important Quranic verse, literally the verse of the [Divine] Chair) inscribed on the main gate and the date of its completion was recorded as 1646. S.M. Latif, the famous historian of Lahore, translated another Persian verse carved at the entrance as follows:

This garden, in the pattern of Paradise, has been founded,
The garden has been bestowed on Mian Bai
By the beauty of Zebinda Begum, the lady of the age.

According to Latif, Mian Bai was Zebunissa's favourite female attendant. The *Shahjahannama* also throws some light on the gift of the gardens to the lucky bai. Since Mian Bai had supervised the laying out of these gardens, the local people called it Mian Bai's gardens. One view is that Zebunissa is buried in Nawankot in Lahore.

Latif also records how Zebunissa used to sit in the marble pavilion of the Lahori Shalimar Gardens and enjoy the soothing rhythm of the waterfall. It was also a place that provided her with inspiration for her poetry. Talking to the waterfall of the Shalimar Gardens, she composed this lyrical quatrain with passion and longing:

O waterfall! For whose sake art thou weeping?
In whose sorrowful recollection hast thou wrinkled thy brows?
What pain was it that impelled thee, like me the whole night,
To strike thy head against stone, and to shed tears?[11]

The *Chinna Katha* (discourses of Sathya Sai Baba) cites a telling incident that reveals Zebunissa's personality. Aurangzeb had gifted her a beautiful mirror. One day while Zebunissa was combing her hair, the mirror slipped from the hands of the maid who was holding it. Seeing the mirror break into pieces, the mortified maid offered herself to be punished. However, Zebunissa remained calm and said how happy she was to see the 'instrument of flattery' broken. She took it as a lesson in detachment.[12]

Only a fraction of Zebunissa's poetry has been translated into English and Urdu. It is a shame that we have rendered her invisible from mainstream accounts of the history and the arts of the Mughal era.[13]

Eventually, it was not her eclectic pursuits but the rebellion of her brother, Akbar, who proclaimed himself emperor in 1681, that hastened the undoing of Zebunissa. While the rebellion was short and unsuccessful, Zebunissa's exchange of letters with her exiled brother caused her to be imprisoned in the Gwalior fortress until her death in 1702. There are many other possible reasons, mainly extrapolated from her poetry. A recent book, *Captive Princess: Zebunissa, Daughter of Emperor Aurangzeb*, by Annie Krieger Krynicki and translated by Enjum Hamid, attempts to examine the causes of her imprisonment and her world view, as well as to reconstruct her life. Such works have highlighted her political differences with her father and shows how alien Aurangzeb's style of governance was to her soul.

Eminent educationist and historian, Sir Jadu Nath Sarkar, writes that Zebunissa died in Delhi and was buried in the garden of the Thirty Thousand Trees outside Kabuli Gate. It is believed that when the railway line was laid out in Delhi, her tomb was demolished and the coffin and inscribed tombstone were shifted to Akbar's mausoleum at Sikandra in Agra.

A poet versified her chronogram in the following words:

A fountain of learning, virtue, beauty and elegance
She was hidden as Joseph in the well
I asked reason the year of her death,
The invisible voice exclaimed: 'the moon became concealed'.[14]

Mir's pensive verses on Delhi contain descriptions about the ups and downs of the Shahjahanabad that was. When he wrote these lines, the Mughal Empire was nothing but a trapped figment of lost grandeur; centripetal forces on the rise were giving way to another relentless spate of foreign invasions. During his exile from Delhi, Mir recited these verses in Lucknow describing the splendours of Delhi that had been ravaged by political events:

Why do you mock at me and ask yourselves
Where in the world I come from, easterners?
There was a city famed throughout the world,
Where dwelled the chosen spirits of the age:
Delhi its name fairest among the fair
Fate looted it and laid it desolate
And to that ravaged city I belong.

In the eighteenth century, Delhi stood out as the finest of cities between Constantinople and Canton. Its mosques, and its literary and artistic fame, were widely known and acknowledged.[15] However, this was to change because of the decline that set in after Aurangzeb, the rise of the East India Company in Bengal and other provinces of northern India. Until 1739, when Nadir Shah ravaged the beauty of Delhi, this city was referred to as the 'Jewel of the East'. Little wonder that, a century later, the city was the jewel of the British Crown.

This was an unsparingly insecure age. Nadir Shah's looting incursions were met with little or no resistance. He plundered Delhi and accumulated the treasures of eight generations of Mughal emperors with relative ease.[16] The decline had actually set in during Jahangir's reign when the excesses and opulence of the state combined with overspending was gradually turning the core rotten. The decline of Delhi became a cultural metaphor and affected the poetry of Mir Taqi Mir and Mirza Mohammed Rafi Sauda (1781)—two great masters of Urdu poetry.

The Persian poetic form, also adapted by Urdu, the 'Shahr-ashob' (cities under distress) was a type of satire that depicted a dark vision of a crumbling urban society, the tumult of daily commerce and social hierarchies that had gone topsy-turvy.[17] Nadir Shah's invasion of Delhi and the twilight of the Mughal Empire were the political impetus for a depressing world view reflecting itself in nostalgic verse. Such poetry satirizes brilliant professionals who are now sad caricatures hankering for a little money, willing to undermine their skills and self-respect. The Urdu 'Shahr-ashob' satires comment on political events without naming the rulers unlike its Persian counterparts that addressed specific rulers. Sauda mourns the loveless state of Delhi:

> Delhi, did you deserve all this?
> Perhaps at one time, this city was the heart of a lover,
> It was wiped out as if it had been an ephemeral drawing.

Thus the poetry of Mir, Sauda and others[18] talks of the economic downturn, pressured societal networks and, most importantly, the dwindling poetics and language betraying a damaged link with the past.

Mir is to Urdu what Shakespeare is to English. A few generations before Ghalib, Mir traversed between the two centres of Urdu poetry, Delhi and Lucknow, but he is identified with Delhi and its crumbling soul during the late eighteenth century. The corpus of his verse, diverse and laden with themes of love, loss and spirituality, also provides a poetic commentary on the times:

> Don't think me a mere poet—no, my verse
> Is made of pain and grief more than you know[19]

Three decades of living in Delhi—from 1740 to 1760 and later, between 1772 and 1782—made Mir a poet of the age. The interlude was spent in Lucknow. His verses speak of Delhi's decline. The city's lost glory turned into creative imagination upon which an immortal reservoir of verse was built. So, in the tradition of the Urdu 'Shahr-ashob', he remarks:

> This age is not like that which went before it
> The times have changed, the earth and skies have changed.

After Shah Jahan, the monarchy lost its rapport with its subjects. Internal conspiracies within the palace led to infighting and the breakdown of governance. Increased taxation imposed on the peasantry after Akbar, increased further by Shah Jahan to finance cities and monuments, left the subjects reeling under an extractive mode of statehood. Aurangzeb broke—at least in the public perception—the compact between a plural state and its subjects. His weak successors could not hold the centre and their extravagance meant that regional defiance of central rule was now a real possibility.

The emergence of small autonomous kingdoms, a replay of Indian history since ancient times, meant that 'Imperius Mughalus' became more of a symbolic signature of Mughal rule rather than actual governance. The absence of a clear law of succession meant that there was a free-for-all competition among crafty nobles. Civil wars were common. Plebeian revolts, lawlessness and land-based struggles also weakened the Mughal Empire.[20]

Accounts suggest that maladministration was an ugly reality in Delhi. In 1757, Delhi's police chief was known to protect burglars in the same way that it sometimes still does in the Delhi of today and, of course in many parts of India and Pakistan. So Bollywood plots wherein corrupt cops are in collusion with criminals exploiting the junta are not new in this region.

Sadat Khan, a nobleman of Oudh, was the precursor of Mir Jafar in Bengal, who goaded Nadir Shah to invade Delhi and plunder its riches. Thus, another invader found a local ally. This goes even further back. Apparently, both Prithviraj Chauhan and Ibrahim Lodhi's downfall happened due to local collaboration with external invaders. But Khan's tragic end was a moral metaphor as he committed suicide after he fell out with Nadir Shah over money. His greed not only destroyed Delhi, but also his life. One wonders if things have changed at all.

Prior to Nadir Shah's invasion of Delhi, Karnal (in modern Haryana) was captured and Dilli-walas waited in anxiety. The local uprising of the proletariat was crushed by Nadir Shah and a general massacre commenced at Chandni Chowk. Some accounts report that about twenty thousand or even more were killed and thousands of women were captured.

At this time, many killed their women using wells as graves of honour. A century and a half later, this was to haunt Delhi and Punjab again when female honour could only be salvaged by unsung deaths. Amrita Pritam knew her history well when she wrote of the tragedies that Punjabi women had to face during the violence of Partition.

The stench of corpses was everywhere. Famine followed in Delhi as granaries were sealed. The emperor's jewels, the Peacock Throne and the Kohinoor diamond were taken away and over 150 million rupees worth of property was amassed.

Nadir Shah, after his return to Persia, waived the taxes of the local population; such was the extent of the loot from Delhi and its adjoining districts. Mir had already moved to Agra a year before Nadir Shah's plunder. Sauda too experienced these seismic changes; his personal fortunes dwindled as the patronage of Nawab Samsam-ud-Daula, who was the imperial paymaster until he was killed in 1739, stopped after the invasion.

However, Nadir Shah was not the last of the invaders. His invasion of Delhi prompted others. Encouraged by the anarchy in India and the shaky seat of Delhi's royalty, Ahmed Shah Abdali, emperor of Afghanistan between 1747 and 1772 of the Durrani

Empire that stretched from Persia and modern-day Afghanistan to Central Asia, also tried his luck. However, he was driven out of India after his first incursion in 1748. But in 1757, he was successful in invading and re-enacting the tragedy in Delhi. In 1760, he came to India again and Delhi suffered another blow.

Before Abdali could succeed, a civil war, from 1753 to 1757, led by Safdarjung of Oudh and his allies, the Jats, plundered Shajhananabad. As always, the poor were the immediate targets of such violence. 'Jat gardi' or hooliganism of the Jats became a menacing term and a living scare in the city. During this time, a young minister, Imadul Mulk, brought peace to Delhi. However, he also was a power seeker who, after winning the confidence of the gullible Mughal emperor, Shah Alam II, reneged on his oath of loyalty taken on the Quran, and betrayed and blinded him. Mir wrote:

> I live to see the needle drawn across the eyes of kings
> The dust beneath his two feet was like collyrium ground with pearls.

Shah Alam II was made irrelevant. He could not even afford food and salaries for his troops. Soldiers' riots within the fort were the natural consequence. Imadul faced public opposition as he turned into a power freak and tinpot dictator. The seeds of public resistance, in a modern sense, were sown in this dark age of Delhi. Imadul had to retreat. Imperial officials encouraged riots.

When Abdali finally arrived in Delhi, the unpopular Imadul and his troops were no match for Abdali's well-organized troops. Abdali's invasions led to massive extortion and large-scale violence. There were so many corpses floating in the canals and other water reservoirs that there was an outbreak of cholera. His collection of riches from the palaces and havelis of Shahjahanabad required Abdali to arrange for 28,000 animals including horses and camels to transport the wealth from Delhi to Kandahar.

In such times, what could poets do other than compose sad verses? Mir's world had been undone. In 1760, Abdali struck again. Mir's lament from his autobiographical account is touching:

> Fires were started in the city and houses were burned down and looted. The following morning was all uproar and confusion … Najib's soldiers started the plunder … breaking the doors … three days and three nights, the savagery continued. The Afghan would leave no article of food and clothing untouched. They broke down walls and roofs of the houses and ill treated and tormented the inhabitants. The city was swarming with them. Men who had been the pillars of the state were left as nothing … family ones bereft of all loved ones … the new city of Shah Jahanabad was ransacked.

Mir then adds:

> I who was already poor became poorer. My house which stood on the main road was levelled with the ground … I have suffered many hardships in this city … perhaps I may find peace and comfort elsewhere. I did not know where I was going, trusting in God to lead me.[21]

A Hindu noble provided him shelter outside the city. Mir wrote:

> Delhi in those days was little better than wilderness which every six months was laid desolate afresh. Besides, a man cannot wander from place to place forever.[22]

When Mir returned to Delhi after taking refuge outside the city, he could not recognize the place:

> The scene of desolation filled my eyes with tears and my mind with the most solemn thoughts and every step my distress and agitation increased. I could not recognise the houses and often lost my bearings. Of the former inhabitants there was no trace and no matter whom I inquired about I was told that he was not there and nobody knew where he might be found. Cloisters and wine shops alike were deserted. Whole bazaars had vanished … everywhere there was a terrible emptiness.

In verse:

> Here where the thorn grows, spreading over mounds of dust and ruins
> These eyes of mine once saw the gardens blooming in the spring.

And again:

I recall the life I used to live, foregathering with my friends in the evenings, reciting poetry and living the life of a lover—weeping at nights for the love of beautiful women, writing verse to them and passing my days in the company of those whose long tresses held me their captive and knowing no peace when I could not be with them ... in those days I had really lived.

> What days were those! Days that are no more
> The days when people loved their fellow men

And what was there now? Not a soul whom I even recognised and with whom I could pass a pleasant few minutes in conversation. I came away from the lane ... and there and then I made a vow that as long as l live I will never come this way again.

Nearly ten years were spent outside Delhi but the decline was pervasive. He returned in 1782, only to see further destruction:

> Live out your life away from men's society,
> For men no longer feel that you are one of them.
> Thousands and thousands were laid low in the dust
> And no one even asked what had become of them.

At the end of the day, Mir knew that his grief was not personal. It was in a sense civilizational, shared and, perhaps, continuing. He wrote:

> My verses are all liked by high society
> But it is to the people I like to speak.

Looking for Mir's house was an arduous task. Mir probably lived in Kucha Chalan (named after *Chehel Amiran*—Forty

Nobles—of the sultanate times. Kucha Chalan was probably beside the present-day Golcha Cinema). The forty nobles were a powerful group within the court of the Delhi sultans. Sir Syed Ahmed Khan, the Muslim reformer, is also reported to have stayed there. While searching for the house, I stumble on the site of Kalan Mahal which served as a temporary residence for Shah Jahan and the royal household while the Red Fort was being completed. Today, a girls' school exists at this site. Its peeling, thick walls speak of their age.

I was caught in a web of oral accounts while searching for Mir's house. The residents of Kucha Chalan were unaware of the poet. Many did not know who he was and confused him with a Kashmiri resident. It was a bizarre experience trying to tell the Muslim underclass that they once had a great poet living near these streets. Some said that Mir also lived in Galli Qasim Jaan where Ghalib's haveli is situated. Of course this is untrue. Ghalib would have mentioned that in the large corpus of letters he had left for posterity.

During the tumultuous events of the eighteenth century, Mir's house was destroyed at least twice. But my meandering is not without some result. The affable local guide takes us to the grave of the only female sultan, Razia. How could I have forgotten that she is buried in Old Delhi, near Turkman Gate instead of in Mehrauli?

Following the cloistered lanes from the Jama Masjid, we walk down the Matia Mahal, pass by Chitli Qabr, clamber up the Pahari Bhojla lanes, enter Bulbulkhana and reach a cul-de-sac. The signboard outside, placed by the Archaeological Survey of India states that one of the two graves lying beyond the gate is believed to be Razia's. The other one is anonymous. It is surely not that of her Assyrian lover, whom she would have liked to be buried with as their love remained unfulfilled. Razia was killed in Haryana and brought here for burial. The place is run down and hardly befitting for the first and only female ruler of Delhi's throne. Centuries would pass before another woman, Indira Gandhi, assumed power in Delhi.

Altamash (1211–36), popularly known as Iltutmish, was the first and the only Muslim sultan to want to appoint a woman, his daughter, Razia, as his successor. But the Turkish nobility, influenced by the clergy who denied women the right to rule, resisted this development. Thus the nobility nominated Razia's brother, Rukn-ud-din Feroze Shah as the sultan. The incompetent and opium-addicted Feroze was unable to keep the central power intact, and within six months, he was killed. The nobility had no choice but to appoint Sultana Razia to the throne.

Razia lived up to her father's expectations. Capable, shrewd and brave, she managed the 'Forty Nobles' with an iron hand. The people of Delhi supported her rule; in due course, she also handled the regional governors by pitting them against each other. But her relationship with Yakut, an Assyrian slave, was unacceptable and enraged the supremacist Turkish nobles. The governor of Lahore reacted to her objectionable love affair which was followed by the rebellion of Malik Ikhtiar-ud-din Altunia, governor of Bhatinda. But Altunia was both a political foe and a jilted lover. According to legend, he had been in love with Razia since childhood.

As quintessential subcontinental love stories proceed, Razia was separated from Yakut when the latter was murdered by Altunia, who imprisoned Razia after winning a battle against her army. Razia had no choice but to marry Altunia to save her life and throne. But the Turkish nobles, in the meantime, crowned Razia's other brother, Behram, as the ruler of the Delhi sultanate. With Altunia's help she waged a rebellion to reclaim the throne but things had changed. Behram defeated the advancing forces and the royal couple lost the battle, and were later executed.

This claustrophobic corner with the two graves, surrounded by decaying ugly buildings with air conditioners jutting out of them, was hauntingly sad. A little slice of sky overhead was a saving grace. Also used as a mosque, there was an odd *namazee* praying in a corner. An unlikely location for a queen's grave, this was a mournful sight. I sat there for a half an hour until the accompanying guide became restive.

So I got up and walked out of the labyrinthine alleys to face the real twenty-first-century Delhi.

NOTES

1. The *Delhi Ode* was written by Bahadur Shah Zafar just before his death and is recorded by William Dalrymple in his book, *The Last Mughal: The Fall of a Dynasty, Delhi 1857*, New York: Vintage, 2008. Also see *Lonely Planet, India*, p. 49.
2. Stephen P. Blake, *Shahjahanabad: The Sovereign City in Mughal India 1639-1739*, Google Books, p. 31.
3. Originally instituted as Madarsa Ghaziuddin Khan, it closed in 1790 but was reopened in 1792. It was reorganized as the Anglo-Arabic College by the British East India Company in 1828.
4. Dastangoi is the art of storytelling. Daastaans were epics, often oral in nature, which were recited or read aloud. They were tales of adventure, magic and warfare. The story of Hamza, supposedly an uncle of Prophet Mohammad, stands out among various daastaans.
5. A chabutra is a feeding table for birds set up in homes and gardens. The practice of putting up these feeding tables is linked to the Jain faith.
6. Stephen P. Blake, *Shahjahanabad: The Sovereign City in Mughal India 1639-1739*, Google Books, p. 66.
7. In their will, called 'waseyya', Muslims are allowed to give out a maximum of one-third of their property. (Quran, 2:180–82, 2:240, 4:33, 5:106–07).
8. Niccolao Manucci wrote, 'it would seem as if the only thing Shahjahan cared for was the search for women to serve his pleasure' and 'for this end he established a fair at his court. No one was allowed to enter except women of all ranks that is to say, great and small, rich and poor, but all handsome.' When he was detained in the Agra Fort, Aurangzeb permitted him to retain 'the whole of his female establishment,

including the singing and dancing women'. Manucci notes that Shahjahan didn't lose his 'weakness for the flesh' even when he had grown very old.

9. This is from the poem 'I Bow Before the Image of My Love' from 'Diwan-e-Makhfi', or *The Book of The Hidden One*, a collection of Zebunissa's writings published in 1724, thirty-five years after her death. Makhfi was also Zebunissa's pen name. In this line she sees herself as an image of divine beauty and worships herself.
10. Translated by Willis Barnstone.
11. S.M. Latif, *Lahore: Its History, Architectural Remains and Antiquities*, 1892; reprinted in 1956, 1972 and 1981.
12. *Chinna Katha II*, p. 208.
13. Some of her poems have been rendered into English and published in the *Wisdom of the East* series, available at http:21persian.packhum.org/persian/
14. S.M. Latif, *Lahore: Its History, Architectural Remains and Antiquities.*
15. P. Spear, *Twilight of the Mughals*, Cambridge, 1951, reprinted Delhi 1969.
16. William Irwin, *Later Mughals*, Jadu Nath Sarkar (ed.). This is a two-volume book published by Oriental Books Reprint Corporation in 1971.
17. 'Shahr-ashob' conventionally described a whole range of professions reflecting the milieu that influenced the lives and vocations of individuals living in a city and who were associated with such professions.
18. Poets such as Qa'im Chandpuri (1793) and Nazir Akbarabadi (1830) also composed such elegies to a city that was evaporating.
19. Ralph Russell, *Three Mughal Poets*, Harvard University Press, p. 233. Most translation in this section have been taken from this book.
20. J. Sarkar, *Fall of the Mughal Empire*, Calcutta: M.C. Sarkar & Sons, 1964.
21. Ralph Russell, *Three Mughal Poets*, Harvard University Press, p. 32.
22. Ibid., p. 35.

7

The Chosen Spirits

After days of waiting and negotiating without an itinerary, I finally go to Sarmad Shaheed's tomb in Old Delhi. His dargah dominates the entryway to Delhi's imposing Jama Masjid. The legendary Sarmad was Jewish by birth but in his own words, 'a follower of the Furqan (Sufi), a (Catholic) priest, a (Buddhist) monk, a Jewish rabbi, an infidel, and a Muslim'.[1] Surely, it is difficult to visualize a mystic with a more intricate confessional identity.

Sarmad's brief but legendary presence in Old Delhi is a fascinating story of eclecticism and its acceptance by people and rejection by the establishment. Sarmad has become a metaphor for the defiance of identities and loyalties, for throwing conformity into the gutter and rejoicing in the ultimate rebellion of wandering the streets as a completely naked fakir.

He was a remarkable figure for his times. In the twentieth century, Maulana Abul Kalam Azad, at the young age of twenty-three, would write a treatise on Sarmad and reflect on how much he was influenced by him. Was Azad, stifled by orthodoxy, yearning to break free of tradition? He was inspired by Sarmad's insistence on not succumbing to the mullah. Sarmad declared that 'a temple and mosque were symbols and expressions of the same reality, God, in which notions of faith and unbelief are extinguished for ever'.

The story of Sarmad is one long progression from travel to love and from populism to execution. Layer by layer, year after year, Sarmad peeled off his identities and found India to be the place his soul was searching for. He arrived in India during Shah Jahan's reign, ostensibly to sell art from Persia. An Armenian Jew by birth, Sarmad had mystic leanings reflecting the complex and layered culture of Persia. En route to mainland India, somewhere close to Thatha in Sindh, Sarmad met a young man who would transform his life forever. Sarmad had started a small business near the Indus and was making a fortune until his encounter with Abhay Chand. His intimate friendship with the Hindu youth transformed his concept of love. He gave up his business and assumed the mantle of a Hindu ascetic. His love for Abhay Chand caused him to renounce the world and shed all the trappings of existence including his clothing. In this nakedness he would sit outside his beloved's door and sing these lines:

> I know not if in this spherical old monastery (the world)
> My God is Abhay Chand or some one else.

Abhay Chand's family, impressed by the purity and intensity of Sarmad's passion, relented and allowed him to associate with their young son. Soon, the two were so attached that they left together to wander the plains of India in order to find meaning and identify their inner vistas of spirituality.

Travels in medieval times were not fleeting journeys but long, arduous forays into unknown worlds and cultures. In this land of Sufis, Sarmad must have heard mystic songs and seen fakirs, leading him to embrace Islam to which he added Hindu tenets. However, by the time he became a fakir, his legendary miracles had entered public memory through popular lore.

The initial abode of Sarmad's turbulent soul was Lahore. He lived for eleven years outside the Shahi Mosque where centuries later, the iconoclastic Ustad Daman was to find his home after the turbulence of Partition. Walking stark naked on the streets of Lahore, Sarmad would compose poetry in quatrains, the classical Persian format, but with unusual themes. He would sing of the Self and deride all conventional institutionalized religion. Sarmad soon began to attain a status equal to that of Persian poets such as Ferdosi, Nizami, Saadi, Hafez and Omar Khayyam. He sang:

> Not only are these temples and sanctuaries
> His house … this earth and this sky are entirely His abode.
> The whole world is mad about His fiction.
> He is truly mad who is mad about Him.

Equally eccentric, though clothed, Dara Shikoh (Shah Jahan's son) became Sarmad's disciple.[2] This close association between Dara and Sarmad was an enriching one and strengthened Dara's quest for spiritual synthesis. One of the letters that Dara wrote to Sarmad inquired:

> My Pir and Preceptor, everyday I resolve to pay my respects to you. It remains unaccomplished. If I be I, wherefore is my intention of no account? If I be not I, what is my fault? Though the murder of Imam Hussein was the will of God, what was the agency of Yazid[3] in murdering Hussein? If it is not the Divine will, then what is the meaning of 'God does whatever He wills and commands whatever He intends'?

Sarmad's reply was terse but emphasized that too much of theological exposition was irrelevant compared to attaining the experiential knowledge of God:

> My dear Prince
> What we have read, we have forgotten
> Save the discourse of the Friend whom we remember again and again.

Sarmad's stories, especially his reverence towards the great saint Mian Mir,[4] are still popular in Lahore. Lahoris believed that the Mughal Empire declined as a result of Sarmad's curse after the execution of Lahore's illustrious citizen, Dara Shikoh. Restless and wandering, Sarmad reached Delhi, where the local population, familiar with his poetry and mystical powers, accepted him with warmth and openness. In Delhi, Khwaja Syed Abu Qasim Sabzwari (known as Hare Bhare Shah), a well-known saint, welcomed and blessed Sarmad. The tragic execution of Dara Shikoh made him extremely sad and he was bold in his condemnation of Aurangzeb and his puritanical governance. Sarmad's nakedness, poetry and views were a direct threat to the court ulema and the emperor himself. When Aurangzeb inquired why he was naked, Sarmad is reported to have exclaimed:

> He who gave you the sovereignty of the world gave me causes of anxiety. He covered with a garment those who had any fault (deformity); to the faultless he gave the robe of nudity.

Sarmad also reinterpreted Prophet Mohammad's ascension to heaven, which became the ultimate excuse for the Mughal court and its clergy to declare him an apostate. His statement was radical:

> The mullahs say that Mohammed entered the heavens, but Sarmad says that the heavens entered Mohammed.

Shahjahanabad's old walls ring with stories about Sarmad. One famous anecdote concerns how Sarmad's open smoking of a local variety of cannabis irked Aurangzeb as he had declared all intoxicants illegal. Hearing from his spies about constant violations, he paid a sudden visit to Sarmad who was sitting amid his disciples and discussing mysticism. The emperor saw the earthen pot with the drugs and inquired what the pot contained. Sarmad replied that it was milk and when Aurangzeb checked the vessel, there was indeed milk in it. His disciples and fellow smokers were astounded and spread the word thus adding to the rich stock of oral accounts of miracles associated with India's saints and sadhus.

Sarmad had little time for ritual. He would ridicule the mullah's sermon outside the Jama Masjid, proclaiming that the mullah's God—the giver—was under Sarmad's feet. His rebellion was short-lived. He was immensely popular in Delhi; his open defiance of the emperor and constant veneration of the late Dara Shikoh was a political threat. Sarmad's charisma and iconoclasm was a direct challenge to the monarchy. Hence the court ulema engineered a fatwa in which Sarmad's nakedness, refusal to recite the full Kalima[5] and denial of Prophet Mohammad's *physical* journey to the heavens constituted the charge sheet and thus a tragic execution took place. Another martyr was born.

Centuries later, I feel overwhelmed as I stand outside Sarmad's flaming red dargah that has two beautiful pipal trees arching over it. The adjacent mazar of Hare Bhare Shah is all green. Given the majestic backdrop of the Jama Masjid, the place turns into an other-worldly painting—red, green and the pink of the sandstone spill on a large canvas along with overcrowding, noise and beggars.

I stand there motionless, unwilling to speak or think. I hear the familiar lyrics of Bulleh Shah exploding through this blank moment:

Bulla! Shah Inayat dey beh boohy
Jis pehnaey sanoon savey tey soohey.

It was Shah Inayat's love
Because of which I have worn clothes red and green.

Red and green symbolize celebration, fertility and revolution. Before crossing the little entrance to the shrine, I find a slim book on Sarmad at the kiosk that sells flowers, incense and other trinkets for visitors. With the book in my hand I enter the dargah and squat on the floor of the quiet little chamber painted red with many red chadars covering the grave and the fragrance of roses.

There is colour all around, intense and lyrical; it is impossible to resist its spell.

When Sarmad was taken to the gallows near the Jama Masjid, the huge crowds gathered there could not believe how a harmless, nearly insane, naked fakir could be murdered in broad daylight. As Sarmad walked through the crowds and waited for the final moment, he composed and recited twenty-four quatrains. The poor low-caste executioner wanted to cover Sarmad's head, but Sarmad stopped him and smiled, uttering these impromptu verses:

> The friend with naked sword has now arrived
> In whatever disguise thou mayst come, I recognise thee.
>
> There was an uproar and we opened our eyes from eternal sleep,
> Saw that the night of wickedness endured, so we slept again.

This extempore gush of poetry would have been lost to us had the court chronicler, Aqil Khan Razi not been present among the onlookers. A well-meaning companion of Sarmad, Shah Asadullah urged him—if only you would cover your nakedness and utter the Kalima in full you might live—but Sarmad just laughed it off remembering Hallaj.[6] He was so filled with divine love that to him, the king, the judge, the executioner, the whole universe, including himself, were the same. His very soul itself merged with the universe. He had no consciousness of himself.

Foreign travellers like Bernier could not understand the Sarmad phenomenon. Disgusted, he wrote about Sarmad's execution:

> I was for a long time disgusted with a celebrated fakir, named Sarmet, who walked in the streets of Delhi as naked as he came to the world. He despised equally the threats and persuations of Aurungzebe and underwent at length the punishment of decapitation for his obstinate refusal to put on his wearing apparel.

The other European, Niccolao Manucci wrote:

> Dara (Shikoh) held to no religion; when with Mohammedans, he praised the tenets of Mohammed, when with Jews, the Jewish religion; in the same way when with Hindus, he praised Hinduism. This is why Aurungzebe styled him a kafir (infidel). At the same time, he had great delight in talking to the Jesuit fathers on religion, and making them dispute with his learned Mohammedans, or with Cermad (Sarmad) an atheist much liked by the prince. This man went always naked, except when he appeared in the presence of the prince when he contented himself with a piece of cloth at his waist.[7]

Abhay Chand died soon after Sarmad was beheaded. His grief was intense and irreparable.

I wished to see the copies of Sarmad's verse in the British Museum, London, and to visit the Oriental Library of Rampur to explore the 'Diwan' of Sarmad that is supposed to contain a portrait of the poet with his loving disciple, Abhay Chand. But life is complicated for Pakistani visitors to India; we cannot get a visa for more than three cities and even that can be a cumbersome process.

On subsequent visits, I would recite these lines by Sarmad for my friend at the dargahs of Sarmad and Hare Bhare Shah:

> Oh King of Kings, I am not a hermit like thee, I am not nude.
> I am frenzied, I am distracted, but I am not depressed,
> I am an idolater, I am an infidel, I am not of the people of the faith,
> I go towards the mosque, but I am not a Muslim.

This mystical tradition did not die with Sarmad and his preceptor, Hare Bhare Shah. Mystics and strange kalandars, or roaming Sufi teachers, have been spotted at Sarmad's dargah on special occasions. One such person was Fateh Mohammed Yasin, who, during the 1960s, was a constant presence at the shrine of Hare Bhare Shah. He would hold conversations with visitors and unearth the mysteries of Sufism, occasionally tapping the ground with his walking stick. Yasin was a junior government clerk in the British era of the early 1940s. His notes were discovered by the charming chronicler, R.V. Smith, who himself is as endangered as Delhi's heritage. Smith has devoted a life to explore and write about Delhi but lives a life of poverty in today's Delhi for he exists on the margins of commercialism.

From the sixteenth century onwards, the Malamatiya Malanti (the Blameworthy Lineage), a school of thought that existed around the eighth century in Iran, and was subsequently absorbed into subcontinental Sufism, emphasizing the negation of all symbols of the ego and deliberately relating to the lowly, flourished due to adherents such as Bulleh Shah in Punjab, Shah Hussain in Lahore and Lalan Shah in Bengal. A rediscovery of the original manifesto of the bhakti movement, this was also a reaction to the co-option of traditional Sufi orders by the Mughal state and regional kingdoms. In many ways, traditional Sufis had become another elite group within the power structure. One could say that, at some level, Sarmad was also an inspiration for the Malamati movement.

I became acquainted with Inder Salim through my blog. He is another Sarmad devotee who lives in Delhi. Inder Salim, who bears a composite, self-constructed name, is a Kashmiri, well ensconced in the Delhi intellectual scene with his frequent and original forays into environmentalism and subaltern takes on culture. He is a performance artist and subverts convention by holding an exhibition of photographs of a Delhi cobbler. As he explains, 'The definition of art-in-public-space is vast … I try to conceptualize my performance with ongoing conflicts, both political and otherwise in my mind, but the *form* employed changes the dynamics of the performance as well.' Inder's view is in sync with the contemporary artistic movement known as 'Stuckism'.[8]

Inder tells me that his fondness for Sarmad began in his native Kashmir. Dara Shikoh had built a garden called Bijebehara in Kashmir and through a strange quirk of fate, Inder's school was located within that garden. 'I have a strange attachment to Sarmad because of this ... not only because most of my dreams are about my school, but my practice of being a performance artist gets constant inspiration from the very idea of Sarmad. Delhi is full of that echo of Sarmad,' adds Inder. He, like Maulana Azad, shares the same regret that Nehru, the first prime minister of a free India, had thought of naming a major road after Aurangzeb instead of Sarmad. 'So I subverted that historical decision through my picture.[9] I think Sarmad is still unrecognized by most of us,' he rued. Inder gave two major performances on Sarmad, one in The Attic in Connaught Place and the other at the Little Theatre Group auditorium as part of the notable Sarai Fellowship Series.

This latter performance by Inder was a subtle introduction of Sarmad and his life in which Inder was nude throughout. In that unselfconscious state, he distributed yellow saffron rice to the audience. And he designed spectacles with green and red for the occasion.[10]

Sarmad, in a way, is a medieval forebear of Stuckism and performative art—global trends which have become increasingly popular since the latter part of the twentieth century. But Inder's naked performance in remembrance of Sarmad is placed within a typical Delhi culture fest which is ironically restrictive as it forecloses Sarmad's limitless search for freedom.

Six centuries of Muslim rule reached its peak during Shah Jahan's reign. By which time the line between orthodox and inclusive elements within the state had been drawn. Mughal rulers wanted public acceptance and legitimacy through their tolerant policies towards their non-Muslim subjects but they also wanted the official sanction of their rule through the court ulema. This duality was to result in a fractured future for the empire and its legacy as well as for the fate of Muslims in India.

The two streams had become well developed over the centuries. The eclecticism of the pluralistic bhakti movement, the Chishti, Qadri and other Sufi schools, Akbar's overt secularism and an ethos of coexistence—all existed side by side with the puritanism and exclusivity of Muslim scholars such as Mujaddid Alif Sani. In such a contested milieu, Shah Jahan's heir apparent, Dara Shikoh, defined and intellectualized the ethos shared by communities across religious, social and geographic divides.

Dara Shikoh was the eldest son of the Mughal emperor Shah Jahan and his wife Mumtaz Mahal. His early education was entrusted to Islamic scholars connected to the royal court, who taught him the Quran, Persian poetry and history. His chief instructor, Mullah Abdul Latif Saharanpuri, inducted Dara into the speculative sciences and Sufism. The intellectual and mystical environment of Mughal India nurtured a unique prince who was interested in the pursuit of knowledge, arts and literature. His vision and contributions to India were momentous. Alas, they remain as derelict and ruinous as the state of Delhi's monuments which everyone likes to talk about but no one wants to adopt.

A young Dara interacted with a host of Muslim and Hindu mystics and yogis, making them a part of his intellectual universe. The notable ones included Shah Muhibulla, Shah Dilruba, Shah Muhammad Lisanulla Rostaki, Baba Lal Das Bairagi and Jagannath Mishra. However, in Mian Mir, the Qadri Sufi of Lahore, who also laid the foundation stone of the fabulous Golden Temple at Amritsar, Dara discovered his Sufi master.

Dara ventured to study and understand Hinduism and learnt Sanskrit. With the help of the pundits of Benares, Dara rendered the Upanishads, the Bhagavadgita and the *Yoga Vashishta* into Persian. This was a grand project, a fine attempt at understanding the commonalities between India's two major religions. Thus wrote Dara in the *Sirr-ul-Akbar* (The Great Secret), his translation of the Upanishads, published in 1657:

> And whereas I was impressed with a longing to behold the gnostic doctrines of every sect and to hear their lofty expressions of monotheism and had cast my eyes upon many theological books and had been a follower thereof for many years, my passion for beholding the Unity (of God), which is a boundless ocean, increased every moment. ... Thereafter, I began to ponder as to why the discussion of monotheism is so conspicuous in India and why the Indian (Hindu) mystics and theologians of ancient India do not disavow the Unity of God, nor do they find any fault with the Unitarians.

Dara's translation of the Upanishads appeared in Latin around 1801 and found its way into Europe's intellectual milieu. Schopenhauer, the German philosopher, termed the book 'the solace of my life and solace of my death'.[11]

The soulful prince was prolific. His body of work, broadly speaking, comprise two streams—first Sufism and Muslim saints and, second, interfaith exchange, focusing on the translations of Hindu sacred texts and the well-known *Majma-ul-Bahrain* (Mingling of the Two Oceans).

The celebrated biography of Sufi saints, *Safinat-ul-Auliya*, Dara's first creative endeavour, was completed when he was barely twenty-five years old. Two years later, he rendered another biographical account of the Sufis entitled, *Sakinat-ul-Auliya*, where he focused on the Qadri[12] school of Sufism in India. By this time Dara and his sister Jahanara were also influenced by Mulla Shah Badakshani, a leading Qadri Sufi.

Another leading treatise of his called *Wahdatul Wajud* was in harmony with the Advaitic (or non-dualistic) message of the Upanishads. *Hasanat-ul-Arifin* or *The Sayings of the Gnostics* comprised the maxims of 107 Sufis. This was an earnest pursuit of knowledge but was also in part, a response to charges of heresy by bigoted theologians who opposed Dara's views on the 'unity of all beings'. This book, where Dara was speaking before his time, was to cost him his life at the hands of bigotry. He attacked the emptiness of rituals and surface understanding of spirituality. One of his verses is revealing:

> May the world be free from the noise of the mullah
> And none should pay any heed to their fatwas.

He constantly chided the ignorance of these self-appointed guardians of faith who were not unlike the fundamentalists of today. Dara wrote that in every age, every prophet and saint had undergone afflictions and torments because of the rigid bigotry of clerics, the mullahs.

The list of Dara's known works is long. *Tariqat-ul-Haqiqat* (Following the Truth) and the *Risala-i-Haq Numa* (The Compass of Truth) are two important works. The first delved into the nature of divine consciousness and the stages that one underwent in order to attain the spiritual mantle of a Sufi. Essentially, he maintained that God was all pervasive in an ultimate expression of non-duality:

> You dwell in the Ka'aba and in Somnath
> And in the hearts of enamoured lovers.
> Thou art in the monastery
> as well as the tavern.
> Thou art at the same time, the light and the moth
> The wine and the cup
> The sage and the fool ...[13]

Dara demonstrated that the Sufi methods of inner cleansing were akin to those of Hindu yogis and tantriks. Meditation and stages of spiritual attainment were also similar in spirit.[14] His poetic collection, the 'Diwan' (called *Iksir-i-Azam* in Persian), was a curious mix of poetry, theology and philosophy, an entire world view that he had imbibed over the years. Another fascinating account was his book, *Makalama Baba Lal wa Dara Shikoh,* documenting seven conversations between Baba Lal,[15] a well-known Hindu sadhu, and himself in Lahore in 1653. These remarkable conversations highlighted the commonalities of Hindu and Sufi teachings and tenets; the text conveys an intimacy and intellectual familiarity between the protagonists, emphasizing the fundamental oneness of their respective spiritual quests. Two quatrains illuminate the essence of Dara's vision:

> Though I do not consider myself separate from Him
> Yet I do not consider myself God.
> Whatever relation the drop bears with the ocean
> That I hold true in my belief, and nothing beyond.

And then again:

> We have not seen an atom separate from the Sun
> Every drop of water is the sea in itself.
> With what name should one call the Truth?
> Every name that exists is one of God's names.[16]

What was once a majestic library. and a centre for dialogue between faiths is now the Archaeology Department of the Delhi Administration. Located close to the Kashmiri Gate in Old Delhi, the original façade and distinguishing marks have vanished. It is now an insipid building, having undergone destruction and reconstruction a few times. The Jamuna once ran close to this library that was built by Dara when the capital moved from Agra to Delhi.

The heir apparent's political need to stay close to the throne must have led to this move. I often wonder how all his books, hundreds and thousands perhaps, were transported to this location. Dara's books were from all over the globe—Iran, Egypt, Turkey and Greece. What happened to his collection of books when Dara was defeated and killed by his brother? Many of the 'heretical' books were allegedly destroyed, but many survived. After his death in 1659, the library was entrusted to the subedar of Lahore, Ali Mardan Khan. The building further changed hands before the end of the Mughal Empire and later, this library became the living quarters of the British resident. This is how some of these books found their way to England.

The present building is an early specimen of Mughal and British architectural synthesis—the basement arches and ornamental pillars are quite 'Mughal' while the exterior is whitewashed by the Raj and its relic, the notorious Public Works Department of India. Sir David Ochterlony, the first resident, may have relaxed in these half-Georgian verandas, reading his files, drafting reports on Delhi and sometimes waiting for a chhota hazree on spring mornings. Noted for his adoption of Mughal ways, Ochterlony is reported to have saved the books and the internal structure that still bears the sandstone signature of the Mughals. Later, the British converted this building into a school that existed up to 1904, but I am unable to gain additional information from the staff. I was not allowed to take photographs by the otherwise courteous attendant. However, I love the jamun trees that have just recovered from fruit bearing. Once again, I remember Lahore the way Dara may have while working on his books here.

Dara Shikoh was equally popular in Lahore and lived in the hearts of the Mughal Lahoris. His Lahori subjects knew him as 'Shah Dara', the rightful heir to the Mughal throne. Lahore's Shahdara, the settlement near the banks of the River Ravi, is named after Dara. His learning and scholarship were widely recognized and Dara's rejection of narrow fundamentalism endears him to the people of the walled city even today. His spirit lives in the detached tolerance of Lahoris towards multifarious points of view. It was after his Lahore sojourns that he settled in Delhi—and spent those intriguing days where I stand today. Rather pretentiously, I fancy tracing his footsteps—after all, like him, I am a Lahori in Delhi. I laugh at myself for such delusional musings and head towards the small museum within the building.

Dara was a keen painter and architect, a skilled calligrapher and poet all rolled into one. The Dara Shikoh album is a collection of paintings and calligraphy which he commissioned in the 1630s as a present for his wife, Nadira Bano Begum, and compiled around 1641–42. After Nadira Bano's death, the album was taken into the royal library and the inscriptions linking it to Dara Shikoh were deliberately, but fortunately, not completely erased. One painting in the album, currently in London, is signed and dated by the artist, Muhammad Khan, AH 1043 (or circa AD 1633). One is glad it is almost intact but it ought to be in Delhi, not London.

By the time I reach the artefacts in the archaeological museum, I am a little tired, not so much physically as psychologically. The two galleries display relics excavated from various sites in Delhi with a timeline as fascinating as the city—the Harappan era walking into the medieval age. The sculptures are interesting but poorly displayed.

Desperate, I finally find a mark of Dara and the sensation is both overawing and sad. I am informed that the room which houses the current library was probably used by Dara Shikoh as his study. I am not interested in the books; it is ironic that British rulers used this space for 'official' purposes (read divide and rule policy), the direct antithesis of what Dara had envisioned for India.

It is a humid morning and there is stillness. But I detect another kind of silence too, the one that has doggedly followed Dara for centuries and permeates the cacophonous noises of hatred and communal discord not just in India but across South Asia.

Dara's love of learning can be traced to his great ancestor Babar. This was transferred to his daughter Gulbadan and to Akbar the Great who, though illiterate, had a library that was unmatched in his era. Carrying the tradition forward, Dara represents the apex of shared learning. In line with many Sufis, he pondered on the possibility of Hindu religious icons being prophets of God as mentioned in the Quran[17] and also on the innate divinity of Hindu scriptures. So, from Dara's point of view, the Vedas and the philosophy of the Upanishads were in harmony with the Holy Quran.

The most well-known of Dara's works is *Majma-ul-Bahrain* completed when he was forty-two years old. It was a pioneering effort to dig out the similarities between Sufism and certain strands of Hindu thought. He describes this treatise as 'a collection of the truth and wisdom of two truth-knowing groups'.

From the veranda, I can see a group of saffron-clad yogis pass by. Dara had written that 'mukti' was closest to the Sufi pursuit of annihilation or 'fana' of the human self in God. Similarly, the Sufi concept of 'ishq' or love was in sync with 'maya' in Hindu terminology. 'From love', says Dara, 'was born the "great soul", alternately known as the soul of Mohammed to the Sufis and Mahatman or Hiranyagarbha to the Hindus.'[18]

The 'great secret' of the Upanishads—the existence of a formless God—was close to the Quranic concept of tauheed. Dara's earlier visits to Kashmir had introduced him to Mullah Shah, whom he referred to as 'the tutor of tutors'. Under the deep guidance of this sage, he delved into ancient scriptures such as the Torah of the Jews, the Gospels of Jesus, the Psalms of David and ancient Hindu texts.

This library, now decrepit, must have played a part. The expansive rooms and inner chambers have altered history but Dara could not change its course. He, however, laid some foundations for a future that could be different from the past. If only his legacy was appreciated in full measure! I think of this impossibility of the possible and leave the grand room.

In 1657, Dara was appointed as regent to look after the affairs of the empire because of his father's illness. But Emperor Shah Jahan's illness became a cue for his sons to begin a war of succession. Aurangzeb quickly made a coalition with Murad and defeated Dara Shikoh at the famous battle of Samogarh. Aurangzeb's superior military campaign, intelligence networks and support from his sister, Roshanara, were the strengths that enabled him to capture the throne in 1658. He then imprisoned his father, Shah Jahan, in the fort at Agra where he died eight years later.

Dara, despite being a brave warrior, was not inclined by nature towards a martial life. Earlier, in 1639, 1642 and 1653, he had suffered defeat in expeditions against the Persians. His final defeat came in 1659 at the hands of Aurangzeb in Deorai (near Ajmer). Dara sought refuge in Dadar (in today's Pakistan) but, sadly, his host, Malik Jiwan, betrayed him and handed him over to Aurangzeb's officials. Aurangzeb humiliated Dara by parading him in disgrace through the streets of Delhi. Bernier, an eyewitness to the scene, wrote:

> When the unhappy Prince was brought to the gates of Dehli, it became a question with Aureng-Zebe, whether ... he should be made to pass through the capital ... that he ought to be seen by the whole city; that it was necessary to strike the people with terror and astonishment, and to impress their minds with an idea of the absolute and irresistible power of Aureng-Zebe.[19]

The hapless residents of Delhi, yet again marginal players in the power game, saw a drama unfold in front of their eyes:

> ... the wretched prisoner was therefore secured on an elephant; his young son, Sipah Shikoh, placed at his side, and behind them, instead of the executioner, was seated Bahadur Khan (one of the royal generals) ... Dara was now seen seated on a miserable and worn-out animal, covered with filth; he no longer wore the necklace of large pearls which distinguish the princes of Hindoustan nor the rich turban and embroidered coat; he and his son were now habited in dirty cloth of the coarsest texture, and his sorry turban was wrapt round with a Kachemire (Kashmir) shawl or scarf, resembling that worn by the meanest of the people.

> ...The people had for some time inveighed bitterly against the unnatural conduct of Aureng-Zebe ... The crowd assembled upon this disgraceful occasion was immense; and everywhere I observed people weeping and lamenting the fate of Dara in the most touching language ... From every quarter I heard piercing and distressing shrieks, for the Indian people have a very tender heart ... men, women and children wailing as if some mighty calamity had happened to themselves. Javan Khan rode near the wretched Dara; and the abusive and indignant cries vociferated as the traitor moved along were absolutely deafening. I observed some Fakires and several poor people throw stones at the infamous Pathan; but not a single movement was made, no one offered to draw his sword, with a view of delivering the beloved and compassionated Prince. When this disgraceful procession had passed through every part of Dehli, the poor prisoner was shut up in one of his own gardens ...[20]

Dara had to die; there was no other choice for Aurangzeb. Dara Shikoh's popular support was formidable and he would have been a constant threat. And, prodded by their sister Roshanara, who hated Dara, the decision was confirmed. Legitimacy was bought through a fatwa by the court ulema who declared Dara to be a heretic punishable by death.

Nazir, a slave who had an axe to grind with Dara, was entrusted with the task of killing him. Anecdotes suggest that Dara's head was sent to the emperor and also to his beloved sister, Jahanara, in Agra, who fainted at the sight. That head, which once dreamt of universal understanding and the seeking of truth, was tossed out as a war victory relic. His headless, wretched body was buried at Humayun's tomb.

Several days later, I make my first trip to Humayun's Tomb. A World Heritage site and the architectural inspiration for the Taj Mahal, this tomb stands in Nizamuddin East bravely facing the winds of time. It is a monument that can make any city proud.

The magnificence of the tomb strikes me the moment I enter via the two-storey gateway. Enclosed by high walls on three sides, the tomb is placed in the centre of a square garden. Intersected by watercourses and woven with gardens much like the Quranic 'paradise', the tomb is calm despite the chattering hordes of schoolchildren. Built by Hamida Begum, Humayun's wife, this was yet another splendid edifice that Mughal rulers and nobles sought to erect in pursuit of an elusive immortality.

Unlike the Taj that radiates cheerfulness, Humayun's Tomb is aglow with melancholy. Perhaps it reflects the tragic lives and deaths of Humayun and Dara Shikoh. A later king, Bahadur Shah II and Hamida Begum are also buried here. This was also the site where Bahadur Shah Zafar was captured nearly a century later and thousands of displaced Delhi Muslims took refuge in 1947.

The tomb, a complex of Mughal buildings, was aesthetically the first Mughal composition of its kind in India because Babar died too early and hardly built anything and Humayun was constantly in wars or exile. The Herat-based architect, Mirza Ghiyas, followed the Chahar Bagh (square garden) style of Persian architecture taking eight years to complete it.

The Aga Khan Trust for Culture has facilitated the conservation of Humayun's tomb and this is what makes it probably the best-preserved Mughal monument in Delhi. Better even than the Red Fort which has served as a symbol of statehood after 1947. The conservation work has allowed for the watercourses to be alive once again, the walkways to appear delightfully intricate and the marble domes to reflect sunlight.

The tomb and the surrounding causeways are magical. Cast in red sandstone, the mausoleum emerges from a seven-metre high square terrace raised over a series of cells which are accessible through arches on each side. The graves are in the centre of this complex. The tomb's elevations are decorated with marble borders and panels. The classic, perforated marble screens or jalis are found at both ends. The arched alcoves, corridors and the high double dome reflect the Persian touch while the kiosks on all sides, endowing it with a pyramidal outline from a distance, are quintessentially Indian.

The central hall is a bit uninspiring. Originally, it was adorned with tasteful furnishings. The English merchant, William Finch, visited the building in 1611 and described it thus:

> ... spread with rich carpets, the tomb itself covered with a pure white sheet, a rich semiane (coloured tent) overhead, and in front, certain bookes on small tressels by which stand his sword, tucke (turban) and shooes.

On the south-western side of the tomb is the interesting structure dedicated to Humayun's barber, aptly called, Nai-ka-Gumbad (Barber's Dome). It stands on a raised platform and is reached by seven steps from the south. The building is square in plan and comprises a single section covered with a double dome. Earlier, Mohammad Bin Tughlaq bestowed his barber with his own fort, Nai ka Kot or Barber's Fort, near Adilabad. Delhi's rulers had their lavish quirks!

South of the main pathway leading to Humayun's Tomb is the pleasing gateway that leads to a walled enclosure called Arab-ki-Sarai. This was supposedly built by Humayun's widow for the 300 Arab merchants she is said to have brought with her from a pilgrimage to Mecca. But another opinion holds that Arab-ki-Sarai might possibly have been an enclosure that housed Persian workers and craftsmen who were engaged in building Humayun's Tomb. Within the eastern enclosure of the Arab-ki-Sarai is Afsarwala Tomb and Masjid. Further west on the main pathway is the gateway to the rather barren Bu Halima's garden. Coloured tiles, traces of which still remain at the entrance facing Humayun's Tomb, combined with the use of sandstone, both set in plaster, make it charming. Further south stands the octagonal tomb of Isa Khan, a nobleman in the court of Sher Shah. At the north-eastern corner of Humayun's Tomb are the remains of the quarters used by Hazrat Nizamuddin Auliya.

The Mughal emperors who reigned after Humayun established a tradition of visiting this tomb. Akbar would visit it almost each time he was in Delhi and the tradition continued until the last king. The garden was a symbol of sovereignty while the tomb denoted the establishment of a dynasty and thus Humayun's Tomb had a profound metaphorical significance as well.[21] It intersects between the two impulses of fortifying sovereignty and the continuation of a dynasty. With the creation of this tomb, the Mughals had established a statement which proclaimed their revival of Delhi and the Muslim empire that frittered away under the later sultans.

Interestingly, Humayun's Tomb was a mixture of Islamic and Hindu elements. Marble merges with local sandstone, arches integrate with temple designs, and astrological features are woven into the architecture. The Mughals were possibly chiselling their knowledge from Hindu astrologers into stone.

Dara Shikoh, the most sophisticated representative of Mughal inclusiveness, is literally and symbolically buried here. Bahadur Shah Zafar's capture by a British captain, leading to the former's dethronement and the subsequent massacres of Mughal heirs started from this point—a moment that also encapsulated the formal end of the Mughal Empire.

NOTES

1. Nathan Katz, 'The Identity of a Mystic: The Case of Sa'id Sarmad, A Jewish-Yogi-Sufi Courtier of the Mughals', *Numen*, Vol. 47, No. 2, Florida International University, 2000, pp. 142–60 (brackets in the quotation are the author's).
2. According to the eminent Persian scholar and historian, Henry George Keene.
3. Yazid was the ruler of Arabia who fought the famous battle of Karbala with Imam Hussein, Prophet Mohammad's grandson. This

epic tragedy is mourned by Shi'ites during Muharram (an Islamic month).

4. Baba Sain Mir Mohammad Sahib (1550–1635), popularly known as Mian Mir, was a Sufi saint who lived in Lahore. He belonged to the Qadri order of Sufism.
5. The first part of the Kalima, in Arabic, means: 'There is no God but God' *(La Ila-ha-Ilallalah)* and the second part, 'And Mohammad is his messenger' *(Mohammad ur Rasool Allah)*. Sarmad refused to recite the second part of the Kalima, stating that he was still lost in understanding the first part—of recognizing that nothing but the Divine existed.
6. Mansur al-Hallaj (c. 858–922) was a Persian mystic, revolutionary writer and pious teacher of Sufism most famous for his apparent, but disputed, self-proclaimed divinity, his poetry and for his execution for heresy at the orders of the Abbasid caliph, Al-Muqtadir, after a long-drawn-out investigation.
7. Niccolas Manucci, *Storia do Mogor*, as translated by William Irvine, Vol. 1, p. 223.
8. 'Stuckism' is a radical and controversial art group that was co-founded in 1999 by Charles Thomson and Billy Childish (who left it in 2001) along with eleven other artists. The name was derived by Thomson from an insult to 'childish' from his ex-girlfriend, British artist Tracey Emin, who had told him that his art was 'stuck'. Several Stuckist manifestos have been issued. One of them, 'Re-modernism', inaugurates a renewal of spiritual values for art, culture and society to replace the emptiness of current postmodernism. The website, www.stuckism.com, started by Ella Guru, has disseminated these ideas, and in five years Stuckism has grown to an international art movement with over 187 groups in forty-five countries. These groups are independent and self-directed (www.stuckism.com/info-html).
9. http:21pics.livejournal.com/indersalim/pic/000ca8cc/
10. http:21pics.livejournal.com/indersalim/pic/000dr81k/
11. Quoted in Abraham Eraly's, *The Mughal Throne—the Saga of India's Great Emperors*, London: Phoenix, 2004, p. 535.
12. The Qadri order, one of the popular Sufi 'silsilas', traces its origins to the Prophet through the twelfth-century Sufi and Islamic scholar of great renown, Sheikh Abdul Qadir Jilani of Baghdad.
13. K.R. Qanungo, *Dara Shikoh.*

14. These include astral healing and concentration on the centres of meditation in the heart and brain. Further, he suggests that the four planes through which the Sufi seeker's journey takes him—nasut, jabrut, malakut and lahut—correspond to the Hindu concept of the 'avasthanam' or the four 'states' of jagrat, swapna, sushupti and turiya.
15. A follower of the renowned Sufi and bhakti saint, Kabir, and founder of a small order, the followers of which were known as 'Baba Lalis'.
16. Translated by Yogindar Sikand.
17. The Holy Quran mentions that God sent 124,000 messengers or prophets and only a few are named. Eclectic Sufis and scholars have interpreted the number in different ways.
18. Yogindar Sikand, *Dara Shikoh.*
19. Francois Bernier, *Travels in the Mogul Empire, AD 1656-1668*, trans. by Archibald Constable on the basis of Irving Brock's version, ed., Vincent A. Smith, Low Price Publications. Slightly edited, and some spellings modernized, accessed through http:21www.columbia.edu/itc/mealac/pritchett/00generallinks/bernier/txt_bernier_dara.html. pp. 68, 69.
20. Ibid., pp. 99–100.
21. D. Fairchild Ruggles, *Humayun's Tomb and Garden: Typologies and Visual Order.* Also in 'Gardens in the Time of the Great Muslim Empires: Theory and Design', Attilio Petruccioli (ed.), New York: Brill Academic Publishers, 2007.

8

Those Who Stayed

In October 1650, Emperor Shah Jahan laid the foundation stone of what he wanted to be 'the finest mosque in the world', the Jama Masjid. Constructed under the supervision of the Persian architect Fazil-Mir-Saman, it was a masterly composition in symmetry and simplicity. An impressive range of cartographers, calligraphers, architects and workers (it is believed that over 5,000 workers toiled for six years) collaborated to create the splendid mosque.

Accompanied by a friend, I enter the mosque from the main gate (presently gate number 1) facing the Matia Mahal market and mount the magnificent red steps that culminate at the grand entrance. The basement wall, over nine metres high, is made of imposing red sandstone. Its delicately crafted domes, minarets, arches and pinnacles, like Lahore's Shahi Mosque, which was built a few decades later, beckon and converse with the visitor. The inlay work, symbolizing the toil of hundreds of artisans, day and night, is delicate. The roof, adorned with honeycomb carving and inlaid within red sandstone, and the perching roof edges on the façade, enhanced further by small arches, symbolize the orderliness of Islam.

I imbibe the grandeur of the main central hall—grand

and echoing—shaded by a vaulted roof and supported by towering pillars and squinches. The central part of the ceiling is ornamented by typical geometrical designs of floral patterns in concentric circles. These patterns typify the multiple strands of Islamic art that evolved in Persia and Central Asia. There are allusions to the Bird of Paradise denoting the migratory nature of souls. Paradise is an artistic landscape, and also a celebration of good deeds done in the temporal world. Unlike other Mughal monuments, the decorations on the arches and minarets are simple and dignified, testifying to the essential simplicity of the Islamic mode of worship.

During the Mughal era, the imam of Jama Masjid was an important imperial appointment. Syed Abdul Ghaffoor Bukhari was appointed as the first Imam-ul-Sultan.[1] Over time, this institution became politicized and adopted an overtly conservative stance. Since Independence, the imams have been a key ally of the Indian state whose patronage ensures a linear hereditary succession and a monopoly over Muslim discourse. Lording it over the ghetto whose inhabitants struggle for survival, these imams want to be in the limelight, issuing fatwas on Muslim women's status and their limits, and dictating the overall conduct of the Muslim population. The struggle to keep medievalism intact is palpably evident, serving thus to only reinforce the Muslim stereotype in popular media and contemporary mythologies.

On one of my visits, I wander into Urdu bookshops, looking for a pictorial autobiography of the Urdu author, Qurratulain Hyder. Behind me resounds the khutba or sermon emanating from the Jama Masjid. Forceful in tone, it articulates a regressive world view and hard-core conservatism. That such stuff is being aired in secular India is remarkable in itself; it keeps the local population intoxicated with a fossilized vision of Islam. The imam is making references to 'non-believers' as if lack of faith was the main reason for the poverty of the population of Old Delhi. His rabid proclamations are aired while customers casually stroll around the Urdu Bazaar that has less bookshops than meat shops. The Urdu Bazaar is as threatened as the language itself, and has come to represent the ultimate stereotype of the illiterate, meat-obsessed Muslim.

Visiting the Jama Masjid is a must if one is in Delhi. The last time I was there with a friend, we dared to enter a little tea stall next to a series of chicken shops that was more a den of flies but promised good tea. The tea as it turned out was not all that bad.

A man sitting next to our table started up a conversation by asking me where I was from. His name was Abdul Ashraf and he was visiting from Gujarat to follow up on a court case. Obviously, this was most interesting—meeting up with a real victim of Modi's Gujarat. So I prodded him to talk of the dislocation, of camps, and of the general state of affairs in Gujarat.

To my utter surprise and embarrassment, (maybe because I was with a Hindu friend), Abdul's lack of coherence and his recourse to a religious theology while speaking about political or everyday-life questions was shocking. Abdul quoted several sayings of Prophet Mohammad which promised 'justice' in the afterlife so that the suffering of the temporal world was somehow the 'fate' of pious Muslims. Our 'pious' Muslim, Abdul, had recently been fired from his factory job and his union had challenged the dismissal in the Supreme Court of India. So 'justice' was perhaps a reference to that and piety, a path leading to wish-fulfilment. I could make little sense of what he said despite the familiarity with theological references. However, Abdul did not mention Modi, communalism and the violence that may have jolted his life. After all, he was living in a big camp when I asked him about the riots.

Perhaps Abdul was too terrified to speak up? Or the violence and personal struggle for a livelihood had impaired his coherence? His inability to rationalize his plight in the context of modern India synchronized with the gems of the retrograde sermon being poured into the ears of 'believers' from the blaring loudspeakers of Jama Masjid.

Sixty years ago, just after Independence, a dejected and wounded Maulana Azad made an impassioned speech on the stairs of the Jama Masjid. He cried:

> Think for one moment. What course have you adopted? Where have you reached and where do you stand now? Haven't your senses become torpid? Aren't you living in a constant state of fear? This fear is your own creation, a fruit of your own deeds.[2]

Despite Azad's exhortations, many Muslims had turned a deaf ear to his views on the two-nation theory. And, as he had predicted, it was not long before upheavals occurred that were to change the destiny of Indian Muslims. Sticking to his position, he reiterated that Partition was a 'fundamental mistake'. He asked whether Muslims were capable of any constructive thinking and if Indian Muslims were going to lead the 'life of escapism' that they had 'opted for in the sacred name of hijrat'. Azad's words in Urdu were lyrical:

> ... where are you going and why? Raise your eyes. The minarets of Jama Masjid want to ask you a question: where have you lost the glorious pages from your chronicles? Was it only yesterday that on the banks of the Jamuna, your caravans performed wuzu?[3] Today, you are afraid of living here! Remember, Delhi has been nurtured with your blood. Brothers! Create a basic change in yourselves. Today, your fear is misplaced as your jubilation was yesterday.

Noting that politics had undergone a major shift, Azad urged Muslims 'to take their cue from history and cast themselves in the new mould'. There were still many 'blank pages in the history of India' and Muslims had to be 'worthy of filling those pages'. That the bright etchings of Delhi all around them were indeed relics of the qafilas of Muslim ancestors. He wanted them to be fit inheritors of this legacy.

I'm struck by Azad's words. The area around the Jama Masjid is, in chillingly real terms, a Muslim's 'own surroundings' and their 'own world'—different and a wee bit cut off from the rest of the city. While Delhi expands outwards and eats into the fields of Haryana and tracts across the Jamuna, the Muslim slum grows inwards and backwards into time and the lost world of fleeting glory.

Azad remained ahead of his times and his prediction that Indian Muslims would end up divided finally came true when, after a bloody war of liberation, East Pakistan became Bangladesh. Now the Muslims of the subcontinent are located in almost equal numbers in India, Pakistan and Bangladesh.

In his 1946 statement on Muslim issues in India, in the classic document of Indian Muslim nationalism, *India Wins Freedom*, Azad had warned:

> Let us consider dispassionately the consequences which will follow if we give effect to the Pakistan scheme. India will be divided into two states, one with a majority of Muslims and the other of Hindus. In the Hindustan State there will remain three and a half crores of Muslims scattered in small minorities all over the land ... They will awaken overnight and discover that they have become alien and foreigners. Backward industrially, educationally and economically, they will be left to the mercies of what would become an unadulterated Hindu Raj ... even if Pakistan was overwhelmingly Muslim in population, it still could hardly solve the problem of Muslims in Hindustan.

He had also foreseen: 'Two states confronting one another, offer no solution to the problem of one another's minorities, but only lead to retribution and reprisals by introducing a system of mutual hostages.' Like Jinnah, Azad was also inclined towards the 1946 Cabinet Mission proposals of creating a confederation once the British left India. But events were unfolding so rapidly that his lonesome voice was drowned in the beating of jubilatory drums for India and Pakistan respectively. Azad, however, remained optimistic and worked until his death in 1958 for the larger secular agenda, especially in education and culture.

Today, much of Azad's 'community', to use the construct we are hostage to, remains uneducated and locked in a different time zone. They evidently ignored Azad's advice to be part of history's advance. Ironically, Azad's fellow Congressmen, even today, continue to use secularism merely as an electoral strategy. Instead of deepening real secular values and education, they focus on the politics of appeasement and patronage. Often, in this process they seek the support of retrogressive clerics, mistaking that for some sort of representation of millions of Indian Muslims.

Decades after Azad's death, his granddaughter, Najma Heptullah, earlier a senior Congress leader, joined the BJP. What could be more ironic than that?

The single most important indicator of the Muslim plight has to do with their educational standards and illiteracy, and that too in Delhi, once home to strong movements towards education.

Aurangzeb, like his grandfather Jahangir, was fond of reading and writing. In the early 1700s, in memory of one of his loyal generals, he established the Ghaziuddin Madrasa near Ajmeri Gate. The well-known nineteenth-century Delhi College now named after India's third president, Dr Zakir Hussain, emerged out of the eminent Ghaziuddin Madrasa. The tradition of madrasas, however, was already well entrenched. The first madrasa in Delhi was established by Firoze Tughlak close to Hauz Khas.

In Shahjahanabad, the emperor's wife (hailing from Fatehpur) built a masjid and therefore it is known as the Fatehpuri Masjid. I could not help but notice that its space looked inwards much like the women's quarters of Shahjahanabad. In 1875, the mosque was converted into a madrasa when Lord Northbrook was the viceroy of India. The fountain of Chandni Chowk was also renamed after Lord Northbrook. In 1878, the madrasa expanded its scope by accepting students from outside Delhi.

Today, this madrasa is locked in time. Young men in topis and ankle-length pyjamas sit on the ground and, with shaking heads, rote-learn Urdu lessons and religious instruction. Like several such madrasas across South Asia, this is a quaint world unaffected by the rapidly changing world. The Fatehpuri Madrasa carries a practice that is increasingly looked upon with fear by non-Muslims who perceive it as a new lexicon of terror and terrorism, and consider it a threat.

The madrasas of Delhi were evolving in the eighteenth and nineteenth centuries. The Delhi College was an innovative example of the re-emphasis of education among Muslims, led by visionaries such as Sayyed Ahmed Khan. A vast network of Muslim scholars, educationists and officials led by Khan, urged the Muslim population to acquire modern education and catch up with the changing times. During the early years of this movement, also known as the 'Aligarh Movement', women's education was not a priority; however, by the twentieth century it would emerge as a pressing one. The famed Aligarh school, college and later the Aligarh Muslim University were concrete results of this movement.

Delhi's intellectual elites joined forces with British zeal to reform Muslim education, resulting in the setting up of the Delhi College, a meeting ground of British and Oriental cultures.[4] By the mid-nineteenth century, the college emerged as a strong institution of quality learning. English and Oriental branches of study existed side by side.

It was the famous principal, Alois Sprenger, who provided much dynamism and intellectual energy to the institution. Leading faculty members, products of the changing times, were

Maulvi Zakaullah, 'Dipty' Nazir Ahmed, Master Ram Chandra and Maulvi Karimuddin. They became the foremost proponents of modern education in Delhi. The poet, Ghalib, was also considered for a job at the Delhi College but he turned it down as he felt that he was not given due respect on his visit for the interview.

Nazir Ahmad was also a novelist and his reformist stories still remain popular in the Urdu language. His works were included in the syllabus at my own school, the Aitchison College, in Pakistan. Munshi Zakaullah, an eminent writer, published over 140 books on diverse topics ranging from history to the rules of chess. The gifted Master Ram Chandra was hailed as a genius because of his groundbreaking work on algebra titled, *A Treatise on Problems of Maxima and Minima Solved by Algebra.*

The British viewed the Delhi College as a modernizing influence on the 'natives' who, with the acquisition of Western knowledge, would form a class that was better acquainted with colonial priorities. Gradually, the curricula of traditional sciences underwent changes. Students were given the option to learn Arabic through compilations of the hadith or via the fables of *The Thousand and One Nights.* But this was also becoming a dangerous trend as the gulf between 'traditional' and 'modern' was to widen, and 'knowledge' became compartmentalized. In South Asia, these parallel streams of learning exist side by side even today, and bridging them has now become a daunting challenge in public policy. The reform of Muslim education, especially to bridge the gap between 'religious' and 'worldly' knowledge, has been a recurrent theme in the writings of South Asian Muslim reformists since the nineteenth century.

This conflict remains unresolved and is now a contested political matter exploited by traditionalists as a bargaining chip for further patronage, and by right-wing Hindu groups such as the Sangh Parivar as another ruse for Muslim bashing.

In Old Delhi, I look for 'Dipty' Nazir Ahmed's house. Nazir Ahmed was a civil servant by profession who had held the post of deputy collector. I have always found such linguistic amalgamation ('Dipty' being the Urdu version of 'Deputy') most fascinating—in the case of Nazir Ahmed it was even more symbolic. Ahmed belonged to the Muslim elite which was trying to save its losing position by aligning with the Raj. So, quite aptly, his title was a combination of the Urdu language and Raj bureaucracy.

Ahmed was given an award of Rs 1,000 and a watch by the British government for his novel *Mirat-ul-Urus* (The Bride's Mirror), authored in 1869, when he was thirty-eight. This prize was for a book, which 'shall serve some useful purpose (and) shall be written in ... Oordoo or Hindee ... Books suitable for the women of India will be especially acceptable, and well awarded.'[5]

Written for his daughters, it became the first Urdu best-seller of sorts by selling over 100,000 copies. In 1903, it was translated for the first time into English. The canvas was a bit like Jane Austen's—dealing with the inner and domestic lives of women. These were tales that were born during the afternoon sunshine, by kitchen lamplights and from the domestic harmony (or turmoil) of Delhi's courtyards. Ahmed thus created a lovely literary work—a miniature of the life of women, timeless and intimate.

I recall many minor details of the novel on my visits to various parts of Shahjahanabad, since the novel is set there—like Turkman Gate sold cheaper grains, and vegetables sold at Chandni Chowk, close to the Sabzi Mandi, were less expensive.

But I am disappointed with Ahmed's haveli. I am denied entry by the current residents of the ramshackle structure which has been rebuilt in a most unpleasing manner. They are not too pleased with a Pakistani visitor making silly inquiries. An old man with a long beard and a cap opens the door but he is hard of hearing. I don't wish to struggle too much, so I give up.

The 140 million Muslims in India have no credible secular leadership and, worst of all, no direction to move out of their 'inner siege' as I find out in Sadia's living room while watching a TV show which reveals some uncomfortable truths. Over 55 per cent of Muslims lived below the poverty line within the national average of 35 per cent. Not to mention that 45 per cent are illiterate compared to 36 per cent of all Indians. Nazir Ahmed would be horrified to know that in 2006, 55 per cent of Muslim women were still illiterate (against the 40 per cent of all Indian women). And the total share of Muslims in the civil services is a little over 2 per cent. Indeed, those sultans and Mughals of yester-empires would never have imagined, while immersed in their splendours and silly little indulgences that, centuries later, over 40 per cent of their inheritors would be called 'Other Backward Castes' (OBC) in postmodern India. Sadia's favourite line would have smacked them with irony, 'The singular places where Muslims are over-represented and constitute nearly 35 per cent are in jails.'

Such a huge underclass provides ideal fodder for electoral politicking and vote-bank swings. Secular parties such as the Congress, the Samajwadi Party, the Bahujan Samaj Party, the Communist Party of India and others find the Muslim community to be a convenient ally in constituency-based politics. The Sachar Committee[6] (2006) is just the latest of countless commissions with the 'correct' recommendations. The demand for OBC reservations that should include Muslims has now emerged. For instance, the Committee's report states that in several states and at the Centre, the Muslim groups 'who are included in the OBC list are eligible for reservation benefits.' The report rationalizes this demand by stating that the condition of Muslim OBCs is 'lower' than other communities in the same category.

I raise this issue with many academics and Delhi intellectuals but have never got a clear reply. There is sufficient appreciation of the problem; erudite additions are made to my skin-deep observations, but the will to publicly advocate this is lacking. This could be a time bomb, politically speaking, I insist dramatically, an impending cleavage that could be a nightmare not just for India but also for the whole region. I am reminded, of course, that the Dalit situation is a priority in the public discourse and this issue is now unwittingly intertwined with the larger issues of the politics of caste and backwardness.

Sadia is always cooking up inventive ways of 'doing something' for the community. From the 'Save Urdu' campaign to employment generation and social work in the Nizamuddin Basti, she has been doing her bit. Delhi was once a place where individuals were tireless in their efforts to ameliorate the condition of Muslims. Today, given that India is a fabulous arena for civic action and leadership, this kind of civic contribution does not necessarily have to be Muslim-centric, but rather, poor or backward-centric.

While in Shahjahanabad, I remember Hakim Ajmal Khan, the eminent doctor and philanthropist. These were times, just after Maulana Altaf Hussain Hali (1837–1914), the poet, had equated the fortunes of the Muslim qaum or community with the fortunes of the city—'Delhi's glory and the glory of the qaum are the same'—Hali mused in one of his pamphlets.

A luminary of pre-Lutyens Delhi, Ajmal Khan, who epitomized such a 'glory', embodied Delhi's urbaneness. Khan advocated the notion that the preservation of Muslim culture was in everyone's interest and this was only achievable through intercommunity cooperation in medicine, politics and culture. Thus he brought together Unani hakims and Ayurvedic practitioners in an attempt to revive traditional medicine and wed it to modernity. While speaking at the first Tibbi conference, Hakim Ajmal narrated how 'Greek medicine travelled from Greece to Egypt, then to Spain from where it reached Baghdad. From Baghdad it came to Iran where it made tremendous progress ... From there it came to India and flourished here.' Both Unani and Ayurvedic systems emanate from the concept of 'the elements' (fire, water, earth and air) in the human body. Thus the remedies are often similar in the two traditional practices which use several common herbs and foods.

From the start of the Delhi Municipality in 1863 to the early twentieth century, various hakims took part in activism and politics. Ajmal Khan and his fellow reformers opposed the misuse of unregulated folk medicines and raised awareness about spurious treatments. However, a century later, quacks still abound and one marvels at the most interesting advertisements in Old Delhi promising miraculous treatments for all ailments.

By early 1920, Ajmal Khan had created three lasting institutions—the Central College in Delhi, the pharmacy to produce indigenous medicines and the Tibbi Conference, which was later renamed the All India Ayurvedic and Unani Tibbiya Conference. Ajmal would visit various princely states to provide medical advice. The nawab of Rampur, who treated him as a general guide, patronized him. Ajmal Khan was a supporter of the Khilafat movement and Gandhi's non-cooperation movement, returning the title 'Haziq-ul-Mulk' given to him in 1907 by the British. After serving as the chairman of the Congress Reception Committee, he was elected president of the Indian National Congress in 1921.

Medicine and politics were his bedfellows throughout his life. Congress included the protection of indigenous health systems as part of its programme. Khan's lasting contribution lay in his vision of evolving the nationalist Muslim school and university, the Jamia Millia.

C.F. Andrews wrote on Ajmal Khan's practice of medicine:

> My first visit to the waiting room brought home a shock to the opinion I carried from England that Hindus and Muslims could not mix. (Ajmal Khan) treated all alike, Hindu and Muslim, rich and poor.[7]

In a similar vein, Nehru wrote in his autobiography:

> He brought the Hindus and Muslims much nearer to each other, for both honoured him and were influenced by his example. To Gandhiji he became a trusted friend whose advice with regard to Hindu-Muslim matters was the final word for him. My father and Hakimji had naturally taken to each other.[8]

In the communal riots of 1919, Ajmal Khan and Swami Shraddhananda saved the city from destruction through their mediation and unity. Andrews testifies, 'I saw the Hakim Saheb in all the true greatness of his character. Night and day, he laboured for peace.'[9]

Ajmal Khan wrote, 'What culture I possess or whether I possess any at all, is a little difficult for me to say. Persian as a language, unhappily, I do not even know. But it is true that my father had grown up in an Indo-Persian cultural atmosphere which was the legacy in North India of the Old Delhi court and of which, even in these degenerate days, Delhi and Lucknow are the two chief centres. Kashmiri Brahmins had a remarkable capacity for adaptation ... Even now there are many distinguished scholars in Persian among the Kashmiris in India ...'

Ajmal Khan's death, ten years before India's partition, was in the words of Nehru, 'a great blow to Congress'. He lamented, 'For all of us, there has been something lacking in a visit to Delhi, for Delhi was so closely associated with Hakimji and his house in Ballimaran.'[10]

Delhi was a poorer place after Ajmal Khan, perhaps never to recover from the absence of such a luminary who blended Muslim heritage with the political reality of his times, and despite his personal faith, upheld staunch secularist credentials.

Contemporary Delhi has its own brand of activism. Lawyers and courts have saved the environment through public interest litigations (PILs). A decade of public activism led to the conversion of public transport to a less toxic compressed natural gas (CNG) fuel. Some hold a grouse against the 'tyranny' of the courts saying that they order demolition of shops and livelihoods. My friend Mayank says, 'They first force tribals to move out from their jungles and when they settle in Delhi's slums, the courts order their slums to be razed.'

In the landmark judgment entitled *M.C. Mehta* vs. *Union of India*,[11] the Supreme Court of India held that air pollution in Delhi caused by vehicular emissions violated the right to life under Article 21 of the Constitution, and thereby directed all commercial vehicles operating in Delhi to switch to the CNG fuel mode in order to protect public health. Taking a cue from this, Pakistani civil society has also been struggling with the courts to save the environment. Though a recent judgment on rickshaws in Lahore has been issued, it calls for a phased shift to a less smoke-emitting variety of autorickshaw.

However, judicial activism has grown in Pakistan. The Pakistani Supreme Court in 2007 came into high-profile conflict with the executive and the president, General Musharraf, who used his definition of 'public interest' to get rid of defiant and proactive judges. The struggle continued as the major political parties, backed by activist lawyers and a nascent civil society, resisted the military dictator, leading to his removal from office in 2008. Consequently, secular and democratic forces in Pakistan won a major victory when the elected government in March 2009, reinstated the deposed chief justice. Never has public pressure been so effective in the country's history.

Firoz Bakht Ahmed, associated with Friends for Education, is another individual who, as a citizen of Delhi, laments the importance given to politics rather than poetry and history. Known as a 'monuments' activist, his mission has been to save and protect the capital's heritage using the modern instruments of justice, media and civil society networks to lobby for the protection of Delhi's heritage. Over the last decade, he has initiated several PILs that have led to the removal of encroachments. The list is impressive—Ghalib's haveli, the tomb of the Mughal poet Zauq, Hazrat Nizamuddin Auliya's dargah, Maulana Azad's tomb, the historic Anglo-Arabic School, Jama Masjid ... and the list goes on.

Bakht has been appalled to see that Old Delhi residents are numb to the fact that the nefarious nexus between land-grabbing colonizers, police and politicians has turned this once beautiful residential city into a colossal bazaar. Many old havelis have metamorphosed into newer structures—petty shops, warehouses, factories and manufacturing units. Public lavatories had been erected on the grave of Sheikh Mohammed Ibrahim Zauq, Urdu master and guide of Bahadur Shah Zafar. Environmentalist lawyer M.C. Mehta helped in filing a PIL, and a progressive judge issued a landmark judgment for the removal of these lavatories. Similarly, Ghalib's haveli was rescued in 1997 through Bakht's litigation. Despite his activism for Ghalib's haveli, Bakht is unhappy that the place has not been conserved in the way it should have been. The available premises are limited to 130 yards as opposed to the original 400 yards. Bakht also involved himself in the Jama Masjid restoration case where he requested the court not to disturb the old culture of the walled city bazaar.

I am back in Nizamuddin East.

After I finish my official work, I move to Sadia's apartment that overlooks one of the many parks in the sleepy little corner where she lives. On a clear day, the tombs walk towards the balconies. The vendors chant in the mornings with their odd business proposals. Sadia is cooking *aloo gosht* with her house help, Sabir, and we all sit to talk or deal with the stream of visitors. Sadia is quite popular among TV channels when they need a quote or two from Delhi's educated Muslim women. The BBC correspondent walks in, followed by the crew, and Sadia hurriedly gets dressed and makes her articulate statements on Indian Muslims.

I have seen her rant on the Muslim personal law, the Danish cartoons, Taslima Nasreen's exile and plans to construct malls next to the Jama Masjid. She talks, writes, entertains and walks up and down, all in one go. I just love it. At last, I have someone who resonates my own eternal restlessness.

There is a girl living at Sadia's place. She's a Muslim, not surprisingly, from Saharanpur, a small town in Uttar Pradesh. Farzana is what we call in Urdu, a 'chanchal'—a boisterous sort born in a conventional religious household. Sadia indulges her. Farzana has been turned into a city girl by Sadia. Farzana, like regular Delhi girls, wears Western clothes, is not bothered about the timings of religious rituals, and is very mobile.

Ahmed Ali wrote in his sad, subtle novel, *Twilight in Delhi*:

> In the world of an Indian home, where the woman is relegated to a subordinate place, love enters very rarely. An unmarried girl is not allowed to chew paan or wear flowers in her hair. She is not even allowed to wear fine and expensive clothes or to use attar. She lives under the threat of going away to strangers when she grows up, who may turn out to be rich or poor or nice or bad. In this atmosphere the idea of love does not take root in the heart. Even if the girl falls in love with a cousin, she cannot speak of it for fear of being punished and looked down upon as an evil thing.

Farzana's transformation in New Delhi was mind-boggling, even to herself! She giggled as she spoke about her brazenness in the big city where she was learning the art of survival. She even managed to get a job at some small business establishment. When we met, there were no barriers. It is the Islam connection that works from Istanbul to Delhi via Islamabad. It is sort of seamless at one level. Farzana and I connected immediately.

In a matter of a few days, a strange intimacy envelops the conversation. This is less to do with lust and more with the ability to understand. She accompanies Sadia and me everywhere—to dargahs, parties and monuments. I notice her vulnerability, especially when the internal hierarchies of Indian Muslims deem her a rural outsider despite the fact that she is a Dilli-wali now. She clings. Sometimes it is too much to handle, for it restricts my urge to communicate with the 'exotic' Indian Muslims. I mean the snooty, artsy, secular types, the ones who have consciously moved away from a fossilized, patriarchal clergy in India.

Farzana was catching up though. Niceties and inanities laced with a few jokes were the social skills that she was not shy to hone. Her sense of humour was terrific. Cracking a joke came naturally to her. So, in a short time, I was declared 'Veer' and she appointed herself as 'Zaara' a la the Bollywood film, *Veer Zaara*, that dealt with a superficial, exaggerated romance between a Pakistani and Indian.

As I leave for Lahore, Farzana asks me to bring back a doll dressed as a bride since she is fond of collecting dolls. Like heroines in black-and-white Indian films who live in a time warp. So there were goodbyes and tears. And they were real.

A year later, I did not find Farzana at Sadia's house. I sort of missed her since she had been such an integral part of Sadia's open-house culture. What happened to Farzana's life and ambitions? I learnt that she fell in love with a Muslim suitor whom she met at work and eloped with him. However, the suitor did not come alone. He came with the baggage of convention and compromise that Farzana impetuously agreed to since she did not want to return to her parental home.

When she came to see Sadia she was dressed in a burqa, the black clothing designed for invisibility in a ritualized retreat within the inner courtyards of Old Delhi's havelis crumbling with time and fighting change. So Farzana ended up exactly where she did not want to be in the first place. Conventions refuse to die; they just come back.

Sadia told me that the veiled Farzana now lives in a cramped space somewhere in the shade of the Jama Masjid. The place is small and dingy. She likes to sing her songs from her native UP but has to keep her voice low since Muslim women are not supposed to be heard loud and that too while singing. The neighbours are all Muslims too. Relegated to Ahmed Ali's zenana or women's quarters, Farzana has swapped centuries.

Ali wrote:

> In the zenana, things went on with the monotonous sameness of Indian life. No one went out anywhere. Only now and then some cousin or aunt or some other relation came to see them. But that was once a month or so or during the festivals. Mostly life stayed like water in a pond with nothing to break the monotony of its static life. Walls stood surrounding them on all sides, shutting the women in from the prying eyes of men, guarding their beauty and virtue with millions of bricks. The world lived and died, things happened, events took place, but all this did not disturb the equanimity of the zenana, which had its world too where the pale and fragile beauties of the hothouse lived secluded from all outside harm, the storms that blow in the world of men. The day came, the evening came and life passed them by.

Ghettos inside, outside, everywhere.

NOTES

1. N.L. Batra, *Jama Masjid: Call of the Soul*, Lucknow: Eastern Book Company.
2. Translated from the Urdu by Firoz Bakht Ahmed.
3. Ablutions before Islamic prayer.
4. Margrit Pernau, *The Delhi College: Traditional Elites, the Colonial State and Education Before 1857*, New Delhi: OUP.
5. Nazir Ahmad, *The Bride's Mirror: A Tale of Life in Delhi a Hundred Years Ago*, translated by G.E. Ward, Permanent Black.
6. The Rajinder Sachar Committee, appointed by the prime minister of India, was a high-level committee for the preparation of a report on

the social, economic and educational status of the Muslim community in India.

7. Jawaharlal Nehru, *An Autobiography*, New Delhi: OUP, 1984, p. 167.
8. Ibid., p. 169.
9. C.F. Andrews, *Hakim Ajmal Khan*, p. 298.
10. Jawaharlal Nehru, *An Autobiography*, New Delhi: OUP, 1984, p. 170.
11. AIR 2001 SC 1948.

9

Centuries of Flavour

Indian Muslims are a strange breed. They may be integrated yet they remain distinctive, not unlike the other ethnic groups that constitute India. Delhi, the Muslim capital of yore, is now a home for many 'pre-moderns', namely, the ones who look towards Central Asia and Mecca instead of Kashi and Mathura. These are neither refugees at Purana Quila nor targets for the extremist Hindu right. They are patriots bearing the legacy of their fathers and grandfathers who consciously rejected the choice of Pakistan. However, they remain, in a sense, victims of their past. Of course, a blanket postulation would be ridiculous, but meeting a cross section of the Muslim 'community' points to the stark uniqueness of this species. All over Delhi, mosques reverberate with azans, a rather astounding phenomenon for a Pakistani visitor. This seems, after all, not the Hindu land that created its binary opposite, the Muslim. Perhaps the Muslims of Old Delhi are more 'Muslim' than many of their counterparts in Pakistan if one were to judge strictly in terms of the observance of rituals.

After the more clearly marked spiritual imperatives, eating mutton is a major marker of identity. Not that the majority of Indians are vegetarians. However, vegetarianism is the standard ethos, a sign of purity as prescribed in the scriptures. However, there are baffling exceptions to the myth of vegetarian purity. The 2006 *Hindu*-CNN-IBN State of the Nation survey that I could lay my hands on to substantiate my casual observations, reveals that only 31 per cent of Indians are pure vegetarians and only 21 per cent of families are completely vegetarian as units.

Women and older people are more likely to be vegetarian than men. Despite the Hindu tenets of vegetarianism, one sees defiant youth eating meat. The vegetarian identity is a construct at best and an inherited cultural rather than religious compulsion. Only 55 per cent of Brahmins termed themselves vegetarians. The Adivasis (indigenous tribal groups) subvert the Hindu Brahmin code, as only 12 per cent are vegetarians. But of course, the stereotype, 'the animal-killing Muslims', are almost always non-vegetarians—at least that is what one hears on Delhi's streets.

The reality is that the Delhi cuisine or, as Sadia Dehlvi puts it, the dastarkhwan places mutton at the centre of this culinary world. Other meats, chicken, for instance, are popular, but mutton is the nucleus of classic Delhi Muslim cuisine. At Sadia's, a meal is not complete if there is no mutton cooked in a classic Dilli style or mince meats such as reshmi, shammi and seekh kababs, and, of course, a meaty nihari. The more health-conscious are aware of the hazards of this culinary pattern. But the gastronomy handed down by centuries of court opulence is still prominent.

Apart from the burqas worn by women in Pakistan and military dictatorship, the Pakistani visitor is also questioned on the meat-fest that defines the idea of eating in Pakistan. The truth is that the meat obsession, especially mutton (for beef, historically, has been the less preferred option), is ever-reflected on Pakistani dining tables. But this is partial and incomplete. The classic Punjabi cuisine of saag and makke ki roti is common to most Punjabi villages. And meat has become out of reach for most Pakistanis, thanks to its soaring prices. But what do we mean by 'Pakistan'? The diverse regions of the north, south, the Sindhi hinterland or the deserts of Cholistan, where a whole range of vegetables (including wild plant leaves) unfamiliar to urban Pakistan are grown and eaten, and where camel meat is stewed perhaps once a year?

My sister is married into a Karachi-based family that had migrated from Delhi. None of the younger members of her in-laws' family have ever seen Delhi. It is a city of their imaginations made up of anecdotes and tales but resurrected each day, almost with every meal. There are endless conversations about the way qeema, biryani and haleem were cooked in Delhi, and vehement distinctions are made between real [read Dilli] biryani and the one cooked in Lahori and other Punjabi kitchens.

So each visit of mine to Delhi has also been a quest to dip into this huge culinary cauldron and taste its various flavours. To know how this gastronomic lineage lives in migrant kitchens and alien stoves, one has to know the city that no longer is immediate or accessible. It was again in Nizamuddin Basti, erstwhile Shahjahanabad and Mehrauli, that my culinary senses started discovering what this fuss over Delhi's cuisine was all about.

A city lives and survives within the intricacies and mosaics of its cuisine. Delhi's culinary legacy is rich and complex. Delhi arguably is an ancient site but not much evidence of its human habitation exists prior to 1000 BC.[1] The Indraprastha of the Mahabharata was probably a small settlement where the Aryans lived. Like many other histories, there is a debate on who the Aryans were and where they came from. Some accounts imply that they were Central Asian or European nomads who invaded India around 1500 BC. Subsequently, many 'Aryan' groups purportedly migrated to Iraq and Iran as the mythologized (yet to be proved) flooding of India forced them to leave the fertile plains and cross the mountains once again.

When they invaded India, the Aryans confronted a decaying Indus Valley civilization and adopted some of their ways, at the same time influencing the local civilizations with their culinary traditions. Once they started to live in the areas surrounding the Indus, the Jamuna and Ganga rivers, the Aryans grew crops, produced oils from different seeds and cultivated diverse ways of cooking which can now be construed as the basis of the 'north Indian' cuisine of today.

An ancient dish of Delhi was made of small split-pea cakes, fried and then eaten with sweet-and-sour tamarind and mango chutney. Potatoes were to replace the split peas leading to the brilliant aloo tikki. It is said that the method of preparation was probably as old as the Aryan lifestyle in India, though potatoes came much later to India.[2] Harappan vessels, the metallic flat pan, or the tawa, various pans and pots were readily adopted by the Aryans.

Delhi's street food is wondrous, a world unto itself, found everywhere and not necessarily in the most hygienic conditions despite court orders. While samosas and tikkis are no novelties for Pakistanis, the chutneys and flavours have subtle differences. The khatti-meethi imli chutney, the moong-dal savoury made with a batter of moong and chana dal and served with hot green chutney with a garnish of grated radish and its leaves are divine. Thelas sell singharas, *Ram laddoos, shakarkandi* and kulcha-chana. Some of them are familiar but Ram laddoos are surely no longer found on Pakistani streets. I remember eating them in Lahore during my childhood but they were called something else; and over time they have vanished not in the least for that obvious Hindu reference.

Sheereen qand and *gajak* are also as old as Delhi. Their ancestral forms have existed in the uncertain narratives of history. The khichdi that one eats now has been there all along—over the centuries it may have been transmuted and adapted by different regions but it is supposed to have emerged during the Aryan era. Delhi-walas of today love khichdi, as did the residents of Indraprashtha, writes Charmaine O'Brien in her loving account of Delhi's cuisine.[3]

Puffed rice is an important ingredient in Delhi's famous chaat which I ate in the lanes of Old Delhi. However, meat is not just a Muslim legacy. The Mahabharata, as I tell my Hindu friends, records that the residents of Indraprastha were eating meat dishes with yogurt and, over time, roasted meat entered their dietary universe. However, around 500 BC, changes began to be seen within the dietary kaleidoscope of Hindus. Charmaine O'Brien, my imaginary companion, says that the later versions of the Mahabharata recorded how grains were the only suitable offering to the gods, while earlier versions listed animal meat as appropriate for ritual sacrifice.

What was it that caused this shift over these five centuries? I let the historians discover that as I muse and enjoy succulent seekh kababs in Delhi. Perhaps the largely agrarian civilization must have discovered that animal slaughter was inimical to the ploughing of fields that were yielding foodgrains for a growing population. Economics may have dictated the spiritual and defined the religious—the kosher and the halal—as clerics love to declare identities and impose them for control. At the same time, modern-day animal activists are opposed to the cruelty involved in halal meat. Others say that halal meat has also been found to be healthier. Personally, I would like to see change in animal slaughter practice and urge for more humane ways to raise and use livestock. Abstinence from meat is another option but ask the Muslims of India and Pakistan how their lives would be without kababs and qeema!

It should be remembered that both Islam and Christianity are desert religions where the land was unyielding for major cultivation. That probably explains the prominence given to meat in both these religions. That, and the Biblical injunction in the first book of the Bible called Genesis, where God is said to give man 'dominion over all the animals of the world', explain the preponderance of meat in everyday diet in these two cultures.

Around 500 BC, the Buddha is supposed to have addressed

Delhi's population about how simple non-animal cuisine was in line with Buddhist principles.[4] Non-violence did not mean pure vegetarianism. Buddhist practitioners have interpreted the Buddha's injunction in a manner that allows them to eat meat provided that the animal was not slaughtered and that it had died accidentally. Mahavira, the Jain guru, had also stopped eating meat. Brahmins, thereon, encouraged vegetarianism. Asafoetida or heeng, a strong-smelling herb, like garlic, also considered a promoter of sexual appetite and aggression, entered into the vegetarian diet despite the fact that it made die-hard vegetarians slightly nervous. Heeng had travelled to India from Afghanistan and also became a replacement for onions, garlic, leeks and other sharp-smelling ingredients.

However, the Tomar Rajputs, valiant warriors, ate meat at Lalkot, the area which now is broadly known as Mehrauli and constitutes pre-Muslim Delhi.

Prior to the eighth century, there is no surviving written or oral account of a place called 'Delhi'. Folklore and legends suggest that one Raja Dhilu was the maker of ancient Delhi in 800 BC. It was the name of the first medieval township of Delhi, located on the south-western border of present Delhi, in Mehrauli. The Persian traveller, Firishta, recorded that Delhi existed prior to Alexander the Great's invasion of India. However, all these theories are perhaps oral histories; endearing yet unverifiable. It is now recorded by historians that Central Asian conquerors created the urban centre that we now know as Delhi. The Turks fashioned Delhi into a Muslim city during the thirteenth century. Essentially nomadic, the Turks were quite basic like their supposed 'grand ancestors', the Aryans, about their dietary habits. Roasted sheep and milk were the main ingredients of their cuisine. Over time, medieval Persia became the inspiration for the Delhi-centred empire. In Persia, food was discussed in poetry and became a vital element of culture. Nuts were used to thicken and enrich sauces; the aroma of rose petals and orange blossoms graced the food cooked in the kitchens of the Persian nobility.

Persian cooks were invited to Delhi. They were surprised to find that the commonly loved spices, supplied by Arab traders to Persia, were present in abundance here. Around Delhi, the fields were green and fertile unlike the rugged landscapes of Central Asia and Persia. A variety of spices and vegetables grew here and there was ample scope for introducing new ones.

A little discovery that I made also subverts the standard associations concerning paneer or cottage cheese, namely, that it was the Turks and Persians who introduced it to the Indian platter. The term 'paneer' is derived from the Persian word 'peynir' and Muslims in northern India used it liberally. Over time, it was also adopted by the Hindus and soon became an integral item and accepted as part of a pure vegetarian diet.

During the sultanate of Delhi (eleventh to early sixteenth century), there was a rudimentary version of the biryani. It evolved during the Mughal era (sixteenth century onwards) and ever since, became a centrepiece of the Indian world of flavours cooked in numerous styles now. The early biryani had cashew nuts and raisins, making it the precursor of what we now know by the name of Kabuli pulau which is a sensation across the world. Ibn Batuta chronicled the minutiae of Delhi life including its cuisine. He records how each meal of the sultans began with rose-water sherbet followed by roast meat, chapattis soaked in ghee, chicken and rice. A medieval version of the samosa was on the menu as well. Fuqqa, a mild alcoholic brew, was also served—so much for the puritanism of the mullah!

As I stood among the ruins of the ASI park, Mehrauli, my wily imagination smelt the rose-tinted sherbet.

Dishes such as halwa and shahi tukda became popular in the sultanate period as did the jalebi. Each time I visited Hazrat Nizamuddin, I could not help but think how the Delhiites of yore would buy what the cluster of shops now sells—naan, kulcha, biryani, pulau, firni and kheer. The same shops are now considered to be in a Muslim ghetto, but are popular among Hindus too. Influential nobles of the sultanate era relished Hindu vegetarian dishes such as saag that is now a permanent feature of Pakistani and Indian cuisine.

Today's 'tandoori' cuisine was perhaps a later development and did not exist in the sultanate era. The sultans were loyal to Delhi unlike the temperamental Mughals who would move between Delhi and Agra, often including Lahore in their capital-hopping sprees. But the Delhi sultans, except Mohammad Bin Tughlaq who created Daulatabad, never left Delhi. It was their favourite grand capital and they kept on adding new sub-cities, courts and, of course, cooks. What was initiated by the sultans was later polished by the Mughals. The splendour of the Delhi sultanate and its court tales caused much envy to outsiders, especially the Mongols. Tragically, internal instability led to the demise of the sultanate, enabling the ambitious and capricious Babar to capture Delhi and add further pages to Delhi's annals of cookery.

In Delhi, the chaat that I loved was made with a combination of fruits and masalas served in a dona, a little round dipped plate made from the dried leaves of the dhak tree. Authentic Dilli ki chaat was reputedly available in the narrow and filthy lanes of Old Delhi or Shahjahanabad. Often, afraid of the lack of public hygiene and the open sewers, I would resist the temptation and then give in, encouraged by the wisdom that sometimes one ought to be unsafe and unpredictable. The chaat-wala's classic touch lies in the sonth, the sweet tamarind chutney, the recipe of which is, more often than not, a family secret and an inter-generational treasure. I wonder what masala is used. The chaat-walas give me vague answers. The spice mixtures taste as if all the world's spices have culminated in the amalgamate—plain to rock salt, roasted cumin and pomegranate seeds buried under *aam choor*. How can commercial chaat masala packets replace this magic mixing and taste intensity found on the streets of Shahjahanabad that may have lost its name but not the flavour?

Funnily, there is even a Chinese version of chaat available in New Delhi's Lajpat Nagar market. This peculiar 'Chinese chaat' at Manik's, a small kiosk, serves chilli chicken on noodles. The Tibetans living in Delhi, on their part, would intrigue even the most qualified anthropologists.

Today, across India and Pakistan, neon-lit fast-food joints serve chaat. Plastic and steel shops boast shop assistants who use polythene gloves, for increased hygiene, to serve unreal chaat. The spicy and sour, green-coloured tamarind water, used in pani puris, is now prepared with mineral water even in some of Delhi's oldest chaat shops. While pani puri often gives the danger signal, 'stay away' (because it is chronically unhygienic), the Delhi version is simply irresistible. We call them gol gappas in dear homeland Pakistan and the tamarind water there is a bit more pungent.

One afternoon under a blazing June sun, Sadia, her cousin and I, devotees of old-style chaat, gather in front of the legendary Prabhu Chaat Bhandar and await its magic in a suffocating alley dogged by the cars and filth of Old Delhi's narrow gulleys. As in Pakistan, one has to sacrifice hygiene at the altar of taste, flies being a mandatory requirement. Prabhu's pani puris, as it turned out, were authentic, refreshing and crisp, making them the best I have had so far.

We ate several portions of the chaat. I remembered the evening when, after listening to Ghalib's exalted poetry with writers, poets and Urdu scholars of Delhi, we stopped near the old State Bank building at Chandni Chowk and gorged on countless dahi vadas. Sadia remains unimpressed with the upmarket chaat joints found in the malls, saying, 'If you want street food, you go to the street.'

Haldiram, a new commercial giant that packages traditional snacks for a contemporary clientele, has raj kachori and the

Bengali Market has pani puri that begs to be as hard-hitting as the ones I am used to in Lahore. Pani puri, as packaged by Haldiram, is sold in sealed plastic bags, which need to be punctured and dipped in the water by the consumer. I see many a yuppie in starched shirts and sleeveless blouses struggling with these packets.

A trendy restaurant called Punjabi by Nature offers an inventive cocktail built around the pani puri—two potato-filled shells are served with a shot of vodka infused with green chilli and lime. The Flame, another eatery, sells chaat with a glass of champagne.

In her memoirs, Babar's daughter remembers that her arrival in Delhi was celebrated with a welcome feast of roasted sheep, bread and fruit. By Akbar's time, the Mughals were well integrated with the local environs and were set to firmly root their destiny within the complex world of India for the next three centuries. Hindustan had become home.

Mughal cuisine developed partly in Agra and Lahore but Delhi created the menu as well as the cooks who shaped its elite sensibilities. The Taj is not the only example of Mughal extravagance; the thin silver and gold sheets that garnished their cuisine also reflect their grandeur. European visitors mention over fifty dishes at a single meal. Akbar took this figure to 500. The Mughals were fond of wild game such as ducks and fowls and added these dishes to the cuisine by the time the court moved to Delhi. Fruits and nuts were essential ingredients in Mughal food, which has now been crudely termed 'Mughlai' cuisine, stuffing an otherwise delicate cuisine with cream and nuts, and sold across the globe as an exotic food experience.

Under the Mughals, the biryani grew to great heights. A multistage cooking process heightened the flavours of each spice as it permeated through cooked rice, nuts, meats, curry and saffron. Haleem (comprising pulses, meat and spices) is another popular dish that still survives. It is a Delhi-Mughal invention, cooked for hours with minute attention to texture, flavours and aroma. They invented combinations of spice use. Chillies complemented indigenous black pepper, and cardamoms, opening up their buds in broths with Persian saffron, unleashed subtle colours and tastes in the same cauldron. With each creative stroke, Delhi found new flavours. Paan was served after meals while imported tea from China was served in cups (a precursor to modernity and an ominous indication of the South Asian tea addiction that was to grow under the Raj).

Restaurants were not common in Mughal Delhi. However, things changed with the decline of the Mughal Empire. The royal cooks, often in organized family units, started popularizing court cuisine within the public domain. This democratization of royal cuisine took place in the same manner as it did in Nizamuddin Basti and Mehrauli where the cooks introduced sultanate flavours to ordinary people during the twilight of the regime. Sad circumstances can sometimes have meaningful results, since this Delhi cuisine now captures world palates.

Not long after this migration of Delhi cuisine, the world started to (perhaps wrongly) recognize Mughal-Delhi cuisine as 'Indian' food. The skewered meats, naan, biryani, meat and vegetable curries in textured and spiced sauces, and a wide array of sweets became the hallmark of Indian food.

My first experience of Karim's was in the late hours of the evening. Karim's is known for its kababs, naans and various types of rotis, roomali[5] being my favourite, as also the brilliant nihari, very much of the Muslim Sultan–Mughal era. Nihari is a healthy, comprehensive meal which was invented for the Mughal army's nutritional needs and often cooked with trotters or mutton. It has now become synonymous with Delhi. There is a branch of Karim's in Nizamuddin as well, but for the original experience one has to go to Old Delhi.

The items on the menu sound exotic—Shah Jahan Kabab, Akbari Murgh Masala, Badshahi Badaam Pasanda (a lean and tender cut) and Nayab Maghaz Masala. It is such an exciting list that I ask for a photocopy to show it to my family back home.

Karim's has a pedigree to boast of. Its present life, technically, began in 1913 but its origins are traced to Emperor Babar. The forefather of the Karim family came to India in the early sixteenth century and became a soldier in Babar's army. But his talent for cooking surpassed his martial prowess and he ended up as Babar's personal cook. And thus, a dynasty of imperial cooks was born. After the Mutiny of 1857, the royal chefs left their jobs to save their lives only to reappear in 1911. During this time many cooks remained in hiding or moved to regional kingdoms in search of employment.

Then came the occasion known as the Delhi Durbar (literally the Court of Delhi), to mark the coronation of King George V. Haji Karim set up a small street stall to serve the crowds gathered for the celebration. He served royal food to the public, aloo gosht being the main dish. Karim's continues to uphold its traditions and even goes to the extent of manually grinding its masalas which are a family secret and mostly done in the dark inner chambers of the establishment.

Later I was to discover the parathe-wali gali, literally, the alley selling parathas prepared with several types of fillings. I ate amazing jalebis—round, juicy and dripping with syrup, nothing like what I have had before.

Whenever I'm in Delhi, I make sure to eat the widely popular dal makhani and countless vegetarian dishes. What I always love to try is *bedmi puri* and aloo found at several places including Nathu's sweet shops. And the delicious, aromatic chana-bhaturas are ideal for those long Sunday breakfasts. I have also attempted to try the wide variety of cuisines from several parts of India. At Dilli Haat, I tried momos (stuffed steamed dumplings) from Arunachal Pradesh in the north-east of India. In fact, I saw momos everywhere sold by street vendors who looked more oriental than the regular 'Delhi-Punjabi'.

Posh restaurants such as the Bukhara at the ITC Maurya Sheraton serve richly marinated and refined cuisine with authentic Mughal flavours. The Clintons ate here and a Clinton Platter is now an item on the menu. The silky reshmi kababs remain the best I have tasted so far.

Shahjahanabad's Chandni Chowk is the hub for sweet sellers. Mughal Delhi perhaps initiated the current ritual of exchanging sweets as a means of social networking and bonding. The royals would frequent Chandni Chowk to eat sweets. Ghante Wallah has been selling sweets since the 1790s, catering, among others, to the later Mughal emperors. I found the famous sweets of Delhi—*piste ki lauz, badam ki lauz* and sohan halwa, which are quintessentially Mughal. Sohan halwa has travelled far. Multan and Karachi are the sohan halwa centres of Pakistan. I wonder if they know the Chandni Chowk connection.

Centuries before ice cream, Akbar's chroniclers were writing about kulfi and the fairly advanced technology that was used to make it. It is believed that relays of horsemen were used to transport ice from the Hindu Kush mountain range to the imperial capital Delhi. Preparation of fruit sorbets in Persian style was common in royal kitchens. Creamy, fragrant and melting, the kulfi is a fine example of Delhi's fine Mughal cooking. Another Pakistani favourite, faluda, also invented for the courts, later reached the streets, many say, leaked by a class of cooks desperate to survive after royal employment was no longer available.

The wide variety of fruits in Shahjahanabad was noted by Bernier during his travels. A passion for fruits gained currency during the latter part of the seventeenth century. Mangoes, mulberries and pomegranates were some of the exotic fruits. Anaar shorba, a soup made with pomegranate juice and spices bearing an intense aroma of the fruit was considered a delicacy. Today, pomegranate juice with a sprinkling of black salt is hugely popular across India and Pakistan. Chai khanas (coffee houses) of Chandni Chowk were the popular forerunners of Khan Market's cafes where the literati and cultured epicurians of Delhi love to flock. Bernier also noted that the non-availability of alcohol was another reason for the popularity of coffee houses.

The (Hindu) Kayasths of Shahjahanabad adopted Mughal tastes and improvised on their meat dishes. However, the mercantile class or the baniyas who ran huge business networks in Shahjahanabad never imbibed Muslim culinary influences. Baniya kitchens were and still remain purely vegetarian, even avoiding china plates as they may contain traces of animal bones. Kadhi, an ancient Indian favourite, is a classic 'moneylender' dish popular across north India and Pakistan.

I was intrigued to discover that the water of the holy Ganga was used to make food in Mughal kitchens and mixed with normal drinking water. Water from the river was constantly replenished by those travelling on royal tours or conquests. Sanctity mixed well with extravagance! We know that Babar gave up onions and garlic while Akbar started his meals with rice and yogurt following Hindu practices. The introduction of vegetarian days at the Mughal court under Akbar indicated the fusion of traditions and perhaps comes close to the reality of India today—sometimes vegetarian and many a time non-vegetarian, myths notwithstanding.

The British first came to India attracted by its spices in the early seventeenth century. Within a century and a half, British residents of Delhi had integrated themselves within the subtleties of the city's culture. Old Delhi-walas tell us how some British sahibs chewed paan in the evenings, smoked hookahs and ate Indian food.

The Raj had its own cuisine, melded from within the well-established and classical Delhi food. 'Kedgeree' is an anglicized version of the Harappan khichdi. Chhota hazree, lunches and dinners were elaborate. The mulligatawny soup is still a splendid Raj relic and served in many of India's restaurants. Pakistan's elite clubs, the last vestiges of the Raj, also serve mulligatawny soup and roast chicken made in the same style invented by British memsahibs. Jalfrezi is another British-Indian dish that is still served in clubs, restaurants and home parties.

In today's Delhi, the Maidens Hotel stands frozen in time. This was also a favourite haunt for Quaid-e-Azam Mohammad Ali Jinnah, who spent many days and nights here. After his marriage to Ruttie, the couple stayed here during their honeymoon. The Curzon Room still wafts the aromas of British India—mulligatawny soup, dak bungalow chicken, gin and lime, and English-style tea with biscuits. After all these years of freedom from Britain, one still finds a popular biscuit brand in India—Britannia.

Events of 1857 broke down the walls to let in an inflow of outsiders into the city. Prior to the Partition, this was a key moment in Delhi's opening up.

My friends, Naina (a college mate at the London School of Economics) and her Punjabi husband Vivek, show me the Not Just Paranthas restaurant that serves over a hundred traditional contemporary versions of new-age parathas. The papad parathas, where lentil wafers make the stuffing, were a great innovation to the traditional chaat that we ate at Chandni Chowk.

Naina and Vivek took me to Defence Colony market for a south Indian meal. Compared to our Defence Enclaves in Lahore and Karachi, this market appeared rather unkempt. The place, called Swagath, was an out-of-this-world experience with the north and the south of India jumbled up with global cuisine. Delectable thalis filled with seafood and prawns and curious sauces from the West can sometimes make meals quite unpredictable.

The old, sometimes smoothly and at other times rather awkwardly, coexists with the new in Delhi. In fact, neither the old is old nor the new is new. The blurring of lines makes it all exciting. The Harappans, the Aryans, the Turko-Mughals and the British, all exist in a manner that would overawe any mortal. Small wonder that India is such an exotic destination for foreign tourists despite the problematic infrastructure and rather inhospitable weather.

NOTES

1. Charmaine O'Brien. *Flavours of Delhi*, Delhi: Penguin, p. 2.
2. Ibid.
3. Ibid.
4. Ibid.
5. Roomali roti, though not an authentic Delhi bread but a stylized version of tender chapatti, is where the chapatti can be so thin that it resembles a roomal or handkerchief.

10

The New Delhis

It was a noisy morning when I arrived at the Central Secretariat, which is rather unimaginatively plonked between the North and South Blocks. In Pakistan too, the secretariats are divided into blocks named after the prosaic letters of the English alphabetical system. For instance, if you wish to reach the Ministry of Finance in Islamabad you need to find 'S' block rather than a particular building. It appears that statehood requires state institutions to exist in an unhistorical, nameless world.

But the North and South Blocks of Delhi are majestic, possibly reflecting the secret yearning of the Raj to follow the earlier empires that it had displaced. Thus came into being Lutyens's Delhi.

The British announced their shift of capital from Calcutta to Delhi in 1911. At a durbar, King George presented himself before his Indian subjects, including my great-grandfather who was present on this occasion, and declared that this '... new creation may be in every way worthy of this ancient and beautiful city'.[1]

This 'New' Delhi took almost two decades to be completed and cost fifteen million pounds, quite obviously paid by Indians through unjust taxation and extracted profits and who had yet to practise the politics of non-cooperation. The chief architects of this imperial splendour were Sir Edwin Lutyens and his assistant, Herbert Baker. Lutyens was son-in-law of a former viceroy, Lord Irwin, thus reinforcing and continuing the imperial traditions of power. This is not to say that he was not a good choice; his creations remain imposing in design and execution. It has been estimated that nearly 30,000 construction workers built this new city. We have little idea how many may have died. Shahjahanabad was also erected on dead bodies, they say.

Lutyens's city was inspired by Washington DC, a planned city. The extravagant Viceregal Lodge, renamed Rashtrapati Bhavan after Independence, was built on the crest of the Ridge. It is said that after Independence, Mahatma Gandhi wanted the building to be converted into a hospital but not many were interested in implementing this radical idea.

The wide sweeping avenue, the famous 'Kings Way', Indianized as Rajpath, winds through the War Memorial arch or India Gate and meanders towards Purana Quila erected on the site of the legendary Indraprastha. The circular colonnade is adjacent to the North Block of the Indian secretariat and leads to Parliament House that is further connected to Connaught Circus, that exclusive space for white men and women to shop and relax and lighten their burden of civilizing the natives so many years ago. The road from Connaught Circus continues towards Shahjahanabad, culminating at the Jama Masjid. In so many ways, the imagined 'New Delhi' connected both the ancient and medieval Delhis with little effort, the design unwittingly facilitating it.

The hexagonal centre point of this new city was Connaught Place. Its concentric rows of colonnaded shops were the commercial part of the city. Now popularly known as 'CP', Connaught Place, named after the Duke of Connaught, uncle of King George V, is a circular plaza, with seven colonnaded sections intercut initially by seven radial roads. CP now barely appears to be the fulcrum it was designed to be, swamped as it is by skyscrapers, not to mention a metro station in its womb. The stand-alone shops are now closing down and retail fast-food chains dot CP. It has lost its unique character and is being converted to a consumer paradise without much identity.

Why should one complain about this? History is shaped by those living today. Let the historians and urban planners of tomorrow decide what comes first, heritage or livelihoods.

On my first visit, my colleague (from the international organization that I was working for then), handled the heavily bureaucracy-controlled entry into the secretariat. Manual entries, paper slips with carbon copies and then a little waiting. I don't mind it at all. The architecture, with its red sandstone arches and long corridors are spellbinding. There are lists of names and some black-and-white images of some Indian politicians and Raj officials of the early twentieth century. The sahibs must have moved freely inside while at the same time, restricting the entry of the natives. I notice that portraits of Indian leaders are also hung on the walls of the long stairways. As we wait for a meeting, I sneak out to walk along the corridors where Azad, Patel and Nehru must have walked in their khadi clothes. These inspired revolutionaries, steeped in both the Eastern ethos and the Western idea of democracy, had chosen to retain these buildings as the hub of a new proud India after 1947. Ironic, some might say.

The offices are grand with huge oval desks where exalted babus sit to implement the destiny of India decided by crafty politicians. How could one not rule from these imperial offices that embody such power? It is only here that one understands why the Central state and its overarching powers were so dear to the founding fathers of modern India. And why the proposals for a loose confederation and a relatively weak Centre were not acceptable to the Congress leadership.

Lutyens made no attempt to hide his contempt for indigenous Indian architecture. An article in *The Telegraph* says that the viceroy's house 'rejected' the Mughal style. Lutyens believed that Indian architecture, including the Taj Mahal, was not meant to be a treasure for posterity. He considered the Taj Mahal 'wonderful, but it is not architecture ... I do not believe there is any really Indian architecture at all, or any great tradition.'[2] To him, the urban landscape dotted with Muslim monuments was a nuisance, and as he wrote to his wife, 'You must sit on your haunches covered with jewels and little else by way of clothing to appreciate these monuments.' His contempt for the Hindu architectural style was equally strong, 'Set square stones and built child-wise ... before you erect, carve every stone differently and independently with lace patterns and terrifying shapes ...'[3]

After 1947, the erstwhile natives assumed charge of the colonial state, changed its nomenclature and trappings while retaining the core of Raj systems and governance. The steel frame of the Raj administration was too strong to be replaced entirely, but over time, politics has made inroads and pierced holes thus rendering it a strange mix of tradition, executive power and political expediency. Across South Asia, the civil bureaucracy continues to rule even after sixty-five years.

According to popular lore, all the Raj buildings of New Delhi have been attributed to Lutyens, rather erroneously. The victim of this misrepresentation has been the unsung architect, R.T. Russell, chief architect to the Government of India, who designed several peripheral government buildings, bungalows and offices of New Delhi. Lutyens built only four bungalow-residences for the viceroy's staff that are now enclosed in the Rashtrapati Bhavan's security zone, as well as the Hyderabad and Baroda Houses near India Gate. The cliché called 'Lutyens's Delhi' is not all that true as many others were part of the new imperial Delhi project.

It was Russell who designed and built Connaught Place,

Eastern and Western Courts, the commander-in-chief's house (now Teen Murti House), Delhi's civil airport, Irwin Stadium (now National Stadium), and over 4,000 government residences that are now occupied by the new elites—judges, politicians and top bureaucrats. Herbert Baker made seven bungalows or 'bungle-ohs' as Lutyens joked, easily forgetting that it was Baker who helped him win the contracts in the first place. I cannot help but laugh when I hear that these same 'bungle-ohs' are now attributed to Lutyens!

My meetings with Indian civil servants at the North and South Blocks and catching up with a few old acquaintances from my stint at the United Nations were pleasurable. The settings were so marvellous that I had to ask one of those exalted babus, a mighty secretary, whose room it was during the pre-1947 days. The mere mention of the Raj brings a twinkle in the eyes of many a bureaucrat in South Asia since it legitimizes a sense of imperial succession. The Indian Civil Service is much venerated even to this day. Later, I took tours with peons who show me the buildings, little rooms, huge corridors and even some old furniture which had escaped the collector's acquisitive eye.

Often, it was a rather strange experience mixed with admiration and sadness. South Asia remains deeply problematic, with deeply embedded post-colonial features that have been debated ad nauseum in political science studies, ironically by the very universities located in the heart of neo-imperialism's darkness.

The towels on the backs of the chairs of babus, both of middle and junior ranks, are part of a tradition that keeps them dry during hot weather. Muted television sets dot their rooms flashing news or cricket. These were all too familiar to me because of their uncanny similarity to the culture of the Pakistani civil services.

Post-1947, Delhi began to acquire a modern, socialist, matter-of-fact look. The National Museum building, built in 1949, retained some colonial elements but it was 'modern'. The new government offices, commemorative buildings and residences built after the British left, were all squares of concrete, shedding the ostentation of earlier times. This is also true for the buildings in Pakistan. The disconnect is severe, not just in terms of aesthetics, but in the shunning of building heritage such as the use of materials like limestone, ideally suited to the arid heat and extreme winters of Delhi or for that matter, Lahore. Generations of skilled artisans were removed from an architecture that became mere structures lacking character altogether.

Heritage is tricky business. Rejecting it served a political purpose as a new history had to be written with a clear script of Independence and visual novelty. Socialist modernism that sprung elsewhere began to take root on Delhi's urban canvas. Yet another foreign style entered Delhi's soul. In the words of Ranjana Sengupta, the brilliant chronicler of Delhi, 'Any main street in Delhi will yield at least two modernist buildings, probably more. This is the look we identify with large government offices, schools and auditoria built through the fifties, sixties and seventies, many of them appearing ramshackle and derelict today ... Shastri Bhavan and Udyog Bhavan, built in the fifties are early examples, as ... is AG's Office near the ITO.'[4]

This trend was to continue till the 1980s with rare exceptions such as the 1962 India International Centre and the 1969 Jawaharlal Nehru Library within the Teen Murti Bhavan. Otherwise, much of Delhi's architecture reflected the rather prosaic permutations of modernism. The Indian Institute of Technology campus and the Jawaharlal Nehru University buildings are ample testimony to this new aesthetic norm. The latter is, however, saved by its rustic environs and a sense of space that gives it a rather medieval feel.

Among the new buildings, the Baha'i Temple inaugurated in 1996, sitting atop the Kalkaji hill in south Delhi, is an inventive architectural statement. A lovingly landscaped garden encircles the chiselled marble edifice. The twenty-seven marble 'petals' arranged in clusters of three form nine sides. The lotus, a sacred symbol of both Hindu and Buddhist faiths, is the leitmotif of the structure.

As I enter the hall, I feel the sunlight splintering into it and caressing my skin. The rays refract through the inner folds of the gigantic lotus petals and create the desired magic of dimension and depth. This diffused effect inside the dome is mesmerizing and I do not want to leave the room. Outside, there are multiple pools in the landscaped garden to provide the necessary ambience to the lotus design. The design also scripts the essential tenet of the Baha'i faith, namely, the unity of religions which is celebrated here through visual representations and architectural innovations.

The New Delhi of Lutyens, Baker and Russell, among others, is no longer new or representative of the urban upheavals that have shaken Delhi since 1947. There is a new megapolis in place of the old New Delhi composed of several new setttlements and 'cities' in their own right. It is home to over 20 million residents.[5] Given their eclectic individuality, these myriad Delhis are often ignored. Compared to the Muslims of Old Delhi and power-obsessed residents of Chanakyapuri, the new clustered Delhis may not care for grand architectures or romantic Persian poetry but manifest the new and the single most tangible ethic: money.

Places like Punjabi Bagh or Paschim Vihar are products of the great historical churning called Partition. These places may not boast of artists or monuments but they are inhabited by people who, with their hard work and clever business acumen, changed the face of Delhi. They represent Delhi's consumerist future and are the economic models for its less affluent. Punjabi Bagh, Rohini (with its Disneyland-like Adventure Island), Tilak Nagar, Uttam Nagar, etc., are the new Delhis that are aspiring to be 'upmarket' with flashy malls, McDonalds and torrents of new money.

Punjabi Bagh is West Delhi's happy haven for wealthy Sikh businessmen and other Punjabi-speaking people. Earlier known as 'Refugee Colony', the neighbourhood was rechristened by Prime Minister Nehru in 1954. Refugees from Pakistani Punjab settled here after Partition and had to prove their worth in the new homeland. These identity-seeking migrants and their descendants have been sheer engines of wealth creation in post-Partition Delhi and brought in 'Punjabiyat' or the Punjabi flavour to the more refined and aesthetic imperial Delhi. Indeed, the old residents, a tiny minority in the megapolis, continue to complain about the 'Punjabification' of a Delhi that has changed before their eyes.

Jangpura's name can be traced back to an obscure Englishman called Colonel Young who acquired an estate on either side of Mathura Road just south of Nizamuddin. Legend has it that many of the original residents of Young Pura were refugees from the village of Raisina, which was obliterated by the construction of the Viceregal Palace. Similarly, Alaknanda, near the hip and trendy Greater Kailash and the Bengali neighbourhood of Chittaranjan Park, is an upwardly mobile middle-class residential area of south Delhi. It emerged as a liveable locality in the late 1970s. The various apartment blocks were built by the Delhi Development Authority after Indira Gandhi's reviled Emergency. There was an imperative to provide comfortable housing for the growing middle-class, resulting in insipid apartment blocks made poetic by naming them after rivers and mountains—Mandakini, Gangotri, Yamunotri, Aravalli and Nilgiri.

Little Lhasa or Majnu ka Tila, near Kashmiri Gate, is a Tibetan ghetto. The name 'Tila' is inspired by the nearby gurdwara, Majnu ka Tila, which was built on the spot where a fifteenth-century Muslim hermit attained enlightenment after being blessed by Guru Nanak. Early Tibetan refugees settled here in the 1960s when their numbers became too large for the Ladakh Bodh Vihara to accommodate. The ghetto houses several hundred families and sells, in Delhi terms, 'authentic' Tibetan food like Gyuma (sausages) and Iowa Khatsa (spicy stuffed lungs) and, of course, momos and noodle soups called thukpas.

Another Delhi is the overwhelmingly Muslim settlement, Nasbandi Colony, situated in the National Capital Region (NCR) in Ghaziabad ('nasbandi' means sterilization). As the friend who took me there put it, 'The world appears to be sterile here. Unpainted houses smacked of aborted undertakings.' The streets were strewn with refuse. Goats and people were scampering along the edges. Flies everywhere—on buffalo meat, overripe mangoes, and infants in hanging baskets. It is just across the border from Delhi and yet it could be from another era.

The underclass of unskilled labour of Nasbandi slum is necessary in order for the other Delhis to flourish. There is no government college here and local children attend madrasas. Nasbandi Colony's past is interesting. Some twenty years ago, Sunehra Khatoon, mother of three children, shifted from Seemapuri to the urban metropolis. Sunehra went to get herself sterilized for birth control and six months later, as promised by a government policy, she was awarded a free fifty-square-yard plot in the neighbourhood. Many joined this scheme through which the government hoped to address the population growth. Thousands underwent sterilization in order to get free plots.

My friend Naina and her husband Vivek lived in South Extension, literally Dakshin Vistaar in Hindi. They moved to Bombay in 2008. Its lanes and tree-lined roads have bungalows made in nouveau architecture which are hybrid structures of modernist flat shapes combined with an attempt to transport American, gothic and Greek features. South Extension has a huge market in the vicinity. It boasts of high-end sari emporiums and jewellers such as Mehrasons. Levi's, Tommy Hilfiger and Benetton are some of the branded shops. Before meeting Naina and Vivek,

I would browse around at Midlands bookstore or Teksons with the rather blunt lady owner. Timeless Art Book Studio is a haven of peace and beauty away from the smog and chaos of the city.

The busy and often clogged Ring Road slices South Extension into half and creates South Extension 1 and South Extension 2. Lying cheek by jowl with the glitzy consumer paradise of South Extension 1 is Kotla Mubarakpur, one of Delhi's seven urban villages. An uppity neighbourhood with natty bungalows lies behind the shops of South Extension 2. Affluent and reeking of wealth, the whole colony is traumatized by the messy parking of the marketplace of South Extension 2. Countless parked cars leave little room to walk around. The posh and opulent can turn into congestion and a municipal nightmare in a minute. The intersections between inner enclaves and the outer reality of the Ring Road combined with the overcrowded side roads are fascinating.

I was often invited to the restaurants in Defence Colony market. This colony, known for its affluent housing, boasts bungalows, big cars and imposing gates manned by uniformed security guards. The colony came into being to facilitate retired army officers. It is also a popular residential place for Delhi's expats who like it for its 'Shining India' bubble. The leafy lanes and well-trimmed parks are charming, but once again, the landscape changes in a few minutes as soon as you hit the busy Ring Road.

Defence Colony market is perennially congested with badly managed traffic. We ate a couple of times at the brilliant Swagath, a South Indian seafood restaurant. On another occasion, we tried Colonel Kebabs which serves some well-done broiled meats, and Sagar, where I was introduced to the wonders of quickly assembled dosas, idlis, and inventive vegetarian thalis. Only in Delhi did I start to appreciate and love vegetarian cooking given the variety of flavours.

Indians have no clue as to what a 'defence' housing area in Pakistan is like. These isolated, opulent and well-managed enclaves are the preserve of the retired as well as serving officials; many affluent civilians also live here. The layouts depict martial orderliness, the architecture loudly nouveau riche (with minor exceptions), and amid the planned streets and boulevards, the city remains culturally anonymous, as if robbed of historical and contextual identity. Such suburbia could be anywhere, outside a big US city or somewhere else.

Modern, consumer-crazy Delhi, where money defines living, gives rise to a paradoxical amnesia and nostalgia about the past. So each day, the media carries a little 'discovery' about the city and its monuments. These crumbling monuments and the desensitization, therefore, paint a melancholic portrait of an otherwise vibrant city. As writer and bureaucrat Pawan Varma puts it:

> One of the peculiar things about Indians is that while they romanticise the remote past, they have little or no sense of history about more recent times … particularly distressing in a city like Delhi where countless monuments languish unnoticed amidst the ebb and flow of a city avalanched by its own municipal concerns. Educated people who live in Hauz Khas have no idea what the monument which gives their colony its name is. The same kind of historical lethargy afflicts most of those who live in and around Masjid Moth, Chirag Dilli, Siri, or Hazrat Nizamuddin.[6]

Many like Pawan Varma, who love Delhi intimately, are pained by the atrophy of some of its most vital parts. A truncated Delhi, no matter how bursting with life it appears to be, will affect the rest of India as it shapes power, culture and 'national' identity. No part of north India, or for that matter, much of what is now Pakistan, can claim not to have been impacted by the happenings in Delhi over the centuries.

Orhan Pamuk wrote in his book *Istanbul*, 'Huzun rises out of the pain they feel for all that which has been lost, but it is also what compels them to invent new defeats and new ways to express their impoverishment.' Huzun, the Turkish word for melancholy, has an Arabic root. Urdu has adopted this term and its derivative, hazeen, to describe melancholy, grief, or a feeling of deep spiritual loss. In his celebrated book, Pamuk describes the mood of his city and that of its collective residents as expressing huzun. But this huzun is a nuanced, often complex feeling signifying positive faith in change as well as a negative sense of resignation. There is melancholy but not morbidity. The residents of Istanbul live under the weight of a grand past, among the vestiges of a towering culture and civilization. However, this culture and civilization are now faded and the Istanbulites do not consider it a living civilization nor do they feel part of a grand continuum but have been severed from it by the adoption of Western civilization.

This disconnect is not resolved. In many respects, the older Delhi, especially the decaying Shahjahanbad with its predominantly Muslim population, reflects the same sense of conflict and wistfulness as Istanbul. This collective melancholy can be seen in some of the old residents of New Delhi too.

With the decay of the Indian Islamic civilization and its irrelevance in the face of globalized Western civilization, many Muslims of Delhi, generally speaking, find refuge in resignation. The Old Delhi-walas cling to memories of their glorious past with a sentimentality that feeds into their melancholy. This clinging defines who they are and gives them a sense of identity and security within a world in which they have been left behind. Similarly, all the sad scenes of their daily lives such as the poverty, squalor, the human drama at the Sufi shrines, beggars, street scenes and lifestyle are perpetuated almost as if these are loved, their melancholy perpetuated as a collective statement of identity. Until the middle of the twentieth century, a 'Dilli-wala' had a distinct identity which expressed itself in speech, manners, habits and pride in the city. This is no longer the case, writes Pawan Varma:

> The Delhi of today is a vast and nondescript aggregation of individual wants. It has no collective soul. It has indeed pole-vaulted beyond the decaying feudalism of the Walled City, and the expansive exclusivism of Lutyen's Delhi, but only to fall in a huge ungovernable sprawl, a victim of its own amazingly haphazard over-reach.[7]

Centuries of British rule created an unrectifiable wedge between modern India and that culture and civilization which immediately preceded the advent of the British. Lutyens was not all that wrong about the natives. Undeniably racist, but in a foretelling manner, his criticism of the 'browns' and their lack of concern for heritage was not too far from the truth. After Independence, crumbling governance, rampant corruption and neglect of planning have contributed to the decline of many a South Asian city.

Old Delhi's melancholy is also about the rise of individual gain and loss of collective identity. This fragmentation could be considered exciting as it can propel entrepreneurship and satisfy the gods of the market, but for a city and its culture Pawan Varma says:

> Those who would have saved Delhi have allowed it to die because they believed that the city could survive even if their only concern was their own well-being. It was a fatal mistake. Cities are sensitive creatures. They have a soul. They can survive periods of neglect. They cannot survive if their patrons are boors, smug in their little fortresses of individual gain, with no sense of pride in where they live ...[8]

NOTES

1. A.K. Jain, 'Delhi—Planning and Growth', *International Journal of Environmental Studies*, Vol. 34, Nos 1 and 2, 1989, pp. 65–77.
2. 'The Genius Who Told Bad Jokes.' *The Telegraph*, 22 June 2002.
3. Christopher Hussey, 'The Life of Sir Edwin Lutyens', *Country Life*, London, 1953.

4. Ranjana Sengupta, *Delhi Metropolitan: The Making Of An Unlikely City*, New Delhi: Penguin, 2008.
5. http:21www.indiaonlinepages.com/population/delhi-population.html
6. Pawan Varma, 'Imperilled Heritage', *Outlook*, 7 May 1997.
7. Pawan Varma, 'The Demise Of Delhi,' *Outlook*, 5 January 1998.
8. Ibid.

11

Rivers of Fire

Somewhere, enmeshed in my yearnings to visit Delhi, lies my overwhelming desire to meet Qurratulain Hyder, the great Urdu writer. I finally meet her in NOIDA, a new suburb of Delhi, officially in Uttar Pradesh, the neigbouring state. The journey to get to Ainee Apa (as she is affectionately known in the Urdu-speaking world) took all these years. The two visits were memorable and extensive, but they remained incomplete. The third meeting never took place. She passed away in August 2007.

Sadia exclaimed, when I told her I wished to see Ainee Apa, 'Gosh, are you an Ainee fan as well? Visitors from Pakistan have two fixations, the Taj and Ainee Apa!' Such was her stature among Urdu readers. Not that she was not known and respected in India—perhaps she was, and more than any other Urdu writer—but it was her Pakistani readership that ironically became the basis for her overawing metaphorical, larger than literary, presence.

She first entered my consciousness when I was in high school and since then I have read almost every word written by her. There was a time at college, when I composed a long letter to her that was never sent. Partly because it was too melodramatic (I had heard of her temperamental disposition) and also because she was allergic to hyperbolic praise. Over the years, I internalized the worlds she painted. Only later did I realize that a part of me has been perennially shaped by the magic of her writings. I still remember that glorious London summer in college when I finished *Aakhir-i-Shab ke Humsafar (*published in English as *Fireflies in the Mist) that* I looked around, and the world, as I knew it, was not the same place. Since then, I have been dwelling in her books.

The *Times Literary Supplement* once wrote that she ought to be counted, along with her contemporaries, Gabriel Garcia Marquez and Milan Kundera, as one of the world's major writers. Her stories deal with the inextricability of Hindu and Muslim subcultures in terms of their literatures, poetics and music backgrounded by the historical forces of colonization, independence and their impact on individual lives. Her magnum opus, *Aag ka Darya* (translated by her as *River of Fire*), undertook a groundbreaking examination of issues of identity within the South Asian civilization. *Darya* is to Urdu fiction what *A Hundred Years of Solitude* is to Latin American literature.

Born in UP in 1927, Qurratulain belonged to an accomplished upper-crust family of writers. Educated in Lucknow, she had a stint in London as a young reporter on Fleet Street before immigrating to Pakistan after the Partition and returning to India around 1962. She was awarded the Jnanpith Award, India's highest literary award and before that, the Sahitya Akademi and Ghalib Awards. Later, she received the Padma Shri, one of India's premier government honours to civilians.

It was no coincidence that she lived for so many years in Delhi and also died in the city though her hometown was Lucknow. She must have felt an uncanny sense of ease here, the city that was so old and yet so new. Her NOIDA house was located in the rather soulless modern suburb of the megapolis. So naturally, Qurratulain's sense of history and her ability to traverse the past and present with equal facility came alive in Delhi.

On my first visit to Delhi, I am invited for lunch at Ainee Apa's house. Travel to NOIDA took some suburban time. Sadia and her visiting cousin from the United States accompanied me. We crossed the Jamuna and headed towards the suburb. Hurriedly, I bought rajnigandha flowers from under a jamun tree, and as I was doing so, I wondered why life was treating me so nicely. Well, I was, after all, buying flowers for none other than Ainee Apa. That was rare good fortune indeed!

We reached a small town house in the quiet and anonymous lanes of Sector 16. These lanes do not know its residents. We made our way somehow. NOIDA's sectors and streets are devoid of a lived history. Does it matter if they are not aware of Ainee Apa? Perhaps not.

Rehana, the domestic help, greeted us as we entered the Ainee sanctum. In her living room, she sat on a large divan in a semi-recline and ferociously moved her pankha. She looked more like a person from the fast-fading Muslim nobility, a character that she would have adroitly portrayed. A guest was reading aloud from an Urdu magazine and she was intently listening to him. As we found out later, her eyesight had also submerged itself into the twilight of her memories and lost visions.

We were warmly greeted and she was excited to see Sadia and her cousin. When I was introduced, she took notice of me and politely asked me to feel at home despite the power breakdown. She apologized repeatedly for the humid afternoon. But she was not the woman I had seen in pictures. Time, an important aspect of her novels, had depleted her energies and her once-celebrated beauty. She was evidently frail but there was nevertheless something electric in her manner and conversation which took me a while to register. Her house was full of books, each room covered from top to bottom with bookshelves. The walls were adorned with her paintings which she had made over a decade, some of which I recognized as sketches in her books and book covers.

Mindful of her celebrated irritation with small talk, I launched into a more flowing dialogue. She hurled several questions in my direction on Indo-Pak relations, the visa policies of both countries and my views on the 'peace process'. I was a bit taken aback and hence unable to offer any coherent replies. Nevertheless, I conjured up some answers that were cautiously optimistic. She appeared amused, saying that her generation suffered incredibly due to conflict. My contemporaries and I have to now rise to the occasion. I can appreciate Ainee Apa's point given that the world she has lived in with its composite Indo-Muslim culture is dead and the RSS and Lashkar, illegitimate children of historical upheavals, are better known than Mir and Kabir.

She wanted to know about the intellectuals of Pakistan and I was once again thrown off balance. But I managed to stutter something about the once historical absence of the Pakistani middle class now changing and growing into an articulate and urban social sector, though I chose not to mention the crass consumerism and the innate conservatism of this new bourgeoisie. I mentioned Kamal, the character from *River of Fire*, who is disillusioned by the aesthetics and the politics of the 1950s but sees no option than to integrate into the changing Pakistan. She smiled and avoided a direct answer by saying that that was an old tale. But it is not an old tale according to me as Kamal's lines are prophetic:

> The joke is that those who raise the slogan of Islam in the loudest voices have nothing to do with the philosophy of this religion. The only thing they know is that the Muslims ruled Spain for 800 years, that they ruled Bharat for a thousand years, while the Ottomans kept East Europe subjugated for centuries. Apart from imperialism, no mention is ever made of Islam's great humanism, nor is it considered necessary to speak about the open-heartedness of Arab seers, Iranian poets and Indian Sufis. There is no interest in the philosophy of Ali and Hussain. Islam is being presented as a violent religion and a violent way of life.[1]

I noticed that Ainee had a terrific sense of humour, her sharp wit unaffected by age and illness. She joked about the idiosyncrasies of Pakistani and Indian politicians, of Muslim backwardness, especially citing a peculiar species that she mentions in her writings—Male, Muslim, Middle Class—MMM, a breed of men, hell-bent on maintaining status quo, nay, sending Muslims into a state of regression.

We lunched in the dining room amidst more of her paintings and books. The atmosphere, despite the sultriness of the afternoon, was cheerful as we talked about the Raj, vanishing Anglo-Indians and Lucknow while the domestics swung handfans as we ate. She held that Zia-ul-Haq's era damaged Pakistan irretrievably. Pakistan, she added, was progressing before Zia took over. She recalled how on the day Bhutto was hanged, everyone in Lucknow seemed desolate. At the Lucknow railway station, a peasant woman crying in the waiting room told her, '*Yeh kaisay log hain ke apnay raja ko mar diya?*' ('What kind of people are these who kill their own king?') I was nothing short of being completely enchanted by her quaint eastern UP Urdu intonations.

Like the great Urdu master, Mir, Ainee also belonged to Lucknow and Delhi, dividing her life between these two cities separated by a thirteen-year long interlude in Pakistan and England. Lucknow, permanent neighbour of consciousness, constantly lived in her psyche and conversation. She insisted that I should visit Lucknow on my next trip, but God (and visa) willing, that is yet to happen. I make a tongue-in-cheek statement about how the 'Lucknow nostalgia industry' is alive and kicking in some parts of Karachi. She liked my blasphemous remark and wondered how I can be a Punjabi given that I speak fairly decent Urdu. But I am now used to this identity crisis.

I began to get a little more familiar and started discussing her books and, a little gingerly, the author herself. Her answers were delightfully original and utterly self-effacing. She said that her parents were born at least a hundred years before their time.

Her father's liberal outlook and her mother's love for the arts were her primary inspirations. She never got married; how could she find a man capable of complementing her? I suppose her rich inner universe made up for the loneliness in exceptional individuals such as she was.

When Ainee moved back to India in 1961, this was not the country she had left behind in 1947. Her world in any case had gone topsy-turvy by then. She accepted the changes with grace and her historical broad-mindedness had prepared her for the transitions that centuries make. In her words:

> What is India all about, what is the problem, why are we so full of problems, why are we like no other country? It's because there's too much history, we have too much of everything, and some of it is excellence but too much of excellence in one country, one period over so many centuries creates problem, it's not a simple story, it becomes a very complicated story ...

Like elsewhere in the subcontinent, history, as compiled, documented and distilled, is the history of rulers and later, the state as ruler. For example, the Indian nationalist discourse had its counterpoint in the two-nation theory—the notion that Hindus and Muslims were two separate 'nations'—used to justify Pakistan's creation. Other narratives, perhaps best typified by the jurist H.M. Seervai's frank interpretation, were, by and large, sidelined. In a contested terrain such as this one, Qurratulain Hyder took no sides and came up with what was later to become a major discipline of historical studies—examining Indo-Pak history from 'below' and from the point of view of people rather than rulers, nobles and court historians.

Ainee's book *Aag ka Darya* was written and published in the highly charged atmosphere of the post-Partition Indian subcontinent, when these two new nation states were rewriting their histories. In Pakistan, *Aag ka Darya* was a sensation right from when it was published in 1959, creating controversies, which in turn, became the hallmark of the book. Several right-wing Pakistani critics and the establishment interpreted the novel to be a negation of the two-nation theory with a subtle endorsement of Indian nationalism. *Aag ka Darya*, for the scale of its canvas, historical consciousness and characterization, surpasses most novels written in any language.

A central and recurring character, Abdul Mansur Kamaluddin of Nishapur, son of a Persian mother and an Arab father, arrives in Hindustan in the fifteenth century. It is Kamaluddin's description of India that sets the contours of modern Indo-Muslim consciousness:

> Leaving the world of kings, rajas and commanders, Kamal saw the other world. This other world was inhabited by labourers, barbers, shoe smiths, peasants and poor artisans. This was the democratic Hindustan ruled by saints who patronized artisans and their guilds. The egalitarianism of Islam was profoundly influencing these Hindu bhaktas. Islam was being spread by peace-loving Sufis—here the sword was irrelevant. Tormented over centuries, the untouchables were chanting 'Ram' with these sankats without the intercession of upper-caste Brahmins ... This was a unique world that was beyond Hindu and Muslim identities. Here love reigned and Kamal was in search of insaan.[2]

By exploring the pain of partition and reiterating that 'civilization' was a larger domain than a 'nation', Qurratulain Hyder made her point in Pakistan and to the limited Urdu readership in India. It was, however, through English translations and Hindi versions of her novels that this point was made in mainstream India. Kumkum Sangari's assessment sums up Ainee's *weltanschauung* well:

> Civilisations were not divisible into nations, national boundaries came and went, civilisations endured. Civilisational unity was perceived as being made up of long-term and contemporary bonds, the textures of lives, memories and friendships.[3]

Qurratulain Hyder's historicity, albeit through fiction, was far deeper than her contemporaries and successors as she explored the complexities and contradictions of the history of Muslims in India. Her emphasis was on the fact that the history of the Indian subcontinent is a narrative of travellers where eras overlap, merge and concur. Her vision has been independently echoed by many historians while writing their own history books. For instance, Irfan Habib's view is that the 'idea' of India as a cultural unity was not a modern secular invention but a much older one; that it was a product of conquest, travellers' visions or a view from outside, while the affect-laden idea of India as a distinctive composite culture or a common heritage emerged from immigrants and converts.

Through her historical fiction, Qurratulain Hyder demolishes stereotypes that emerge from the particularism of religious identities. Her writings are not a set of propaganda tools that invoke the 'one India' stereotype. Instead, there is immense complexity that confronts communal versions of history and the Partition saga. In this complexity, the nationalism of Pakistan or India becomes a secondary issue. The religious or communal narrative also becomes a 'constructed' reality. The reader can see through it, feel with the author and flow with her grand sweep.

Not content with writing fiction, Ainee Apa set about rediscovering the essentials of the Indo-Muslim civilization. She dug out, what she claims, is the first subcontinental modern novel as we know it, entitled *Qissa-e Rangin*, authored by a late nineteenth-century East India Company official, Hasan Shah, in Persian. This invaluable Persian manuscript and its 1892 translation into Urdu as *Nashtar* were lying neglected and Qurratulain translated it into English and published it under the title *The Nautch Girl* in 1992. There were critics and sceptics, but she held her ground. This is an outstanding contribution to the corpus of South Asian, and indeed, world literature.

Posterity will treat it as a major landmark in the evolution of subcontinental literature.[4]

When I met her the second time, Qurratulain, pre-empting my about-to-be-enacted melodrama, warned me, 'Now don't you do the conventional thing … It was great that I finally met you as I have been dying to meet you for so many years.' She said this in pure Hindi. We laughed and laughed and I told her that all the clichés are true and need to be expressed shamelessly.

During this meeting we spoke extensively about *The Nautch Girl*. She was angry that no one bothered to find and study this novel until she unearthed the manuscript from the Patna Library. In fact, her rejection of contrarian views that this was not the first modern Urdu novel was emphatic. She recalled how a small-time official of the East India Company writing in those times, had such a fine sense of plot, dialogue and characterizations, exclaiming, '*Arrey yeh novel nahee hai tau auṛ kya hai?*' ('What is this if not a novel?')

Then we talked of one of her characters, the Calcutta-based singer-courtesan Gauhar Jaan (who died in 1930), from her novel *Gardish-i-Rang-i-Chaman*. I told her that a musicologist friend had discovered some rare thumris sung by her in her original voice. I presented these CDs to her during my second visit and when we listened to them she was in a state of disbelief. She asked me to search for the music of Janki Bai, another luminary of the early twenteith century. I called my musicologist friend to request him to dig out Janki's music and he was stunned when I told him whom I wanted it for. In addition to painting and writing, Qurratulain Hyder was also fluent in the language of music. She co-authored a book with Malti Gilani on Ustad Bade Ghulam Ali Khan and, in her heyday, played the piano and the sitar.

As I left, I promised that I would return very soon to present her with Janki Bai's music. I wrote about my meeting with this legendary woman in my journal which later turned into a piece for *The Friday Times*, a Pakistani weekly. 'My undelivered letter to Ainee Apa is getting longer. I shall need a lifetime to complete it,' I wrote. The letter was never completed and still lives somewhere in me.

A third meeting was never to take place. I remember that languid day of August 2007 when my friends from across the globe called me to commiserate on her passing away, as if I was related to her. I did not know what to do so I wrote this in my blog:

> I have been upset the entire day. Perhaps it does not matter in the larger scheme of things. But this is a sad, sad day. Qurratulain Hyder, the literary giant of our times, is no more. At a personal level it is not just the death of another literary figure but it is far greater and deeper than that. She inspired generations of Urdu readers and there is not a single Urdu writer of the post-independence era who has not been influenced by her.
>
> Hyder primarily wrote for herself but reached out and made her mark, and in the process she connected with millions of readers. And I am just one of them. My friends and I have talked today and we knew how she shaped our inner lives. I have at least avoided regret … I met her after years of longing to do so …
>
> But there will be nobody in that NOIDA house, though that little temple opposite her house will remain and the sound of azaan from a neighbouring mosque will also be heard. But the hearty laughter, quick repartee and inimitable writings have ended. However, as a friend said, 'Writers die, their stories don't' makes me a little happy.

Several months later, when I visited Delhi, I was among her admirers, critics, researchers and the Urdu-walas of Delhi at the Jamia Millia University to read a paper on her work. In order to avoid a clichéd review of her work, I chose to speak on the enigma of Qurratulain's dual belonging and her popularity among Pakistani readers. She lived in India, but was immensely popular in Pakistan as she presented an alternative view of history and selfhood. She remained a unique bond between India and Pakistan until she died.

On a chilly February morning, I was in a session chaired by the towering littérateur of Urdu literature, Gopichand Narang, who incidentally is not a Muslim, which is yet another defiance of stereotypes. At the same symbolic site of Jamia Millia that passionately attempted to merge Hindus and Muslims only to see the splintering later, I recalled Qurratulain's remarks in her acceptance speech at the 1991 Jnanpith Award function:

> My concern for civilisational values about which I continue writing may sound naive, woolly-headed and simplistic. But then, perhaps, I am like that little bird which foolishly puts up its claws, hoping that it will stop the sky from falling.[5]

I wonder what her legacy is after all. Is it just another woolly-headed, quaint vision of a secular India? Such a cliché will not do justice to her magnificent writings. They are beyond the labels of 'secular', 'Muslim', 'Indo-Muslim' and so on, arresting as they are for their complexity and richness, and the inextricability of Muslim and non-Muslim cultures in terms of literature, poetry and music, colonization and Independence. But, above all, her writings depict her quest for humanism, love, belonging and a search for enlightenment. This is what most of her characters end up doing in the vast canvas of her books.

Adjacent to the Jamia Millia Islamia University, the settlement of Jamia Nagar has a small graveyard where Ainee Apa is buried. The Jamia Millia Islamia University of today is a bustling, growing campus where thousands of students from all over India study modern disciplines. Its Urdu department is well staffed and plays a vital role in the growth of the language as well as its literature in India.

Jamia has its own way of paying tribute to great people. A small lawn is called Baagh-i-Ismat Chughtai, named after an iconoclastic and progressive Urdu writer. A Dabistan-i-Mir or the literary world of Mir, the poet, is under construction. There is a Munshi Prem Chand Museum to honour his powerful writings both in Urdu and Hindi. Prem Chand exemplifies Jamia's ethos of blending tradition with modernity and a strong, secular world view. Most recently, Jamia has established a museum in memory of Qurratulain Hyder where her personal belongings, including her collection of books and paintings, are displayed.

Rakshanda Jalil was my guide to this little shrine for Qurratulain with its neatly arranged shelves and glass cabinets. The paintings and the books reminded me of those monsoon afternoons spent at her house in NOIDA. There was an old painting of her Dehradun home—a fireplace, book-lined teak shelves and a velvety couch. Little did she imagine that one day, this vision of domestic bliss would end up in a nondescript gallery of sorts as memorabilia.

Jamia Millia Islamia was originally established in Aligarh in 1920 and moved to Delhi fifteen years later. Its present campus in Okhla came into being in 1936. Nationalist Muslims like Dr Mukhtar Ahmad Ansari and Mufti Kafayattullah of Delhi, including Allama Iqbal, Pakistan's national poet, were instrumental in its creation. Other luminaries like Maulana Shabbir Ahmed Usmani, Maulana Husain Ahmad Madni and Chaudhury Khaleeq-uz-zaman from UP were members of its foundation committee. Most of them were to become freedom fighters and torch-bearers of modern Indian nationalism.

In 1920, Delhi's well-known renaissance personality Hakim Ajmal Khan was elected the first chancellor of Jamia while the firebrand Mohammad Ali Jauhar became the first vice chancellor. Allama Iqbal did not accept the offer of vice chancellorship. I asked the Jamia-walas about his refusal. They said that Iqbal did not want to move from Lahore. Quite plausible as we all know that Iqbal was a homely man and a dreamy poet, not exactly cut out for executive humdrum.

Jamia's silver jubilee function in 1946 was indicative of the split among Muslims. On the dais, Jinnah and Liaquat Ali Khan were seated on one side of Dr Zakir Husain, the vice chancellor, while Jawaharlal Nehru, Asaf Ali and Sir Rajagopalachari sat on the other side. It was a miniature painting that foretold the events to come, echoing Azad's prophecies about Muslims splitting and losing the plot. Well, that is what the Indian nationalist discourse would have to say. As a Pakistani, these postulates appear so remote and academic. I come from a country that actually *exists* and is as real as life itself. One has to move beyond the notion that a country of 180 million can just be a historical aberration. Pakistan is a reality now and the burgeoning youth relates with this 'identity' alone.

Post-Independence, Jamia grew as an academic institution, but its journey to getting recognized as a Central university ended only in 1988. NDTV newscaster, Barkha Dutt, Bollywood star Shah Rukh Khan and cricketer Virender Sehwag are the better-known alumni of Jamia. This institution is perhaps one of those few places in India where buildings are named after not-so-mainstream thinkers like Noam Chomsky and Edward Said.

Quite poignantly, the seminar I attended was held next to the Yasser Arafat Hall. But outside Jamia's little world, in the politics of New Delhi, the Palestinian issue is no longer that of an 'occupation' but more in line with the global media consensus that it is an issue of 'terrorism' against Israeli citizens. And names such as 'Chomsky' sit strangely marginalized as the mainstream Indian corporate media collaborates with the ultra capitalist Fox News. This is something about India that hit me each time—the relatively illusionary comfort with which opposites seem to coexist.

But somewhere in the large campus, amid the old and the new unappealing buildings and manicured lawns, there remains something of its original beginnings. The 'missionary' purpose of Jamia has acquired a plural and multifarious colour compared to the pre-1947 years. That is evident from the many Muslims in the faculty and students, but a larger number of non-Muslims, validating the secularist vision that led to Jamia's creation in the first place.

Jamia's tarana composed by Khaleeq Siddiqi reiterates the essential spirit that has been described by him in a rather quaint fashion:

> Different are the dancing cups
> And different is their dance
> Here drinking begets thirst anew
> And different is this tavern's call

'Tavern's call' might be a little too romantic for those studying dentistry, but it manages to reinforce its commitment to knowledge. Jamia has survived, like Indians, the multiple crises of existence, revolutions and geography.

The first time I met Rakhshanda Jalil was on the shores of the Bosphorus in Istanbul. We bumped into each other in the sprawling Topkapi Museum. Her Urdu was crisp and eloquent and echoed amidst the arches. We exchanged our personal contacts and like innumerable such encounters, forgot about it. It was not until a couple of years later that we re-established contact. Rakhshanda, it so happened, was the moving hand behind the creation of Jamia's little museum in memory of Qurratulain Hyder.

We met in Delhi again on the Jamia lawns on a sunny December afternoon where the little group of persons included the former vice chancellor, Mushirul Hasan and Sadia Dehlvi. Rakhshanda, in those days, worked at the Jamia Millia Islamia University as media and cultural coordinator and had infused youthfulness to the office by constantly breaking the clichéd boundaries that a media relations office entails. Instead of merely issuing press releases, Rakhshanda organized substantive discussions, co-authored books with the Jamia staff and innovated on Jamia's outreach within India and outside.

This impromptu lunch, which was primarily made up of sandwiches, pakodas and fried fish, followed a special viewing of the numerous calligraphic works of Ameena Ahmed, who had donated her choicest selection to the university. Dressed in a flowing silk sari, Rakshanda appeared to be completely professional with a quick wit and an amazingly sharp memory. Her jokes about Pakistan were a little sharp at times but since it was all in good humour, I took them in my stride.

Rakhshanda, prior to joining Jamia, had taught English at the universities of Delhi and Aligarh. Her special contribution to languages has been the introduction of Urdu literature to a wider English-speaking audience within India and abroad. She has translated renowned Pakistani Urdu writers such as Intizar Hussain among others and has several publications to her credit. Her interest in Pakistan is not in its geopolitics but in the politics of its language(s) which is, in some ways, similar to India. She says, with a twinkle in her eyes, 'Except that in India, we rue the "oppression" of Urdu whereas in Pakistan, it is Urdu that is the oppressor!'

Our exchanges on literature resumed when we met at her apartment in Okhla. She had a full house as her sisters were visiting from Mumbai and London. Three confident, modern women in charge of their lives coexisted with their lesser privileged and conservative Muslim counterparts elsewhere in India. Chaste Urdu intermingled with public school English. I saw how traditional Delhi-Muslim cuisine was as popular here as were cucumber sandwiches. The proximity to Jamia was the key reason to live in Okhla; most people may wonder why an educated, well-to-do Muslim couple would choose to live in the cleaner part of a large Muslim ghetto.

Rakhshanda had prepared a lavish dinner. There were various types of mutton dishes from bhunna gosht cooked in the

Shahjahanabad style to the ubiquitous nihari, from a traditional meaty stew to a tenderly cooked biryani, bringing together the quintessential Dilli menu. Indeed, mutton dominated the spread, and in fact defined it. After dinner, we sat around the heater in her cosy living room attempting to warm ourselves in the cold wave that grips Delhi during the winter.

Najmi Waziri, Rakhshanda's husband, is a leading lawyer at the Delhi High Court and also an activist. Tall and athletic, he is passionate about exposing the mafia groups around the Jama Masjid, Hazrat Nizamuddin's dargah and other places where the self-serving Muslim clergy exploits their 'minority' privileges for personal gain. At the shrines, small groups appropriate for themselves the financial contributions made by the devotees. Similarly, the outer precincts of Jama Masjid are also used as an income-generating device for the family of the Shahi Imam instead of the community at large.

Najmi has therefore invoked the ire of the conservative sections of the Muslim clergy which has resulted in threats to his life, making it necessary for the government to provide him with security. He told us all this with a chuckle and a lawyer's eloquence.

Our conversations, as always when Indian and Pakistani Muslims meet, lead to the thorny issues of Partition, identities and contemporary politics. Indeed, Partition creeps into discussions much more in Delhi than in Pakistan where the subject is closed at least in the public domain. I hear jibes about Pakistan and how the Indian Muslims are better off than their counterparts in Pakistan. The educated and liberal Muslims are more likely to articulate their nationalism compared to those who live on the margins of subsistence. I am never in a mood to enter into a polemic, but I do my little speech on Pakistan, on how it is progressing despite the turmoil of recent years and how wrong the perceptions in the media are.

Of course, I have no definitive judgements to pronounce except that I am a Pakistani and proud of it—the only country I have. But I emphasize that heritage and cultures, languages and civilizations can be shared beyond national boundaries. Why is there an exclusivism and a hankering after final solutions when nationalisms encounter each other?

If anything, those who understand Delhi can see how states and boundaries, glories and kingdoms are ephemeral. What is permanent is the indomitable human spirit and shared civilizational values that need not be boxed in or limited to labels.

India's eminent historian, Mushirul Hasan, was Jamia's vice chancellor for a long time and consolidated Jamia into a formidable institution. Mushir is erudite, a prolific writer and an inspirational figure. His refined UP mannerisms blend in with a modern sensibility—the sort of figure that Azad may have envisioned as a model Indian Muslim. He speaks in a mellow tone but with force of conviction. A formidable intellectual, his writings, more often than not, discuss contemporary communal issues as well as they take on the daunting task of rewriting the histories of India, and by default, that of Pakistan. Mushir has over a dozen books to his credit and countless papers and articles.

In his recent book, *Moderate or Militant: Images of India's Muslims,*[6] Mushir investigates the complexities of pluralism, secularism, jihad, discrimination, education and all that afflict the Muslims of India. In particular, the book brings together several of Mushir's earlier works on Muslims, their place in twenty-first-century India, their fears, deprivations and potential to play a role in the future of Indian society and polity. India's Muslims are neither moderates nor radicals, but plain Indian citizens who could be secular or non-secular as any other community. He writes, 'India will remain quintessentially secular and pluralistic as long as there is intercommunity intermingling, and if the Muslims manage to shape their lives in a democratic India even if secularism is undulating.' Could it also mean that they must reconcile with the mainstream or perish?

Mushir lambasts the hidden and not-so-hidden biases of Nirad C. Chaudhuri and V.S. Naipaul who lived far away from either the subcontinent, or for that matter, the Arab world. For instance, according to Mushir, Nirad could only see the ruins of the Hindu temples that the Muslim invaders had destroyed and 'the facts of history mattered little, if at all.' Naipaul, the self-appointed authority on Islam and Muslims defended the destruction of the Babri Masjid by terming it as 'an act of historical balancing'. Mushir reminds one of Gandhi and his role in stopping the rampaging mobs around Jamia Millia Islamia on 8 September 1947, 'Gandhi came to the campus to inspire confidence; General Cariappa, the Commander-in-Chief, the Prime Minister and the Health Minister followed his visit.'

What I find most inspiring about Mushir is his candour. On Jinnah, Mushir holds: '... his attempts not to wreck secular democracy were frustrated by the inability of the Congress to overcome the influence of the Hindu Mahasabha or a sizable section of its own communalized membership.' The hasty preparation of the 'Partition Plan' of 2 June 1947, with its utter disregard for India's people and their plight, still needs a careful re-examination, as we agree. The singular focus on Jinnah in the narratives of Indian history is, at best, misleading; some responsibility for the violence and uprooting of millions needs to be shouldered by the Congress as well.

Mushir's is the strongest of mainstream voices in India, since many fellow voices emanate from Western academies. As he reminds us, six decades after Independence is the opportune moment to 'revise and reconsider established theories on Partition, introduce a more nuanced discourse, and stay clear of the conventional wisdom that we, the generation born after Independence, have inherited as the theme of "communal" politics generally and the Pakistan movement in particular.

As old orthodoxies recede before the flood of fresh historical evidence and earlier certitudes are overturned by newly detected contradiction,' this is the time to heal what historian Ayesha Jalal calls 'the multiple fractures which turned the promised dawn of freedom into a painful moment of separation'.[7]

Mushir also has a lighter side to him. A tremendous sense of humour is evident from the engaging chit-chat that he musters. He also has a wide repertoire of poetry, anecdotes, quotes and qissas in the limitless memory store. The UP culture has a definitive mark on his persona that is faithfully cosmopolitan.

During the Jamia seminar on Qurratulain Hyder, the Urdu-walas—poets, writers, critics and engaged readers dotted the Jamia campus with a 'forced' optimism about Urdu and its literature. Mushir constantly challenged this melee of Urdu lovers. He participated both as a history guru and vice chancellor. He provoked us discussants by questioning Hyder's political moorings or why she was not as radical in condemning Partition the way, for instance, Amrita Pritam was. He challenged the conventionalism of the Urdu world steeped in an eighteenth- and nineteenth-century rhetoric of glory. To me, this was of immense symbolism in Delhi and India at large—modernity confronting the limits of a language that has politically and scientifically not progressed despite the innovativeness and richness of its literature.

The Urduwalas were invited for a dinner by Jamia University. We arrived early, taking Mushir's advice to 'hang out' before the formalism began. The rooftop of the India International Centre is a secluded, open space. Standing next to a glowing coal stove on that chilly winter night, Mushir held forth about India and Pakistan as we waited for the guests to arrive. He makes a few profound statements, spreads a dose of optimism about the future and then in a flash, recites the oft-quoted lines from the great Urdu poet, Ali Sardar Jafri:

You come from the garden of Lahore laden with flowers,
We will come bearing the light of a Benares morning

With fresh breezes from Himalayan heights
And then, together we can ask, who is the enemy?[8]

Later at Sadia's house, Mushir recites a few lines in Persian from Rumi as the little gathering slowly turns into a cultural soiree. A culture of spontaneous verse and a delightful inter-ethnic and inter-religious bonding emerges in the evening's moments, moments that have become distant in both India and Pakistan. This was a farewell dinner for me as I was leaving the next day.

Among the attendees were Oroon Das who plays Rumi in Delhi's theatre production, former diplomat Rangacharya and his wife Kokila, and the civil servant Parveen Talha, who after a long stint in the civil services, retired as a member of the Union Public Service Commission. Eclectic as the gathering was, Mushir's presence charged the atmosphere and his jokes and poetry were most entertaining. Mercifully, a running commentary on Pakistan did not enter the conversational ring. No contests created, no comparisons made and no contrasts drawn.

The way it should be. At least, sometimes.

NOTES

1. Translation found in 'The Vision of Qurratulain Hyder' by Khalid Hasan, *The Friday Times*, Lahore: Vanguard Publications, 2008.
2. Translated by the author from *Aag ka Darya*, Lahore: Sang-i-Meel Publications, 2007, p. 128.
3. Kumkum Sangari, 'Qurratulain Hyder's "Aag ka Darya"', *Muse India*, No. 14, p. 2.
4. In my meeting with her, she elucidated how modern this novel was in terms of its characterization, mood and technique. There were traces in it of what was to be known, at least a century later, as the stream of consciousness technique.
5. *Outlook India*, web version, translation by C.M. Naim.

6. Published by OUP.
7. Ayesha Jalal, 'Secularists, Subalterns and the Stigma of Communalism', accessed in January 2010 at http:21www.tufts.edu/~ajalal01/Articles/partition.ieshr.pdf
8. Translated from the Urdu by Khushwant Singh.

12

Ghalib's Delhi

The Red Fort stands in the heart of Shahjahanabad, like a relic that someone forgot to worship. Imposing in its presence, it emerges into one's vision from nowhere. Still used as a symbol for state power and sovereignty, the prime minister speaks, each year, on India's Republic Day from this grand, sad monument. Its upkeep is as tragic as the Lahore Fort. Before we enter the fort, I remember what my Delhi friend Rana quoted from an article sometime back, 'Ignorance of one's history is a prerequisite for patriotism'. He had forgotten who had written it though.

As is the case with the Lahore Fort, the Red Fort is immensely enchanting and instantly casts a spell on the visitor. My Delhi visits would not be complete without extensive explorations of the monument. But it is only in Agra that the majesty of a fairly well-preserved Mughal fort impresses you with its elaborate and sophisticated architectural and aesthetic nuances. However, both in Delhi and Lahore, the fort meanderings are mere exercises in visual delight.

Flanked by a group of Americans, my most detailed tour was a part of a heritage walk. We started off rather early on a chilly December morning, mixed with the anticipation of warm sunlight and the good-natured blabber of tourists.

Entering the fort through scanners reminded me once again of the word 'terror' juxtaposed with the word 'Muslim'. The Indian media keeps whipping up these words periodically. But is it not a dangerous alienating game? I shrug off such questions and move forward with the little group amid the sound of clicking cameras.

The walkways to the main buildings in the fort complex were clean and quiet as the stream of tourists had not started flowing in. The Diwan-e-Aam (public gallery) is our first major halt. This was the site of the royals' durbars including the ones organized by the British. The lonely throne made of marble with intricate inlay work can be spotted behind the protective screens placed around it. I imagine what the Delhi Durbar must have been in all its glory. After wandering through the Diwan-e-Khas which were the royal chambers, bedrooms and interconnected courtyards, we reach the little gate that provided the escape route for Bahadur Shah Zafar, who perhaps had no idea that this exit would be his final one and that the world inside the fort was going to crumble and disappear with the brutal end to the 1857 Mutiny by the British. The little wooden gate is locked.

On the night of the fall of Delhi in early 1858, General Wilson, the commander of the British forces, celebrated his victory with a festive dinner in the Diwan-e-Khas, the innermost sanctum of the three-centuries-old Mughal reign in India. The dinner would be an eclectic mix of Victorian cold cuts, canned fish and meats, and general army mess cuisine. In the days to follow, twenty-one Mughal princes were condemned, hanged and eliminated in a flash. Many more were shot dead and their corpses were displayed in Chandni Chowk to inform the public as to what would happen to rebellious subjects as well as to remind citizens about the brutal capabilities of the new imperial order. The British contemplated demolishing the Jama Masjid and the Red Fort. However, the exquisite Fathepuri Mosque was sold to Lala Chunna Mal, a Hindu merchant, as his private property and the Zinatul Masjid was converted into a bakery. Buildings within a radius of 500 yards of the Red Fort were razed to the ground. Structures around the Jama Masjid were also cleared in the name of martial orderliness. Quite symbolically, the buildings blocking the new wider roads and the planned railway line were also demolished.

The kuchas, galis and katras erased in the process represented a larger metaphor—the erasure of not just bricks, mortar and marble, but a centuries-old way of life. An entire tehzib[1] was dismantled and replaced. For Delhi this was nothing new though; each episode of human suffering is real and unique. Delhi's melancholy was to stay, but counterpoised by the inner zest of its residents who had seen much worse and reinvented themselves like their beloved city.

The negligence of the fort as it stands today is quite monumental; in particular, the latter-day additions of iron grills and fences which are completely out of sync with the place. The government departments in Pakistan and India are incapable of appreciating fine aesthetics and the buck, as usual, stops at 'lack of resources'. Many walls of the fort have been tastelessly white-washed for purposes of 'conservation', and the shoddy patchwork amid small Mughal bricks or sandstone conspicuously mars the impact of the old structures. In many ways, the Red Fort is modelled after the Lahore Fort—the public and private quarters, gardens, Sheesh Mahal and the underground chambers. The differences can be attributed to the innovations of Shah Jahan and his highly refined female companions, the queen and Princess Jahanara, as well as its proximity to Chandni Chowk and the city of Shahjahanabad.

The American tourists in our group are not particularly gripped by the grandeur and myriad architectural styles unfolded by our charismatic companion, Sadia Dehlvi, as she attempts to unravel the centuries of evolution, glory and destruction that the fort has experienced. She explains how the fort was a self-contained city, an elite version of the Shajhanabad outside, that even provided for residential and training spaces for the troops, servants and royal staff. There were spaces too for local commerce for the royal ladies. I wonder if I could visit the fort alone at night when there is no one else.

As we reach the sandstone chabutras designed for musical soirées and for poetry sessions or mushairas, the cloistered spaces open up. How magical it must have been! I attempt to explain the concept of mushairas to the Americans but feel inhibited by the impossibility of translating the inner language of culture. Mushairas were the high points of Delhi's literary culture. Young as well as more seasoned poets recited their verses with elegant etiquette in the late evenings; these sessions continuing well into the dawn. Kings and nobles, patrons of the Delhi poets, would be the chief guests, adding decorum to these events. Despite many internal and external attacks, by the early nineteenth century, the fort grew into a hub for poetry and its experimentation, especially in Urdu. The finest Persian carpets would be unrolled for the poets. A roving candle would light up the poetry in front of the bards. Ghazals, a genre of poetry, expressing love for the temporal and divine with doses of existential rambling, were popular.

The ghazal is uniquely structured in that each couplet is a universe of meaning and there is no compulsion, despite the formalism, to build on a single theme. Even the mood varies with each couplet and so does the theme. Disparate yet whole, the couplets of a ghazal are connected.

As the comforting sunlight added little patterns on the red sandstone, I mused about how the eminent poets of Delhi—Ghalib, Momin, Azurda, Sahbai—would all gather during a typical mushaira presided over by Bahadur Shah Zafar. The poets would play games with Ustad Zauq, the king's favourite poet, by paying compliments to his rivals and by overrating lesser poets.

Such was the cultural climate of Shahjahanabad that a

Frenchman, Alexander Heatherley, adopted the nom de plume of 'Azad' and became a pupil of Delhi's Urdu poets, finding a place at royal gatherings. He was already composing high-quality verse at the age of twenty-one. Trained in medicine, he loved poetry, and would travel to Delhi from his various postings. A unique combination of a white man dressed as a military officer, a mushaira buff and speaking in chaste Delhi Urdu!

I dream up an imaginary portrait of Nawab Mustafa Khan 'Shefta'. Shefta was another master poet who had received his coaching from the legendary Urdu poet, Momin. Such was Momin's aplomb that for his one couplet, Ghalib was willing to forgo his entire collection of Urdu verse. Momin's couplets were simple. When translated they lose their stunning impact:

> When you are with me, it is like
> Nothing else is there.

Modes of praise during these poetical soirées were also quite formal. The younger poets had to be encouraged while the senior ones were praised with artistic restraint. The masters disliked it if their couplet was extolled beyond its worth; they themselves being aware about which of their creative rhymes deserved appreciation and to what extent.

But Mirza Ghalib was the odd one out. His Persian poetry was outstanding even as his Urdu ghazals were not always accessible to most listeners in a degenerating environment. The range of subjects and the countless moods and styles that he experimented with were not prevalent in such an ambience. He lamented at mushairas that there was no one who could truly appreciate his worth. There was sarcasm in this verse:

> I seek no praise, nor care for rewards
> If there is no meaning in my verse, so be it.

I recall a vivid description of a mushaira in Farhatullah Baig's book, *Delhi ki Akhri Shama* (The Last Lamp of Delhi). Baig's evocative portrayal of the mushaira at the Haveli Mubarak-un-Nisa Begum, where the last mushaira under Zafar was arranged, deals with the ethics, aesthetics and refined cultural nuances of this institution. This was the age of Urdu's popularization and its entry into the mass media.

Lithographs were introduced to Delhi around 1840 which popularized the written script and reach of Urdu to those who were not a part of the exclusive elite cultural extravaganza. Poetry collections or 'diwans' of leading poets started to be published and Urdu newspapers came into being. In 1841, Ghalib's printed Urdu diwan was available to the public and four years later, his Persian collection of verse was published in Delhi. Notable Urdu newspapers like *Aina-e-Sikandar* and *Jam-e-Jahan* commenced their printing in Delhi. They carried printed news of India and the world. Urdu had finally reached its zenith though its glory was to eclipse after the traumatic events of 1857 and afterwards.

The mushaira continued as a popular participatory poetic event well into the twentieth century. After 1857, regional kingdoms and other dispersed centres of power patronized poets and Urdu poetry. The late-nineteenth century witnessed a new realism in Urdu poetry that narrated the tales of ordinary people and their everyday lives. Nazeer Akbarabadi and other such poets experimented more with the medium of the 'poem' rather than the ghazal. However, the classical style was to continue as a mark of purity and cultural ascendancy in Delhi, Lucknow, Aligarh and elsewhere.

It was in the early decades of the twentieth century that Urdu literature began to shed its self-conscious and indulgent classical trappings by adopting a modern, particularly Leftist orientation. The birth and subsequent evolution of the Progressive Writers' Movement was the finest moment in Urdu literature as it endeavoured to bring various Urdu writers and poets from all over India to buy into the concept that literature should not be created just for its own sake but should have the larger goal of social change. These were the heydays of the anti-colonial movement. The Progressive Writers' Movement had some of the best poets and writers as its vanguards. Faiz Ahmed Faiz is the best-known torch-bearer of this tradition whose poetry was to provide a moving expression of the public sentiment and political movements in Pakistan. The other luminaries of this movement were Sajjad Zaheer, M.D. Taseer, Rashid Jahan, Kaifi Azmi, Ismat Chughtai, Sahir Ludhianvi, and Ahmed Nadeem Qasmi, to name a few.

The Progressive Writers' Movement continued in post-Independence Pakistan and became a threat to the post-colonial state that carried on with the old style of ruling through a well-developed steel-frame bureaucracy. The ones who migrated to Pakistan faced a new reality that, in the words of Faiz, was not the dawn that they had hoped for:

> This blemished light, this dawn by night half-devoured
> Is surely not the dawn for which we were waiting.

They say that poetry flowed easily before modern life occupied all the major intersections and filled cultural life with concrete. This is why the mushaira is now a dying institution in both India and Pakistan. Such events are regularly held but they are ritualistic, often lacking in imagination, and rather removed from the prevailing cultural environment. For the young, e-forums and dedicated websites have overtaken mushairas. Earlier, in Pakistan, state-owned television had provided much impetus to the coverage and even sponsoring of mushairas on all important national occasions. Since the 1990s, the supremacy of the market and the 'sale' of airtime have taken that away from the viewers.

Urdu was created by Delhi for its imperial efficiency and social amalgamation. Its variegated vocabulary from Turkish, Arabic, Sanskrit and Persian provided immediacy and connection to all.

Urdu was a marker of social mobility, a measure of refinement and urbanism, and found votaries in Delhi and several towns and cities of northern India such as Lucknow, Aligarh and Allahabad. Later it gave way to English, while in Pakistan, it, ironically, became what English is to India.

The eclecticism of Delhi over centuries provided the catalytic impetus for the sophisticated development of the Urdu language. Though the Mughals made Persian the language of the court, Urdu remained the language of the masses. Even the elites spoke Urdu at home. The Sufis also used Urdu to communicate with their devotees. Several poets changed their idiom from Persian to Urdu. Leading lights such as Wali Daccani (1668–1744), Hatim (1669–1734), Mir Dard (1788–1843), Mazhar (1700–81), Sauda (1730–80), Mir (1722–1810) and Insha (1778–1838) were the modern agents of this linguistic evolution. It is said that, once, Mir declined to recite his poem in Lucknow saying that only knowledge of Urdu, as it was spoken on the steps of the Jama Masjid in Delhi, will enable them to understand what he wrote!

By the 1850s Urdu had almost completely replaced Persian as the popular literary medium. India and Urdu's fortunes were to change after 1857—the watershed year.

The constructed identification of Urdu with Muslims and later with Pakistan led to its gradual abandonment by the Indian state and the elites. History testifies to the fact that it was a language that connected all and was used by everyone in pre-1857 India. 'Hindustani', another version of Urdu mixed with Hindi, still survives in Bollywood and its songs, and is the popular language of TV soaps and the streets of northern India. The purist Doordarshan (national television of India) anchors who talk to their guests in shuddha Hindi are replied to in chaste Hindustani that highlights what the state channels are trying to do—remould identity and language using a nation-state filter.

As I find out, Urdu is not extinct in Delhi mainly due to its inherent value, and one could surmise, its cultured past. Partition and the biases that it created have receded in the decades and no longer find a place in contemporary Delhi.

For instance, Indira Varma, a Sikh migrant from Pakistan, runs the Sham-e-Ghazal Society that sponsors mushairas on a regular basis. Indira also composes verses in Urdu and has a few collections to her credit. I spotted her recent book, *Shafaq Ke Rang* at the Makataba bookshop in the Urdu Bazar. In Delhi, I picked up a copy of the enjoyable and profound novel *Ka'i Chand The Sar-e-Aasman*, authored by the eminent critic Shamsur Rehman Faruqi, and published by Penguin. *Ka'i Chand* is Urdu's major novel in the last two decades. Once again its theme deals with Delhi, the decline of Indo-Muslim culture as represented by its central character, an eclectic singing woman remarkable for her culture, emotion and tragedy. There is also a revival of the medieval tradition of Dastangoi by the energetic duo of Mahmood Farooqi and Danish Hussain. Mainstream theatre also keeps Urdu alive and thriving.

Delhi's relationship with Urdu is intimate and seminal. In particular, the Urdu ghazal, notwithstanding the immense contributions made by Lucknow, evolved and flourished in Delhi before anywhere else.

High literature in Urdu grew in three different centres—the Deccan, Delhi and Lucknow. The Deccan emerged as the earliest centre for the Urdu ghazal, due to the linguistic interaction between the local people and Muslim conquerors from Central Asia who settled there in the twelfth and thirteenth centuries. From the mid-fourteenth to eighteenth centuries, Urdu poets flourished in northern India and the Deccan. Quli Qutub Shah (1565–1611) is known as its first major poet, like Chaucer is in English, with a volume of significant poetry in a language later named 'Urdu'. Wali Deccani (1635–1707) and Siraj Aurangabadi (1715–63) followed Shah in the Deccan. Delhi was concurrently experimenting with the Urdu ghazal and, by the eighteenth century, had turned into a major centre. Lucknow followed suit as the third literary capital of Urdu in the nineteenth century. The Urdu ghazal reached its zenith with Mir and Ghalib of Delhi, *qasida* with Sauda in Delhi, mathnawi with Mir Hasan of Lucknow and *marthiya* with Anis and Dabir, again in Lucknow.

> Ghalib, you write so well upon these
> mystic themes of love divine
> We would have counted you a saint, but
> that we knew of your love of wine.

Our Urdu teacher at school, Dr Jaffri, was the only doctorate holder. His area of study was Ghalib and his metaphysics. This was rare even in the Urdu universe that Pakistan is. Dr Jaffri's mentoring initiated a personal journey for me into Ghalib's world. Ghalib cannot be classified as a 'subcontinental' poet; his rank and stature need to be further assessed. The obstacles of translation and communication render this task difficult; impossible, perhaps. Ghalib's Urdu verses are widely available in Devanagari script in Delhi, but even then it remains 'too difficult' as many a reader tells me.

This is what Dr Jaffri used to warn me about as I asked him questions on the complexity of Ghalib's poetic universe. He would insist, 'Once you break the initial barrier, hundreds and thousands of paths will appear before you; you can wander and navigate as you wish.' Undaunted, I have been treading these multiple pathways into an Indian garden with Persian flowers and still, at times, I wonder how little I understand.

Ghalib lived within the decline, fracture and eventual dissolution of Mughal rule. He had moved to Delhi around 1810 from Agra where he was born into a family of Turkish aristocratic descent. Coming to this city was an important event in the life of this thirteen-year-old newly married poet who desperately needed material security, who was set on a long literary career, and who was later to be declared a genius.

In Ballimaran Street in Shahjahanabad, Ghalib lived a life of relative ease despite his continued struggle for patronage and financial solvency. His early works were steeped in the classical Persian style. However, within a few years, he was to adopt a personal idiom which was unrivalled for its originality and iconoclasm. He continued the traditions of Mir and Dard (other two eminents poet of Delhi) in composing verses that were embedded in the Wahdatul Wajud philosophy that evolved from the Sufi thought of Ibn-e-Arabi on the one hand, and local Indian streams of Vedantic cosmic-personal reality on the other.

Constant financial insecurity, not unlike that faced by many poets and writers of that age in India and outside, merged with an underlying sense of personal inadequacy. This defined his existentialist world view. There are references in his letters as well as verse, how liberation from the constant search for a means of livelihood could bolster the creativity of an artist. By 1847, Ghalib gained access to the royal court and his dabbling in Urdu was encouraged by the emperor's penchant for the language. But he always remained at the margins of power, both native and imperial, except during a brief interlude when he became the poet laureate. He wrote:

> I used to attend the durbar, and receive a robe of honour; I cannot see that happening now. I am neither one of the accepted nor one of the rejected, nor a culprit, nor an informer, nor a conspirator. Well, tell me yourself, if a durbar is held here and I am summoned, where am I to get an offering to present?[2]

His rivalry with Zauq, the king's ustad, emanated from this competitive view of access to patronage. But there was also some arrogance and a belief in the immortality of his verse that made him complain about the king's patronization of a lesser poet such as Zauq. Bahadur Shah Zafar, the last Mughal king, a distinguished poet himself, was not enamoured by Ghalib's personality that, at best, remained defiant despite his show of outward obedience. Ghalib perhaps felt that subordination to the court was a little belittling, and his astute understanding of the world made him realize that the Mughal court was a mere twilight of what the empire was. Nevertheless, after the demise of a pliant Zauq, the emperor had no choice but to appoint Ghalib as the leading court poet.

Another royal assignment for Ghalib was to document the official history of the Mughals—the *Partavistan*—in two volumes. *Mehr-e-Neem Roz*, the first volume, was completed with much boredom (as gleaned from the tone of his letters). The second volume could never be completed as the world changed with the uprising of 1857 and the end of the empire itself. Ghalib was too disinterested to do it anyway.

Ghalib never owned a house in an age when everyone lived in personal abodes. He was overwhelmed by the imperatives of paying rent or accepting a house from a patron on a temporary basis. He was also strikingly not into possessions either. Most of the books that he read were borrowed. None of his children survived except the two sons of his wife's nephew. The nephew died at a young age in 1852, leaving Ghalib with the onerous task of raising the young boys.

Ghalib's one wish, perhaps as strong as the wish to be a great poet, that he should have a regular, secure income, never materialized. His relationship with his wife was not a happy one and bordered on an indifference not uncommon to those times. Deprived of the security of having a father in a male-oriented society, he had looked for material and moral certainties. His poetry is thus filled with his vulnerabilities.

Ghalib's complex poetry transcends time and boundaries of human thought. Here are some verses that bring out his myriad facets where he indulges in a fascinating postmodern 'unpacking' of the self:

I have nothing to do with the rosary
Or with the wine bowl
In a dream, I am as one
Whose hands have been cut off.

Being most humble
I bear enmity to none
I am neither a fallen grain
Nor a stretched-cut share.

In the circle of the pious
I am contemptible,

But in the company of sinners
I am the most select[3]

Finding Ghalib's haveli in Kucha Ballimaran, where he died, was not a problem. Passing through various lanes and the overpopulated corners of Shahjahanabad, I reach the legendary haveli, distinctive for its rather ordinary appearance. For one, it is only a partial space recovered by the government from encroachers, victims of circumstance themselves. There is a little parking stand that one had to cross to get into the structure. The architecture is also not that spectacular but there are sad efforts to celebrate the great poet by adorning the walls with his framed poetry and some photographs. One poem reads:

Even in captivity,
I have fire under my feet, ablaze
Every loop of my fetter melts
like a hair in front of a flame.

I am alone that afternoon and sit on the entrance stairs for quite some time trying to create in my mind, the mood of this era—intimate, personal and yet so affected by power struggles. The night before I was browsing through the pages of a new work by a devoted Ghalib scholar, Ralph Russell, who describes the relative stability of Delhi[4] despite the shrunken size of the Mughal Empire:

> The city itself was prosperous, being the distributing centre for the northern trade to the east and south. By 1852, it had about 160,000 inhabitants. Within it there lived the merchants, the financiers, the learned and the dependents of the court. Of the 2014 salatin or descendents of the emperors listed in 1852, a considerable proportion lived outside the Fort walls.[5]

Mughal pre-Mutiny pageantry was best represented by grand festivals that were a matter of public excitement. The emperor would 'parade the streets on his elephant, the ministers, the heir-apparent and the Mirzas in their places. A straggle of foot soldiers went in front and behind; musicians sounded trumpets and rhapsodists recited the imperial praises—a slightly tarnished and tawdry assembly perhaps, and raucous to the ear, but cheerful and colorful and much appreciated.'[6]

Every landmark recalled an authentic association with individuals or events. Localities such as Habash Khan ka Phatak, Bangash ki Sarai, Haveli Haidar Quli, Gali Qasim Jan, Jarnail Bibi ki Haveli, Begum ka Bagh, Kucha Ghasi Ram, Baradari Sher Afgan, Namak Haram ki Haveli, all represented snippets of an urban life that was personal and intimate and which accorded due recognition to individuals and their lives.

Ghalib's Delhi and its nobility engaged in a colourful variety of sports. The sandy slopes of the Jamuna near Delhi Gate, Mahabat Khan ki Reti, was the kite-flying arena with its colourful contests. Kabutarbazi was another popular game. It was a common sight to see the nobility go about with their prized quails and partridges perched on their shoulders. Several akharas operated in the city as did chess competitions and satta. On the steps of the Jama Masjid, Dastangohs always attracted large crowds.

Phoolwalon ki sair were held during the monsoons and gardens would be frequented by families during winters. Bhands, Bahrupias and Bhagat Baaz (street performers) and Kathputli Baaz (puppeteers), were sources of popular entertainment.

Cultured courtesans were central to a prosperous man's life, allowing the latter to mingle with women other than their wives and indulge in a poetic language of longing, union and separation from the beloved. Urdu literature was full of these themes and its proponents, such as Ghalib, idolized the courtesan figure. Ghalib's poetry has references to his beloved courtesan who tragically left him lonely after her untimely death.

At the parallel Mughal centre, Lahore's Hira Mandi was also flourishing right under the shade of the grand Badshahi Mosque built by Emperor Aurangzeb. The prevalent culture of the time spilt into the regional centres. The fabled Umrao Jaan Ada in Lucknow was also a metaphor for this decadence.

The loss of masculine (dynastic) power generated a feminized renaissance, and to be creative and powerful it had to be free of institutional bonds such as family, honour and respectability. These islands of free interaction between noblemen and highly cultured women therefore came about in kothas that smacked of courtly elegance and yet suitable enough for the continuation of patriarchal relations.

In Ghalib's Delhi, Hindus and Muslims shared common saints, pirs, mazars, dargahs and even popular gods. C. F. Andrews, the renowned British historian, describes his meeting in 1904 in Delhi with Munshi Zakaullah, a well-known younger companion of Ghalib, who recounted this feature of those times:

> The intimate residence together side by side in the same city of Mussalmans and Hindus had brought about a noticeable amalgamation of customs among the common people. The art of living peacefully with neighbours of a different religion had reached a very high level during the reign of Bahadur Shah Zafar ... Influenced by this milieu, Ghalib proclaimed:
>
> In the Kaaba I will play the shankh (conch shell)
> In the temple I have draped the ahram *(a robe worn during pilgrimage to Mecca).*

The verse above describes the Sufi concept of 'fana' or dissolution of the self into divine reality, similar to the unity articulated in Vedanta. Ghalib's secular person and society were shaped by the crystallization of a centuries-long evolution of coexistence, of a culture that was inclusive and beyond the rigidities imposed by clergies. Ghalib wrote:

> A free man does not hide the truth; I am half a Muslim, free from the bonds of convention and every religion; and in the same way have freed myself from grief at the sting of men's tongues.

The most haunting and immortal testament of this spirit was expressed through the Persian mathnawi *Chirag-e-Dair* (Temple Lamp) which is a tribute to the temples of Benares. This was not the first or the last poem to be inspired by the ambience of Benares, but for a Muslim poet to compose it was phenomenal. Ghalib was tempted to settle down in Benares. He had broken his journey to Calcutta where he was headed to plead for the renewal of his pension with the British authorities. Ghalib stayed in Benares for a month or so and imbibed the temporal and spiritual beauties of the ancient city. The mathnawi of the symbolic 108 verses[7] depicted a subversive (from the Muslim point of view) idea that Kashi was *Kaaba-e-Hindustan* or the Mecca of India:

> Where autumn turns into the touch of sandal
> On fair foreheads
> Springtide wears the sacred thread of flower waves,
> And the splash of twilight is the crimson mark
> of Kashi's dust on heaven's brow.
> The Kaaba of Hind,
> This conch blowers dell
> Its icons and idols are made of the light,
> That once flashed on Mount Sinai.
> These radiant idolations naids,
> Set the pious Brahmins afire, when their faces glow
> Like moving lamps on the Ganges banks.[8]

As I muse on that entrance staircase, the temperamental humidity of July interrupts my reverie with a rather heavy downpour. Half wet but pleased with the rain, I take shelter in the nearby dhaba that pretends to be a restaurant. It is evidently Muslim from its name and its offering of various meat dishes. I wait for the rain to end and reopen Russell's brilliant book. I read, 'Long after Delhi had ceased to be the Paris of power, it continued as the Versailles of good manners. Secondly, it continued the royal tradition of patronising the arts … The most favoured, however, was poetry.'

I recall this verse as I wait for the rain to stop:

> Look not upon me slightingly;
> Though I am dust beneath your feet
> Men honour your capital because I dwell in it.

Many people did not share Ghalib's unconventional views in his time. But there must have been some sort of acceptance of unconventionality enabling Ghalib to have a Hindu pupil and friend, Hargopal Tufta, or to pronounce Shivji Ram Brahman as his son.[9]

In 1857, the year of the Mutiny, Ghalib was fifty-nine years old and had lived for more than forty years in Delhi. He had also visited Calcutta where the British were in full control. He astutely observed the inner rot and decay of the old Mughal order which was powerless to resist the new force of British imperialism. In one of his letters, prior to 1857, he had predicted that the Mughal court would not survive many more days. In a post-Mutiny letter (dated 1859) Ghalib cried:

> My friend, what a question to ask! Five things kept Delhi alive—the fort, the daily crowds at the Jama Masjid, the weekly walk to the Jamuna bridge, and the yearly fair of the flowermen. None of these survives, so how could Delhi survive? Yes, there was once a city of that name in the realm of India … Only three Muslims are left—Mustafa Khan (Shefta) in Meerut, Maulvi Sadr-ud-din Khan in Sultanji and that slave to the things of this

> world, Asad Ghalib in Ballimaran. And all three are despised and rejected, destitute and distressed.[10]

In a ghazal, that was more open than his cautious verses for public consumption, he laments:

> Now every English soldier that bears arms
> Is sovereign and free to work his will.
> Men dare not venture out into the street
> And terror chills their hearts within them still ...
> The city is athirst for Muslim blood
> And every grain of dust must drink its fill ...[11]

The nobility of Delhi became paupers following the 1857 uprising, ending in the final control of the British in 1858. In an 1859 letter to his disciple Tufta, Ghalib wrote:

> Hakim Ahsanullah Khan, one of the senior ministers of Bahadur Shah is living in the stable of his own mansion whereas the English are occupying the main house ... The moon faced begums of the Red Fort are wandering the streets in filthy clothes, ragged pajamas and broken shoes.

During the revolt, Ghalib remained pretty much confined to his house, undoubtedly frightened by the rampant massacres in the city. Many of his friends were hanged, deprived of their fortunes, exiled from the city or detained in jails. By October 1858, he had completed his diary of the Revolt, the *Dast-Ambooh*, and presented copies of it to the British authorities, mainly with the purpose of proving that he had not supported the insurrection. Although his life and immediate possessions were spared, little value was attached to his writings; he was told that he was still suspected of having loyalties towards the Mughal king. During the ensuing years, Ghalib's main source of income continued to be the stipend he got from the nawab of Rampur. *Ud-i-Hindi*, the first collection of his letters, was published in October 1868. Ghalib died a few months later, on 15 February 1869.

During my many visits to Delhi I came across a wealth of literature on Ghalib. Walking through the old lanes of Delhi, I discovered how the greatest of his woes was the crumbling of a civilization before his very eyes:

> But for that I should not have been in Delhi now. Do not think I am exaggerating; everyone, rich and poor alike, has left the city, and those who did not leave of their own accord have been expelled. Nobles, grant-holders, wealthy men, artisans—none are left. I am afraid to write you a detailed account. Those who were in the service of the fort are being drastically dealt with and are harassed with interrogations and arrests, but that is only those who entered the service of the court during these months and took part in the revolt.[12]

And again:

> If Ghalib sings in bitter strain, forgive him,
> Today pain stabs more keenly at his heart.

Post-1947 Delhiites, like Ghalib, complained of the transformation of their city. They could not find many friends and people they knew. But then this is what makes Delhi so resilient and oblivious to the shocks of time.[13]

In the decade that followed 1857, Ghalib witnessed the British-led reconstruction of a city they had ravaged. The famed Phoolwalon ki sair was revived in the 1860s; classes in Delhi College were resumed in 1867. The Town Hall was built opposite the railway station in 1863, a Post and Telegraph Office and a dak bungalow were built near Kashmiri Gate. A clock tower was erected in Chandni Chowk. The new Victorian architecture emerged as a counterpoint to the rest of Shahjahanabad that was Ghalib's spatial universe.

A year later, on a freezing December evening, I marched in a procession from Chandni Chowk to Ghalib's haveli to celebrate the 210th birth anniversary of the great poet. The procession began from the Town Hall and terminated at the haveli in

Gali Kasim Jan. The poet Gulzar who had flown from Mumbai to attend the birthday celebrations of Mirza Ghalib, led this literary pageant. Such was Gulzar's charisma that even Delhi's chief minister and the local member of Parliament seemed like ordinary guests at the event. Several Urdu-walas, an endangered species in India, were also there in their closed-neck achkans, carrying its lost glory. Ghalib's brilliant and most recent biographer, Pavan Varma, introduced me to Gulzar, and what an exciting moment that was!

The haveli, with its characteristic semicircular brick arches supported by square columns, was illuminated for the occasion. A group of hip-hop reporters from TV channels wanted to know why Ghalib was so great. I was also asked to speak and this marked my first TV appearance in India. I spoke about Ghalib's humanism, relevance and universal appeal. Local poets, including Iqbal Ahmed Khan, who lives in Ballimaran, and who has, for years, recited Ghalib's verses befriended me and treated me to chai later.

For a Pakistani whose identity is wrapped around Urdu, this was a confusing moment. Pakistan does not claim Ghalib; the 'enemy', that is, the Indian state, owned this archetypical Urdu bard.

At Ghalib's haveli, I talk to Pavan Varma about the all-round decay. This was not our first meeting. Long before, I had met him in person. His book on Ghalib, *Ghalib: The Man, the Times*, had acquainted me with his rather direct style. This was Varma's first book published in 1999 and was later translated into several Indian languages. A distinguished Indian Foreign Service officer, he is also one of the last remnants of the 'Ganga-Jamuni tehzeeb' that values India's past in its entirety instead of picking and choosing what would suit a particular power narrative.

Varma approached the Sahitya Akademi to publish his manuscript, but they were rather unhelpful. A common friend asked him to meet the famous writer, Khushwant Singh, who liked the draft. Singh sent it to Penguin who loved it and called it 'A' class. It has now acquired an evergreen shelf life and its nine editions were printed in English.

After several stints in foreign missions, Varma became the director general of the Indian Council for Cultural Relations in 2007. He continues in the tradition of the eminent men of Delhi who have undertaken the onerous task of advocating cultural preservation, valuing heritage and the Urdu language. His outspoken laments on the state of Urdu are also well known:

> I have often met people who want to enjoy the meaning of an Urdu couplet but are unable to. Others come out with the conventional 'wah, wah!' when a poem is recited, but have not, I am pretty sure, understood its meaning. There are understandable reasons for this inadequacy. For at least two generations now, Urdu has not been studied by most of our educated, simply because it is not part of the school curriculum. People don't know the script, and, increasingly, very little of the vocabulary. The result is the neglect of the good Urdu poets, and the proliferation of the mediocre ...

Varma's second book, *Havelis of Old Delhi*, is a tribute to the architectural and cultural legacy of Shahjahanabad. *Havelis* highlights 'age' and transports the reader into a lost world. This book provided me with the formidable reference material that I had been looking for. I owe it to his insights, the range of his inquiry and his accessible style to further discover the lost havelis and their stories.

Gulzar, whom I met at Ghalib's birthday celebrations, is India's finest poet in Hindustani and Urdu. He has gained both critical acclaim and commercial success. Gulzar (Sampooran Singh), like many other Punjabis, is heavily inspired by Urdu poetry. His film songs are an instant hit for they are not just forced lyrics; most often they are not rhymed but modernist in their structure, tone, symbols and unconventionally simple images. His work has been published in Pakistan as well. The late master of Urdu poetry,

Ahmed Nadeem Qasmi, hailing from the same region of Upper (Pakistani) Punjab, accepted Gulzar with open arms and their relationship grew strong. Gulzar, thus transcended the label of 'Bollywood lyricist' and entered the Pakistani Urdu world of poetic imagination.

Gulzar's lasting contribution to Ghalib was his presentation of the poet's life and poetry on national television. Hailed as one of the finest literary productions, this audio-visual production carried Ghalib's story and verse into millions of Indian homes and abroad.[14] Gulzar's love for the poet finds expression in his words:

> I always say Ghalib had three trusted servants who were always with him. The first was Kalloo, who was with Ghalib till his very last days. The second was Wafadar who had a lisp. The third is me. They lived their time. I am still in service of him.[15]

The hallmark of Gulzar's *Ghalib* was its attempt to explore the iconoclastic vision of the poet. We see Ghalib's sense of humour despite the tribulations of life, uncertain financial conditions and the loss of seven children who never lived to provide a family to the poet. Most importantly, Gulzar's rendition highlighted Ghalib's utter lack of pretence and rejection of worldly appearances, 'Nothing about him or his life was put on.'[16]

In 2008, Varma rendered forty-five of Gulzar's verses into English in a collection entitled *Selected Poems.* The last four lines of one of his poems, 'Rape', read:

> Just a woman, weak, vulnerable
> Four men, only because they were men,
> Pinned her against a wall and raped her!
> Stark. Chilling.

In Jamia Millia's quaint, modern ambience, Rakhshanda Jalil and I discuss Ghalib's attitude towards the British conquest of and subsequent rule in India. He had a range of attitudes that are often conflictual and contradictory. His journal-monograph of 1857, the *Dast-Ambooh* was, on balance, evidently pro-British. He cited British excesses but also expressed dismay at the ruthlessness of the resistance. On the other hand, his letters, addressed to his close friends were critical and frank. There were occasions where, apprehensive of a leak, he requested his friends to destroy his letters. A few written to the nawab of Rampur made such requests. Thankfully, not all the addressees followed Ghalib's advice. They seemed to know the value of these letters.

Ghalib's awe of the British was to some degree undone by the events of 1857 and the brutalities that the people of Delhi, especially Muslims, had to face. The hangings, according to one estimate, of 27,000 persons[17] in a single year shook his sense of humanity. Rakhshanda reminds me that the Muslims were allowed to return by November 1859, more than two years after their expulsion.

Ghalib soon understood the new realities. In response to an 1858 government order, he wrote:

> All well-wishers of the British are to illuminate their houses, and there are to be illuminations in the bazaars and on the Deputy Commissioner sahib's bungalow. Your humble servant, even in this state of penury, not having received his appointed pension for the last eighteen months, will illuminate his house, and has sent a poem of fifteen couplets to the Commissioner of the city.[18]

At Jamia Millia Islamia, I am introduced to Professor Sadiq-ur-Rahman Kidwai, the secretary of the Ghalib Institute. Professor Kidwai is a mild-mannered critic and academic reminding me of a more genteel past. Within a couple of days I find myself riding a Delhi autorickshaw, searching for the Ghalib Institute in response to a lunch invitation. I struggle with Delhi's chaotic and mercurial traffic. The auto driver has never heard of the institute and, to make matters worse, he takes a wrong turn past the India International Centre. As we were groping for the way, we pass the well-known Sai Baba temple, packed for a pooja ceremony. Helped by the traffic jam, I have time to quickly peep into the temple. I cannot help but notice how the dargah culture—the chadars, the flower sellers and incense, not to mention the greedy clerics collecting donations—has influenced the temple. I vowed to visit the temple again.

Finally, we reach the Ghalib Institute. The lunch has been hosted for a group of visiting Pakistanis; quite a few Delhi-based Urdu writers and critics have also been invited. Eminent writer and critic, Shamim Hanafi, the Karachi-based Dr Asif Farrukhi, editor of *Dunya-zaad*, and several others are chatting as I reach the room where a pre-lunch discussion is concluding. I see a large number of guests from Pakistani universities. Is this the result of a more liberal visa regime, I wonder.

The former Indian president, Dr Zakir Hussain had launched the idea of setting up this institute during Ghalib's centenary celebrations in 1969. Two years later, the institute became functional. Now a thriving centre for research, it is managed by a trust of eminent people. The institute, known as Aiwan-e-Ghalib, has an impressive library, a museum commemorating Ghalib's life and a decent auditorium. Each year, Aiwan-e-Ghalib holds an international seminar and maintains a myriad network of scholars and researchers. It also awards achievements in Urdu prose, poetry, criticism and drama. Qurratulain Hyder was also an awardee of the institute.

We sit in one of the visitors' rooms and enjoy the hospitality of the Urdu-walas of Delhi. The conversation traverses common ground—happenings in the Urdu world, sentimental and not-so-sentimental remembrances and, of course, Ghalib. Urdu's binding force momentarily suspends Indo-Pak differences and the politics of separateness.

The other hunt for Ghalib memorabilia leads me to the privately managed Ghalib Academy located in the congested Nizamuddin Basti. This is an uninspiring site for an institute focusing on the life and works of such a great poet. The alley leading to the building is thronged by Ghalib-illiterates—unemployed boys, burqa-clad beggars and hundreds of pilgrims on their way to the Hazrat Nizamuddin dargah. His tomb is always unvisited even though it is situated in a very busy lane, probably the way Ghalib may have wished. He had no pretensions of being a people's person despite his innate humanism.

Inside the Ghalib Academy, the first impressions are disappointing—paan-stained walls, cobwebs, walls with peeling plaster and emptiness. This is a privately supported institute established to promote Urdu poetry by Hakim Abdul Hamid of the Hamdard group. Interestingly, this academy receives no funding from the state. Hence the worn-out state of affairs, including, some would say, the language and its appeal.

On the brighter side, this auditorium hosts important events and the library proudly offers books free of cost and for reference. There is also a little museum on the second floor showcasing kaftans, caps and portraits of Ghalib's life and times. An art gallery with paintings by M.F. Hussain, Anis Farooqui and Satish Gujral is a bonus. Ghalib Academy also publishes books on Ghalib in English, Hindi and, of course Urdu (*Diwan-e-Ghalib* is the perennial best-seller). To serve the local community of unskilled youth, a computerized calligraphy training centre boasting of 'exhaustive lab practice and very low fees' also prepares Urdu typists. The library is a little treasure of thousands of archived newspaper clippings, which makes it quite a treat for Ghalib fans.

In one of his letters Ghalib wrote about what his Delhi would become in the twenty-first century:

> It grieves me to hear of the desolation of Lucknow, but remember that there this destruction will give way to creation—that is, the roads will be widened and the bazaars improved, so that everyone who sees it will approve of what had been done. In Delhi, destruction is not followed by creation, and the work of destruction goes on all the time. The whole appearance of

> the city, except for the street of shops that runs from Lahore Gate of the Fort to the Lahore Gate of the city ('i.e.,' says Mihr, 'Chandni Chowk and Khari Baoli') has been spoiled, and will go on being spoiled ....[19]

A random walk around Urdu Bazaar and several parts of Shahjahanabad today would bear witness to these prophetic words. But Ghalib never lost his zest for life or his sense of humour. Even on his deathbed he was composing poetry and writing letters. He could not see properly, could not write and sought the help of his disciples to create new masterpieces in modern Urdu prose. Such were the poets of Delhi. Such was the city—even in its ruins it glowed like a splintered, uncut jewel.

NOTES

1. Arabic word that encompasses the concept of civilization, culture and etiquette.
2. Ralph Russell, *Ghalib: Life, Letters and Ghazals*, New Delhi: OUP, p. 164.
3. Natalia Prigarina, *Mirza Ghalib: A Creative Biography*, New York: OUP, 2000.
4. During the period—1800 to 1857—the population of Delhi was stable and smaller than that of Lucknow (350,000) and much smaller than the other urban centres such as Calcutta, Bombay and Madras.
5. Ralph Russell, *Ghalib: Life, Letters and Ghazals*, New Delhi: OUP, p. 274.
6. Ibid.
7. Hindu rosaries have 108 beads.
8. Translated by Pavan Varma from *Ghalib: The Man and the Times*, New Delhi: Penguin, 2008.
9. Ibid.
10. Ralph Russell, *Ghalib: Life, Letters and Ghazals*, New Delhi: OUP, p, 165.
11. Ibid., p. 131.
12. Ibid.
13. Delhi College had kick-started the Muslim Renaissance in the middle of the nineteenth century. Munshi Zakaullah was one of the best-known representatives of that age as well as Sayyid Ahmad Khan.

Munshi Zakaullah in his old age declared, 'People speak of the "good old times", but those times, as a whole, were not good, when compared with the days in which we are now living. They were full of corruption and decay. But the afterglow was extinguished by a thunderstorm of violence; the Mughal dream ended in nightmare.'

14. Gulzar has directed several offbeat films in Bollywood that remain distinct for their originality and rejection of stereotypes.
15. Gulzar, *Mirza Ghalib, A Biographical Scenario*, New Delhi: Rupa & Co., 2003, Preface.
16. Ibid.
17. K.M. Ashraf, 'Ghalib & The Revolt of 1857', in *Rebellion 1857*, P.C. Joshi (ed).
18. Russell and Islam, *Ghalib: Life and Letters*, p. 149.
19. Ibid., p. 179.

13

Love's Labyrinth

Professor Amita Singh is an accidental friend of mine. We had met in Beijing in a high-sounding conference in 2006 where we were delegates from our respective institutions. As is the case with South Asians, especially those from the two constantly squabbling neighbours, the bonding is instant, almost predestined.

There was a large contingent from India at the conference. Ideologues from Universities in West Bengal, the marketists from Maharashtra and Gujarat and, of course, Dr Amita Singh from the firebrand, left-leaning Jawaharlal Nehru University, or JNU, comprised this assorted group. Exuberant and passionate, Amita, a public administration expert, is not the archetypal academic living in an ivory tower. Imbued with a sense of the real, her communication skills are terrific. Dressed in ethnic-chic saris, her intelligent eyes not willing to miss anything, Amita is an engaging character. In a short conversation, she can traverse subjects and paradigms, experiences and anecdotes often not without a sense of humour. We spent several days in the sub-zero temperature of Beijing and her energy kept the conference and its various sessions animated.

Our interaction turned into friendship. There was also a self-conscious attempt to break political divides and historical gulfs.

Amita has a large number of Pakistani friends and her frequent visits to Lahore and Karachi have also erased the commonly held media-inspired prejudices.

A year later, I pack for a trip to Delhi to attend a conference at the JNU. Dr Amita Singh heads the Centre for the Study of Law and Governance. She makes sure that I confirm my plans and arrive at the venue. A little ado and I also get a visa! At Lahore airport I once again face the immigration official who asks me why I am visiting Delhi. The man, imbued with textbook patriotism, also warns me that there is no stamp on the visa form (an additional layer on the passport-visa-embassy quagmire). Our conversation, as I recall from the corner of my memory, proceeded along these lines:

Me: (fake-polite) I have a legitimate visa, why would you not let me go?
Official: (earnest) Sir, they send many people back due to the stamp not being there. You know how Indians are ... don't believe their high-sounding rhetoric!
Me: (rankled) Well, I really have to reach there. I am supposed to speak tomorrow morning.
Official: (irritated) At your own risk, jaiye jaiye!

Panicking, I call Amita from the airport who also gets disconcerted by this piece of news. Within minutes she has called the liaison officials and assures me that JNU will arrange for the airport pickup and that I should call Mr X and Mr Y at the university. Not a little perturbed, I board the flight. The Lahore–Delhi route is one of the smallest rides in the South Asian airspace. Within minutes of take off, and even before one tries to finish the newspaper, the announcement for landing hits the ears.

I am grilled with equal suspicion and subdued ferocity at the Indira Gandhi International Airport in Delhi. The visa, alas, had been issued in a different country. So I was a Pakistani, sporting an Indian visa issued in a third country; all of this was quite confusing for the linear red-tape-obsessed officialdom. I register at a separate desk, of course, and then answer some odd questions on the number of days, the credentials of my host and more. The address and the relatively unknown name of the JNU guest house is also checked by a superior who, thank heavens, is far more good-humoured than his underlings.

By the time I came out of the arrival section of the airport, I was exhausted. This was arguably the most trying journey to Delhi. The winter sun was soothing and cheered me up instantly. At the airport, a graduate student of JNU, Chetan Singai, received me. Chetan was born and brought up in Bangalore, once the 'Garden City', as he informs me. However, it was now the Silicon Valley of India. Extremely polite and deferential, I stopped him from calling me 'Sir' and insisted that he was free to address me by my first name.

Crawling in the frustrating traffic, we talked a lot. Chetan had come to Delhi in 2004 to pursue a masters degree in political science. His first visit at the age of twenty-two was in connection with a SAARC 'Budding Economists' competition where he represented the South Indian region. With a twinkle in his eyes, he described his first visit to the sprawling JNU campus and how he just 'fell in love with the place'. A distinguished student, he made it to the masters programme. In the process, he landed at the Centre for Law and Governance to do an MPhil. He praised JNU's flexible academic policy which allows for such freedoms for students to chart their own course of study.

'From the Garden City to spacious JNU, I felt at home,' remarked Chetan. 'I don't feel like moving outside the campus for any reason,' he said with a broad smile. Before he moved here, he was always in awe of the historical significance of this city, 'In Delhi, I have revisited many of the historical monuments. They are stunning, of course! I was not overawed by them, but everything here has a unique aesthetic that is quite different from what I grew up with,' he said. At JNU, Chetan discovered only in his second year, that the Qutub Minar was literally in his backyard!

Chetan, like a responsible host, provides a running commentary as we enter the broad arched gate of JNU. This was a different Delhi—calm and scenic, the noise level inside the campus, incredibly low. JNU's 1,000 acres have been carved out of the wild Aravalli Hills. We crossed forest areas that would have been a delight for birdwatchers and tree lovers.

The *Imperial Gazetteer of India*, 1881, had noted that the rocky and undulating hill spurs close to Mehrauli were dotted with keekar and beri bushes, while the soil glowed with mica. The *Imperial Gazetteer* informs us that the hills of Delhi used to provide a pleasing scene when looked at from the other side of the Jamuna river. Apparently, in clear weather, even the Himalayas could be spotted. No such luck now. But the hill spurs are vaguely visible even in the December smog much like an impressionistic painting.

I am a guest at the Chintan Guest House managed by the Indian Council of Social Science Research established in 1969 by the state to promote research in social sciences. This is a typical government guest house with a large retinue of staff and austere rooms. The waiter, who salaams me as he deposits my luggage, is, as I find out, a Muslim. I am tempted to talk with him but I need a rest after a long haul with ferocious bureaucracies.

The emergence of JNU in the early 1970s was a milestone in the educational landscape of India as it launched cutting-edge disciplines and introduced fresh perspectives within the Indian university culture. JNU has always been considered as one of India's most politically aware and active educational institutions with Marxist student politics ruling the campus for years.

The academics at JNU proudly claim that the university and its campus life is a microcosm of India, drawing students from all parts of the country and from almost every strata of Indian society. JNU's annual admission tests are conducted at three dozen or so centres across the country simultaneously. There is affirmative action for under-represented ethnic groups including the 'unmentionable' castes; almost a quarter of seats are reserved for them. Students from overseas are also encouraged and, each year, nearly 10 per cent of the students are from abroad.

During my stay at Chintan, the television coverage of student elections was most interesting. Some local channels commented, patronizingly, how JNU was time-warped. The Left had died in the world but the JNU faculty and students were keeping it alive almost artificially. I could not help notice the extraordinary politicking in the campus. All four key posts—president, vice-president, general secretary and joint secretary—were won by the AISA (All India Students Association). AISA, at least then, was closely affiliated with the Communist Party of India (Marxist-Leninist). Even more intriguing was the fact that the CPI(ML) had won only five seats in the state legislative assembly in Bihar and one in Jharkhand and, quite clearly, was not a widespread movement in populous India. The media also played up CPI(ML)'s support to the Naxalite movements in areas around Bihar, Chhattisgarh, Jharkhand and the Andhra Pradesh–Karnataka border.

True to its reputation, JNU was a mini-India space. The political contest within the campus was a close reflection of national politics. Eight parties within the campus were contesting. My head swirled as I tried to keep up with this heightened pluralism. As a foreigner, despite my desire to learn more about student politics, I was whacked up by the confusion caused by so many acronyms.

Chetan was a little sceptical about the AISA's victory in 2006, saying it was contradictory. 'While anti-globalization was one of the major planks of the AISA election manifesto, JNU students are not shy of crawling the glitzy shopping malls of

Delhi wearing brands like Reebok, Nike, Levi's, and so on. Some even work part-time in the call centres of Gurgaon.' He said that this schizophrenia was probably an offshoot of aggressive corporate dreams sold via the media. Another student told me at the conference, that the faculty was confused. The same neo-liberal international institutions which are vehemently criticized during academic sessions end up supporting the seminars and knowledge events at JNU. Wither their politics? But at JNU, it is difficult to remain unaffected by the sheer enthusiasm and life on campus. Elections or no elections, most of the students are so politically aware that even plays and other entertainment activities centre round issues and political positions.

The conference and related discussions were lively, and thankfully devoid of the strangulating formality typical of public sector events. I made my two-bit contribution and chaired a few sessions. Amita Singh ran around the place, arranging and rearranging sessions, negotiating with the egos of the VIPs who came to lecture at certain sessions. Amidst the mayhem, Amita would not forget to introduce me to the participants and JNU staff. She would give long, embarrassingly laudatory introductions and end with the phrase 'and he represents the younger generation that will change India–Pakistan relations'. Sometimes I would squirm or smile, cough or even laugh loudly. When I was introduced thus to Dr Karan Singh, eminent statesman and the then chancellor of JNU, he was quite realistic, saying, '*Woh kabhee na kabhee to hoga*, but you tell me, which Pakistani city are you from?' We began chatting and Dr Karan Singh, as I found out, was a Doon School alumnus and his immediate interest was in my school, the Aitchison College, that was the Pakistani version (albeit less exclusive) of the post-Independence Doon School.

Dr Karan Singh is a wry politician, published author and also the titular maharaja of Jammu and Kashmir. He is the son of the last ruler of the ill-fated princely state, Maharaja Hari Singh. Steeped in letters, he holds a doctorate from Delhi University. Singh has had a long consistent political career. He also served as governor of the state of Jammu and Kashmir from 1965 to 1967. Thereafter, he was a minister, an ambassador, a Lok Sabha MP, and a Rajya Sabha member since 1996.

Knowing his background, I refrained from any political discussion. Dressed in an achkan and pyjama, he was quite a charming figure typical of black-and-white faded photos of a past era. During our brief interaction, he spoke of peace and missed opportunities.

Involved students and researchers took care of the guests besides managing little stalls commonly known as 'information kiosks'. There were a few publishing houses as well on the veranda with books and countless titles related to the myriad disciplines exhausted during the conference.

JNU is stimulating, often breaking notions of conventional wisdom on poverty and development. In fact, it tackles the 'captive mind' syndrome head on. The tendency of Third World scholars and academia to be influenced by Western theories and concepts gets a thorough thrashing here. Corporate India loves to mock JNU calling it passé or at best naive but the reality is that in spite of the watering down of its past ideological exuberance, JNU and such other hubs of thought and activity provide the necessary impetus for equitable change and respect the diversity of entitlements. It provides that essential, if only a little, digression from the linear view of progress that India has espoused since its liberalization which is now bolstered by high growth rates masking inequality and poverty.

As a Pakistani, this is even more inspiring. Our public sector campuses have been held hostage by the right wing and the best of academics are abroad or in private sector universities. Pakistan's marriage to neo-liberalism has been accepted at large—by politicians, parties and unelected institutions of governance. A few individuals and some NGOs have challenged the ascendancy of the market and blind faith in its workability. But there are few institutions and spaces that can provide sustained resistance or, at least, present alternatives. Even the best of private universities in Lahore cannot say what JNU can. This is the difference, an essential one, which I felt in Delhi.

I met a wide range of earnest, eccentric and highly gifted researchers at the conference. A lady from Heidelberg talked about farmer suicides in India with passion; an Australian academic made startling revelations about slums and issues of justice, and so on. I was delighted to meet Kuldeep Mathur, former head of the Centre of the Study of Law and Governance. Professor Mathur has written extensively on the environmental campaigns of Delhi. I happened to read his paper on the politics of the environmental clean-up in the wake of civil society's movement against air pollution. Delhi has been a success story in some ways, but achieving this has not been a smooth process. It has deep implications on the tendency of the executive to take refuge in court edicts.

Sometime, in those few memorable days spent at JNU, my dynamic hosts, led by Chetan, introduced me to the Ganga Dhaba (tea stall) close to the Ganga Hostel. This dhaba is not just another tea stall but a popular joint famous for its late-night student congregations. Tea is but an excuse for political discussions and laughter. However, the dhaba is in effect, a small, dusty place. What makes it unique is the energy of the students. We too sip masala chai and talk about the campus and how it has evolved over the decades.

Pawas, a south Indian student, tells me how the social atmosphere of the campus has transformed since the 1990s. Echoing him, a younger academic explains how the teaching community has also changed. It is not necessary that members of various faculties are card-carrying Leftists. The government has subtly tried to align JNU with the changing times, read neo-liberalism. Competition is rife. The cultural life of JNU, which once held mushairas and kavi sammelans, has also changed. Even social integration has been thwarted with the increased use of the Internet and now special campaigns are required for cosmopolitanism. Ironically, as I find out, more and more JNU students are not looking for causes. Instead, they are busy preparing for competitive exams for entry into the civil services.

One of the students in the organizational team was Nazia Khan, a Delhi girl. Demure yet articulate, Nazia is a dynamic young woman who intends to enter the civil service. Her decision is backed by her family and as she tells me, her parents have strongly encouraged her to pursue graduate studies. Nazia's family is from Old Delhi and she spent her early years near Ballimaran. Her immediate family moved out of the area as it was getting congested and the better schools were situated in the farther corners of 'New' Delhi.

Nazia was exceptionally beautiful. The infiniteness of her eyes made her even more charming. But above all it was her art of storytelling, undoing the ordinariness of simple events, the tales and places of Old Delhi that one had heard already. During our splintered conversations, at tea breaks, lunch hours and the several mindless official dinners, we squeezed a few moments to discuss the obligations expected out of her as a Muslim woman. Nazia is very much a product of her age. She is not defiant about conventions but believes in tailoring them to the present.

Two women lawyer activists from Lahore are also objects of much curiosity. For mainstream Indians, Pakistani women are burqa-clad Taliban creations or at best, Muslim typecasts from Indian cinema. Western perceptions are material for a long and sordid story. Irum Ahsan and Saima Khawaja have been at the forefront of environmental movements in Pakistan and have been pursuing public interest litigations.

Irum laid out the pros and cons of alternative dispute resolution, particularly the jirgas in the tribal and rural areas while Saima traced the trajectory of public interest litigation and the corresponding judicial activism for environmental protection in Pakistan. They are the new faces of Pakistani womanhood—confident, conventional yet modern and extremely articulate. Saima covers her head and her dupatta moves in a Benazir-esque fashion while she talks or makes speeches. While we were at JNU, a horrible incident took place. A Muslim woman who was raped by her father-in-law faced further discrimination by the mullahs in India who declared that her marriage ought to be annulled due to this sexual act. Therefore she had to seek a formal divorce and marry her father-in-law. Saima Khawaja held a press conference and spoke vehemently against this bigoted understanding and application of Islamic jurisprudence. In a few days, she made a mark at JNU.

JNU provided this space and encouraged Saima to speak up. 'We feel like celebrities here,' remarked Saima when we chatted at the farewell dinner. Irum was sorry about how such an environment of relatively free expression has yet to take root in Pakistan. I remind them that this is JNU, a little island of enlightenment, and may not be taken as the norm in contemporary India.

Saima has another mission too. She would have been a Delhiite had Partition not taken place. Her mother lived at Akbar Road, in a bungalow where the Congress party office exists now. Her father left Shahjahanabad in 1947 never to return. Such is their sense of loss that they do not want to look back or even converse about Delhi. Muted memories came back from Saima's childhood as she related the migration tale. Her grandfather rose to the position of governor of West Pakistan in the late 1950s. Pakistan augmented the family's privilege and status like other sections of the Muslim elite that migrated to Pakistan. For instance, Saima's family speaks proper Urdu, biryani and other culinary delights are cooked with a touch of authenticity, innate pride and perhaps nostalgia, a wistfulness that needs to be fostered, lest it empties the memory.

The venomous Naipaul had, for a change, made some relevant remarks on the cities of India. By extension, these words are equally applicable to most cities which evolved during British India:

> All the four main cities in India were developed by the British, but none has so British a stamp as Calcutta. Lutyens's New Delhi is a disaster, a mock-imperial joke, neither British nor Indian, a city built for parades rather than people, and today given a correctly grotesque scale by the noisy little scooter-rickshaws that scurry about its long avenues and endless roundabouts ... Calcutta alone appears to have been created in the image of England, the British here falling, unusually, into the imperialist practice of the French and the Portuguese. And what has resulted in Calcutta is a grandeur more rooted than that of New Delhi ...[1]

Driving out of JNU, the taxi driver, evidently a novice, missed a turning and drove aimlessly. He was not that perturbed despite my protests. I wanted to reach the Hazrat Nizamuddin dargah before it was late. Having lost our way, we passed a conglomerate of shanty towns where the Delhi underclass, shunted out to cleanse the metropolis, lived. The sight intrigued me, so the next day I returned to the huge slum that provides shelter to a small fraction of the millions who live in squatter settlements across India.

In Delhi alone, there are over 800 slum clusters. Each is said to have between 100 and 1,000 huts with a total population of about four million. I learn at JNU that around 800,000 housing units were required to accommodate slum dwellers so that they have access to basic health, education and other facilities. According to an old estimate of the Ministry of Housing and Urban Poverty Alleviation, India-wide, there was a shortfall of over 169 million dwelling units. Perhaps it is growing at the same pace.

This is not different from Pakistan. A simple formula is to divide each figure by eight and one can safely apply it to Pakistan.

A copy of the *Forbes* magazine that I picked up rates Delhi as the twenty-fourth dirtiest city in the world with the filthy waters of the Jamuna and other health hazards.[2] As expected, the city authorities deny the charge. Such rankings take into account levels of air pollution, waste management, water potability, hospital supplies, medical services and the presence of infectious diseases. While the municipal authorities have taken several measures such as landfills and sanitation improvement, the situation is far from satisfactory and even a casual visitor cannot help but notice that. Like several other South Asian metropolitan areas, this state of affairs can be traced to the 'multiplicity of authority' or overlapping jurisdictions—drainage maintenance is the responsibility of the Municipal Corporation of Delhi (MCD), sewage control that of the Delhi Jal Board (DJB) and so on.[3]

Delhi's urban sprawl is mixed seamlessly with its rural hinterland. The 275 'revenue villages' of Delhi are no longer peripheral but are a part of the capital though not always officially acknowledged. Once, as I walked by the posh Kailash Colony to Zamrudpur, ugly concrete urbanity effortlessly merged with lazy old men smoking hookah on a khaat. If one visits the trendy Hauz Khas village, there are hardly any signs of the urban–rural divide; everyone looks wealthy amidst the swanky art galleries and charming curio shops. Rangpuri village that borders Radisson Hotel, has Haryana's Jat kids driving flashy cars and dancing in National Highway 8 clubs, thanks to the urban real-estate demand as more and more Haryana villages are being sucked into Delhi's urbanity.

Out of 33.60 lakh households in Delhi, 1.79 lakh live in rural areas.[4] Lucky Peck, author of the book, *Delhi: A Thousand Years of Building*, notes that during the colonial era, the expansion of the city swallowed up nearly fifty villages and during the first decade after Independence another fifty were pulled into urbanization. Some of the villages like Malcha and Raisina survive only as street names. Raisina, of course, was shifted to build the Viceregal Lodge, later renamed Rashtrapati Bhawan. The exact site of the village is said to be where the Delhi Press Club houses busy journalists.

During the construction of New Delhi, the British cleared away entire villages. Post-Independence, the city expanded and was planned around these villages. The villages remained, while the farmlands sprouted residential apartments instead of crops. Vasant Enclave next to Vasant Gaon, Khirki Extension next to Khirki Village and Nizamuddin West next to Nizamuddin Basti were all villages that are now core constituents of metropolitan Delhi.

Similarly, the villagers of Kotla Mubarakpur, next to South Extension I would herd their cows to graze in what is today the coveted and bustling Defence Colony area. The residents of Shahpur Jat village, now a hub of chic designer boutiques and basement workshops, had their farmlands spreading from today's Hauz Khas and Andrewsganj to as far as Greater Kailash and Malviya Nagar. These developments were similar to that of Pakistani cities. For instance, Lahore city also spreads out into the rural hinterlands and even posh areas such as the Defence Housing Authority area were very much rural in their origins.

The case of Defence Lahore is another story. Given the high demand for real estate by Pakistan's new-rich classes and expatriates, it has now expanded towards the Indian border. Serving and retired army officials, once wary of such a location, are keen to be there and promote the housing. Atal Bihari Vajpayee, former prime minister of India wrote in a famous poem, 'Now there shall be no war'. Cynics in Pakistan ask which Pakistani general would risk a war when he has so passionately built his farmhouse or plush bungalow in such close proximity to the Indian border?

Coming to know Dr Shreekant Gupta, a former director of the National Institute of Urban Affairs (NIUA)[5] and a thorough Delhiite, has been fated by the stars. My meeting with Dr Gupta who allows me to call him 'Ali' (a testament to his composite Delhi identity), was initially arranged on email. Earlier, I had read his letter to the editor published in the UK-based conservative *Economist* magazine. The writer, a political leader of Britain, in an article in the magazine, a harbinger of doom for Pakistan, had described the country as 'The world's most dangerous place.' I was not surprised. I was struck by Gupta's empathy and directness:

> Sir, the title (of your article) by your leader about Pakistan—*The World's Most Dangerous Place*, January 5, confirms the old adage in journalism: when it bleeds it leads. Yes, Pakistan is going through trying times, but it is far from being the world's most dangerous country. Having just returned from Pakistan, which I traversed without hindrance, with my Indian passport and Hindu name, I can say emphatically that its people are warm and friendly and passionate about democracy and the forthcoming elections.
>
> Parts of my own country (and Nepal and Sri Lanka) are racked by Maoist guerrilla warfare and violent separatist movements. I do not recall you designating India as the world's most dangerous place when Rajiv Gandhi was assassinated during electioneering or Indira Gandhi for that matter. The latter's killing was followed by a brutal and murderous pogrom against the Sikhs and Delhi burned for days. The truth always contains shades of grey.

I made a note of it but never remembered to follow up. Then Dr Gupta visited my blogsite *Jahane Rumi* and left a comment. We corresponded and developed a cyber friendship that turned into a real one within months. Exchanging ideas, stories and anecdotes were our cyber, and sometimes, real pastime. As a fellow South Asian, Dr Gupta's proud challenge to Western perceptions appeared to me a testament of his intellectual honesty. In Dr Gupta I found a friend, but more importantly, my country has another well wisher in the neighbourhood.

Another piece written by Dr Gupta, based on his visits to Pakistan, was entitled 'Dholaks Drown Gunfire' and had these memorable lines:

> ... if there was one country in the world where I could blend and not feel out of place and where I was welcomed with open arms it was Pakistan. Having been there on four previous occasions, once with a group of students from the Delhi School of Economics, traversing the country for two weeks, I had ample experience of the legendary Pakistani hospitality.

One of his accounts was of a Pakistani (Punjabi) wedding saying how he had to remind himself that he was not in Delhi. He wrote:

> As the evening air acquires a nip and woollens gradually start appearing, houses in Pindi and Lahore and Delhi and Amritsar are echoing to the sound of dholaks ... female cousins are busy every evening practicing Bollywood dance numbers for mehndi night. I am told that the most popular number to be choreographed this season is *'maujan hee maujan'* from the recent Bollywood hit *Jab We Met*. A couple of years ago it was *'kajra-re'* from *Bunty aur Babli* (and at a mehendi in Lahore I had to remind myself I was not in Delhi) ...
>
> [In Pakistan] ... people are going about their daily lives and marrying and meeting and yes, trying to have a bit of enjoyment in their lives. While columnists and think-tanks dissect the events and pontificate over the future of Pakistan it is the people who

are affirming their resilience and that of their nation. Indeed, the sounds of the dholak may yet drown that of guns.

Dr Gupta holds that as the world becomes increasingly urban, South Asia will account for five of the world's ten biggest cities by 2015, namely, Delhi, Dhaka, Karachi, Kolkata and Mumbai. By then, a total of about 700 million South Asians will live in towns and cities, a colossal number by any yardstick.

Shreekant Gupta had an eventful stint at the NIUA. After 1962, the government prepared the draft of Delhi's Master Plan 2021, and issued it for public comment in 2005. A little over a year later, Dr Gupta led a team at NIUA that presented an alternative called Perspective Plan for Delhi. Delhi Development Authority (DDA) was rattled by the alternative as it challenged the notions of conventional official planning. Earlier too NIUA had sent in its comments which were not given much importance. It therefore concluded that the proposed master plan for Delhi had become 'a compendium of concessions and amendments rather than a lucid and tenable road map for the future development of the capital of India'.

Dr Gupta and his associates noted that the draft Master Plan 2021 failed to address the on-ground spatial and physical character of Delhi—its size, built form, settlement patterns and ways of life. In so many ways, it had ignored the innate purpose of a master plan, namely to 'establish an evolved system of spatial and physical order as a manifestation of the needs and aspirations of city-dwellers and constrained resources that are a natural fallout of unplanned urban expansion'.

Delhi in the twentieth century found itself littered with illegal constructions, encroachments on public land, crumbling infrastructure and local bodies and agencies with conflicting mandates working in a haphazard manner. And of course, the all-pervasive corruption reported in the media. Land-use planning had been neglected by the DDA and the actual use was nothing like the planned usage.

Dr Gupta was keen to prepare a base map of the ground conditions in Delhi using satellite imaging. Such an investigation revealed that almost 60 per cent of the total land area of NCT Delhi (148,300 hectares) was built up. Covert land transactions and market forces had converted most agricultural land into built-up areas. Dr Gupta says that Delhi is nothing compared to what was envisaged in the land-use plan of MPD '62 and its amended versions. 'More than 75 per cent of urban development in the city is in violation of the Master Plan. DDA's land use plan is an abstraction in that it matches reality only in terms of the road network and the layout of planned colonies.'

The quality of the life of Delhiities had been impacted in this process. For instance, the area at the northern tip of East Delhi, shown as a green belt is actually a concrete jungle. Likewise, in the south-west, the mini city of Najafgarh is shown as vacant space in the land-use plan!

The possibilities of new and newer Delhis are ever-present in the metropolis. In this faster-than-life pace, defined by fast-moving urban frontiers, conservation and protection of heritage must find a space. Not just in Delhi but in Lahore, Dhaka, Karachi and Kolkata. Otherwise anonymous cities will continue to emerge whetting the ahistorical ethos of globalized greed.

The Delhi Metro had commenced its services when I was in JNU. From chaotic New Delhi, it is now possible to travel to the back lanes of Old Delhi in a few minutes. To reach Ballimaran I had used the metro. The old-world Shahjahanabad residents were quite indifferent about the futuristic metro beneath the ground that they stood on.

Delhi's Metro is now a multi-line network that connects the huge city or the National Capital Territory and is still expanding. Sites are always dug up somewhere and road signs announce that the metro will pass hither very soon. This has been a capital-intensive success though its critics are many and doubt whether it would help the congestion in a city where about 30 per cent of commuters still walk.

Travelling to Old Delhi was quite comfortable, fast, clean and efficient. It is a different matter that when one leaves the metro at Chandni Chowk and takes the back alley that has still to adjust to the metro age, horses and their smelly leftovers greet us with an alarming reality.

Initially the Delhi Metro was financed by the Japanese Development Assistance to the tune of 60 per cent, but Indianization of the system and its adoption by the government seems to have worked out. Pradip Krishen, a tree lover and author-photographer of the acclaimed book, *Trees of Delhi—A Field Guide*, has complained in an interview:

> … I don't know, when the history of New Delhi is written I wonder whether the building of the metro will go down as a major cause of the destruction of thousands of trees. The metro pushes on and one day it'll be appropriate to take stock of what it achieved and the price that was paid. I really don't have a handle on the number of trees that were felled for the metro, but it's a little bit like going into denial. Besides, I think in some ways the worst is still to come … I've just seen a horrific plan to build an underground highway through Sundar Nursery that will uproot over a thousand trees. I went and counted the trees that lie in the zone of destruction—114 species, more species than the most carefully cultivated patch of garden in the whole city, Lodi Garden. It's appalling!

It is only after browsing through the excellent compendium *Trees of Delhi* that one marvels at Delhi's uniqueness. It is a city that borders the edges of the desert and yet the number and diversity of trees is mind-boggling. Over the centuries, Delhi has been home to over 252 species. Krishen informs us that New York only possesses a maximum of 130 species. The range of tree species in Delhi makes one forget that it is not part of a rainforest, nor perched on the equator but sits in an arid zone. Admittedly, there are several exotic trees, grafted from other climes by its foreign rulers and planners. This is what Delhi shares with Lahore—a thousand blooming flowers and myriad species of trees that refuse to die despite all the machinations of time and urban changes. I still have to undertake a tree walk to spot Delhi's trees along the hilly ridges of Dhaula Kuan, Vasant Vihar and the Tughlaqabad ravines. But the comfort zone of Lodi Gardens has quenched my curiosity to a great extent.

There is an unspoken acceptance of the Dalit[6] reality in India. The caste system, with a history of more than 3,000 years in India, has deepened the social segregation rooted in the dehumanizing principle of purity and impurity. Dr Ambedkar had postulated that the caste system came into being long after the different races of India had co-mingled in blood and culture. Caste divisions are not distinctions of race and to view them as such would be an unforgivable perversion of the historical process.[7]

The caste system is not restricted to Hinduism as is commonly believed. Muslims, Sikhs and Christians also practise it as it is a deeply ingrained social system. In Pakistan, Punjabi and Sindhi villages have another version of the system, based on different names with different excuses but follow a similar principle. Kumhar (potter), Chamar (hide worker), Choora (janitor), Mochi (cobbler), Nai (barber)—are still derogatory terms common in elite parlance. Menial jobs are still reserved for the lower tiers of society while land tillers and landowners are exalted in social hierarchy. Islam and its egalitarian ethos have not been able to dilute these divisions.

Dr Ambedkar was instrumental in outlawing the practice of untouchability formally through the Constitution of India in 1950. Still, Dalits continue to be subjected to extreme forms of social and economic exclusion and discrimination. The Dalit reality in India mars India's achievements and casts a shadow over its potential future.

The Dalit population, a few years ago, had been estimated at around 16 per cent of the total population of India. More than one million Dalits are said to be manual scavengers who clean public latrines and dispose of dead animals (we have a similar underclass in Pakistan). The data also shows that the overwhelming majority of Dalits live in rural areas who are more often than not landless and work as casual labourers.[8]

'Dalit' in Marathi literally means 'broken' or 'cracked' but Dalits are now redefining the word and with it their struggle. They are making sense of their existence through political struggle, education and activism. In the past few decades Dalits have crossed several barriers and have articulated their political position in a most unequivocal way. Nevertheless it requires decades for rural India to overcome centuries of embedded segregation and the associated violence.

A few months earlier, I had read a moving poem, 'Which Language Should I Speak', by Arun Kamble, a Marathi poet:[9]

> Chewing trotters in the badlands
> my grandpa,
> the permanent resident of my body,
> the household of tradition heaped on his back,
> hollers at me,
> 'You whore-son, talk like we do.
> Talk, I tell you!'
>
> Picking through the Vedas
> his top-knot well-oiled with ghee,
> my Brahmin teacher tells me,
>
> 'You idiot, use the language correctly!'
> Now I ask you which language should I speak?

Visiting the famous Dalit Colony, close to Gole Market, in Delhi, was quite an experience. Other than wanting for myself the much-talked-about Dalit experience, my interest had been piqued due to Gandhiji. Mahatma Gandhi used to live here during 1946–47. He had selected this place so that he could live alongside the 'untouchables'. The small room where he stayed hosted crucial meetings of the Congress. It was here that the Cabinet Mission met the Mahatma. But I was more curious about the present than the past. Popular Dalit voices are not too flattering about the Mahatma's word 'Harijan' (People of God) for the Dalits who saw it as his rather diluted resistance to mainstream Hinduism.

Unlike its past state, today this locality has apartment blocks, a paved road and a fairly well-sized park for children. Much to my surprise, the place seemed to be an ordinary middle-class Indian locality rather than anything else. This was not what I had expected. Pictures of India's Dalits living an abject life of desperate poverty were rudely challenged. I met a couple of young men sitting on the pavement. They introduced themselves with only their first names and I, on my part, did not insist on their full identities. I confess I was a little uncomfortable when I uttered the D word and was not sure how the boys would take it. And I did sense a little discomfort among them but it was just a ripple that soon disappeared. I was reassured by their laughter.

But the surface 'normalcy' of the Dalit Colony that I initially sensed gave way to cynicism. The opportunities for many young men and women are limited as my subsequent visits informed me. But India is changing and has come a long way with Dalits championing their causes through the ballot box and by winning 'reservation' in government jobs. We in Pakistan have invisible Dalits too. Among the Sindhi Hindus, among the Christians and Muslims as well. Casteism is not dead in South Asia and India is not the only country where it persists. Pakistan's hierarchy of biradaris and village society still maintains old divisions despite the Islamic faith and its emphasis on equality.

Lower-caste people and Muslims have been allies in Uttar Pradesh. The Dalits are quite out of the Hindu–Muslim communalism politics. I heard about a popular anti-communal song '*Mandir-Masjid*' composed by a Dalit poet, which essentially reminds how God stands divided in temples, mosques and gurdwaras and how human blood is often sacrificed to win religious arguments and struggles.

But V.S. Naipaul, whose views are unfortunately widely heard, holds that there can be no reconciliation between Islam and other faiths in the subcontinent. He writes: 'There can be no reconciliation. Islam is a religion of fixed laws. This goes contrary to everything in modern India. Also, the convert's deepest impulse is the rejection of his origins.'

My friend Mayank has a vast collection of magazines and books. He gives me several articles on Naipaul. While reclining in the back seat of a Delhi cab, I read an intriguing interview. Naipaul on the 'fractured past, fissured present' of India corrects the interviewer and calls India's past a 'calamitous millennium' that commenced with Muslim invasions:

> This is such a big and bad event that people still have to find polite, destiny-defying ways of speaking about it. In art books and history books, people write of the Muslims 'arriving' in India, as though the Muslims came on a tourist bus and went away again. The Muslim view of their conquest of India is a truer one. They speak of the triumph of the faith, the destruction of idols and temples, the loot, the carting away of the local people as slaves, so cheap and numerous that they were being sold for a few rupees.

Present in Delhi and witness to this calamitous millennium, I find his rant chilling. He wrote about the absence of Hindu monuments in the north and lack of Hindu records of this period indicating the 'grinding down of Hindu India'. Not just that, Akbar for the first time is referred to as the 'terrible Akbar' who destroyed Orissa. And hear what he had to say about 'useless' Mughal buildings:

> They are a carry-over from the architecture of Isfahan. In India they speak of the desert. They cover enormous spaces and they make me think of everything that was flattened to enable them to come up. Humayun's tomb is, I suppose, the chastest and the best. The Taj is so wasteful, so decadent and in the end so cruel that it is painful to be there for very long. This is an extravagance that speaks of the blood of the people.

Naipaul denied the almost universally accepted tenet of Indian secularism by writing that India did not have a secular character. He also states that Partition was the right choice; otherwise an undivided India would have found it difficult to deal with a huge minority. And India's espousal of nuclear weapons was also welcomed by the great author: '... I actually think that the subcontinent is safer now.' Quite logically, therefore, Gandhi, 'uneducated and never a thinker', was summarily dismissed by Naipaul. The cleverly packaged and eloquently written revisionism is one of the many reasons for an anti-historical attitude to Delhi's Muslim past.

As the taxi passed through the jam-packed roads squeezed by brazen encroachments, I wonder about the signages on modern boards—Kidwai Nagar, Hazrat Nizamuddin, Jain Mandir, Okhla, Jamia, Saket, etc. Delhi is a multi-petalled lotus like the Baha'i Temple and should be nurtured. This city belongs to all South Asians; those who are in a perpetual state of self-hatred may leave it alone.

NOTES

1. Excerpted from *The Writer and the World* by V.S. Naipaul.
2. 'Forbes gives Delhi the "dirty" tag', Times News Network.
3. The Indian Right to Information Act is also celebrated at JNU as a major step towards making citizens powerful. Delhi leads the country

in terms of applications moved under the Right to Information Act. Over time, thousands of applications have been filed with various state authorities to seek information and transparency. The isolated Mughal courts and Raj durbars have finally given way to a more accessible environment.

4. According to the Directorate of Economics & Statistics.
5. Delhi-based think tank. Visit www.niua.org
6. In South Asia's caste system, a Dalit, formerly known as 'untouchable' or 'achhuta' is a person outside of the four varnas and considered below all and polluting. Dalits include people such as leather workers, scavengers, tanners, flayers, cobblers, agricultural labourers, municipal cleaners, gymnasts, drum beaters, folk musicians and street handicraft persons. Like upper castes, Dalits are also divided into various sub-castes. Visit www.nacdor.org/TEXT FILES/Dalit.htm
7. Dr B.R. Ambedkar, 'Annihilation of Caste' in writings and speeches, Vol. 1, p. 49.
8. Dalit Foundation.
9. Translated from the Marathi by Priya Adarker.

14

Familiar, Unfamiliar?

On a sunny, wintry morning in 2007 I was introduced to S. Irfan Habib, a Delhi-based historian who has the same name as that of the Aligarh-based legendary historian of India. Professor Habib instantly clicked with me, a Pakistani, and told me about his pleasant experiences during his visit to Lahore, and, of course, made some insightful comments on India, Pakistan and their shared histories—three characters that always accompany me in Delhi. I was meeting, for a change, an 'educated' Indian Muslim who was not making snide remarks about Pakistan and how it was not secular and how wonderfully secular India was. How easy it is to adopt a nationalistic identity! Irfan Habib's integrity when he talks of the Indo-Pakistani reality or any other issue stems from a curious mix of old-world ideology and an objective sense of history.

As we talked, I was awed by Habib's doctoral thesis on Bhagat Singh and his comrades. He taught history for several years in UP until he moved to Delhi in 1982 and absorbed himself in the capital buzz. He worked for years at the National Institute of Science, Technology and Development Studies. His research interests therefore shifted to the history of science.

Habib's ancestors, the Saiyads of Barha from UP migrated

from Persia in the early medieval period and were known to be vanguards in the Mughal armies. This reminds me of Ghalib and his insistence on his warrior lineage. In the twilight of the Mughal era, soon after the death of Aurangzeb, the famed Syed brothers, Husain Ali and Hasan Ali were known as the kingmakers. They acquired unlimited power after Aurangzeb's death and installed and removed Mughal emperors at will. They were Habib's ancestors. His grandfather, Hakim Syed Habib Hasan was a prominent student of the celebrated Hakim Ajmal Khan and among the first batch of students graduating from Tibbia College, Delhi, in 1919. The younger hakim, Habib's grandfather Syed Habib Hasan, spent a few years working in Ajmal Khan's matab (clinic) in Ballimaran before setting up his own medical practice in Jansath, Muzaffarnagar.

When we met, Irfan Habib was preparing to go to Lahore to launch his book on Bhagat Singh. The book was extremely well received given the resonance of the shared hero of both countries. The enigmatic and brave Singh is beyond a research 'subject' for Habib. Habib wrote, Bhagat Singh 'was not only against communal and divisive politics, he hated and mocked the Indian caste system which makes people untouchable on the basis of their birth in a particular caste. He reiterated that all exploitations—economic, social or cultural—had to go if we want to build a strong nation.' As my knowledge of Bhagat Singh gets refreshed by a first-rate researcher, I am reminded that his sacrifice 'has the potential to enliven millions of struggling lives'. Our own South Asian Che Guevara, 'Bhagat Singh continues to inspire all those who are committed to secular socialist values and reject caste-based hierarchical society.' The most intriguing discovery for me was that despite his marginalization, Bhagat Singh, found a supporter in mainstream politics in Jinnah. We read that Jinnah, isolated and dismayed by the encroachment of religion in politics at that time, rose in support of Bhagat Singh. In his incisive speech to the Constituent Assembly on 12 and 14 September 1929, Jinnah harshly condemned criminal colonial rule and the government's actions against revolutionaries. He said:

> The man who goes on hunger strike has a soul. He is moved by the soul and he believes in the justice of his cause; he is not an ordinary criminal who is guilty of a cold-blooded, sordid, wicked crime ... It is the system, this damnable system of government which is resented by the people ... And the last words I wish to address to the government are, try and concentrate your mind on the root cause and the more you concentrate on the root cause, the less difficulties and inconveniences there will be for you to face, and thank heaven that the money of the taxpayer will not be wasted in prosecuting men, nay citizens, who are fighting and struggling for the freedom of their country.

In Pakistan, we have conveniently forgotten the nature and trajectory of our freedom struggle. All non-Muslims are grouped in one single category which is completely rejected by the rulers of Pakistan irrespective of their message and their history. The same fate met Bhagat Singh. That he was supported by Jinnah is a fact never mentioned in the corridors of power or in the textbooks of Pakistan. It is not surprising, though. Bhagat Singh, a symbol of resistance, could never be the hero of a government that, for decades, has not represented the will of the people.

The other area that Habib has been active in concerns communal harmony and dialogues around this thorny theme. His voice is undeniably strong and direct:

> There has been a lot of noise about rethinking in Islam, particularly post September 11, 2001. I feel it is long overdue and September 11 has just given us a rude shock to get into action. Within India, Godhra and the ensuing Gujarat carnage has added urgency to the question of rethinking, making us conscious of the fact that there is something seriously wrong somewhere. If September 11 and Godhra are the ugly faces of Islam, then the burning of Graham Staines and his children and

> the ongoing Gujarat carnage is the depraved and distorted face of Hinduism. Both are threats to the secular and pluralist fabric of India.

Habib's frustrations are not academic. He is also an activist, and, of late, has been using Twitter to speak out. He rightly says that Islam did not undergo any meaningful reform to cope with the challenges of modernity. Attempts at ijtihad, a reasoned struggle and rethinking to reform Islam, have been sabotaged by woolly arguments saying that Islam is beyond time and context, thus any talk of 'rethinking' is un-Islamic. This was seen during the nineteenth century when Syed Ahmed Khan, Jamaluddin Afghani, Mohammad Abduh and others gave a call for ijtihad.[1]

Habib quotes Alam Khundmiri, a thinker from Hyderabad (1922–83), who argued that most Muslim social reform movements have been trapped by the flawed reasoning that equates medieval religious tradition with Islam forgetting that Islam itself revolted against the superstitions of the age. In a piece that Habib shared with me he writes:

> Another much talked about feature of Islam is the shariah. It is being interpreted in its most revile form by the believers themselves and in the process inviting ridicule and scorn of the civilised world. The shariah is perceived as a divine code of conduct applicable forever without any spatial or temporal constraints. This has led to serious complications with respect to women's rights. It is unfortunate that in Islam religiosity and morality have become synonymous with legality, while in fact legality should be subordinate to a moral and ethical vision. There is an urgent need to make necessary changes in the shariah under the Quranic gaze so that it conforms to the moral fervour of the Prophet and the ethical vision of Islam.[2]

This rare and candid self-examination is counterpoised by his analysis of what happened to Hinduism and 'its vulgarization at the hands of Sangh Parivar'.

As we talk and exchange letters, I get a better understanding of Habib's insight. He calls the Parivar a cohort of 'rabble-rousers' who have appointed themselves as representatives of Hinduism and all its followers. While the cohort is quick to condemn its '*bete noire*, Islam', it ends up echoing and mirroring what the Islamists do. As Habib puts it, they 'have brazenly adopted the most un-Hindu version of Hinduism called Hindutva, propounded by Vir Savarkar in the early last century'. I am even more fascinated when Habib informs us that Savarkar was an avowed atheist and 'had no qualms in defacing Hinduism to suit his politics of social engineering'. This brand of politicking masked as faith was shunned for years and decades until L.K. Advani regurgitated it in the 1990s 'providing it legitimacy and respect', complains Habib.

The construct of 'cultural nationalism' promoted by Advani was also rooted in the 'the mischievous ideology of Savarkar who unabashedly made Hindutva and nationalism interchangeable'. Little wonder then that such a narrow vision made Maulana Azad, Bacha Khan, Ajmal Khan and other Muslim luminaries shun the concept of cultural nationalism pushed by the Sangh Parivar.

This particularist world view was in direct opposition to the nationalism articulated by Jamaluddin Afghani, who in the 1880s, identified the composite 'strength of Indian nationalism' where myriad communities were united against colonial rule. Afghani highlighted the notion of a shared secular heritage of a grand civilization not unlike Qurratulain Hyder's romantic view of the Indian past forerunning the Nehruvian concept of Indian history in *The Discovery of India.*

This unique, commonly experienced and lived heritage was not mired in religious discourse or exclusivism. Habib holds that Hindutva is 'unfortunately rooted in the revival of a sectarian past and not the common past of all Indians. It seeks to construct an unadulterated Indian past after a careful sifting of icons and ideas, leaving out a large section from our heritage as something not only alien but also defiling.' A more serious lament by my erudite friend is the simmering reality that Hindutva's 'concerted hammering of lies' has engulfed a sizeable number of Hindus. The electorate's verdict, however, has been clear in the elections—extremist ideology should stay far from matters of national governance.

Jihadi Islam, or what many Western academics have referred to as political Islam or Islamism, plays a similar game. The Hindutva and Islamist discourses denude personal and collective spirituality and rob them of their intrinsic humanity. Hatred thus invokes the constructed pasts of glory, virility, victory and war. The present therefore is perverted and the future turned into a nightmare. Little wonder then that Naipaul, the hero of global adulation, keeps drumming away that reconciliation is not possible. These narratives, as I suggest, rather humbly, to Habib, are embedded in our past but are not at all insurmountable.

The best counterpoint to harking back to an exclusivism dusted in gold is to revive what we have shared and continue to share—namely our civilizational and cultural values.

And creative dastangohs[3] of the twenty-first century are doing just that.

Once upon a time, the gullies and kuchas of Shahjahanabad must have echoed with stories of dastangohs or storytellers. The crowds gathered in front of kabab stalls, chai khanas and masjids, must have listened awestruck at the wonderful tales of kings, lovers, vazirs, poets, khwajas, seducers, hakims and fakirs. The storyteller would impersonate each character—his voice regal when he is the emperor, high-pitched when depicting the romantic longing of an imprisoned princess and shrill when describing the nagging of a toothless old crone. When the story needed a description of a bazaar, the dastangoh would use the coarse dialect of commoners and, for the royal chambers, a sophisticated Persian with unparalled elegance.

That world, which has disappeared, is now being lovingly resurrected in Delhi. Not under the shadows of the Jama Masjid, but in air-conditioned playhouses of the India International Centre and the India Habitat Centre. It was this zest for the text, good old-fashioned narration, the fantastical details and scope for improvisation in performance that attracted Mahmood Farooqui and Danish Husain to the world of Dastangoi.

I first saw Farooqui performing Dastangoi on a soft winter afternoon in an auditorium in Delhi University. That was also the first time in my life I was watching Dastangoi. I had missed their performances in Pakistan. The words of the daastaan had been one-dimensional for me until this evening, much like reading Shakespeare but never actually getting an opportunity to see his plays on stage, the original reason for which they were written. So it was a pleasantly giddy feeling to finally watch and not read a daastaan. Those words which I had encountered on pages earlier sprung to real life.

Both Farooqui and Husain wore white kurtas and pyjamas with muslin caps and looked as if they were part of the audience, seated on a simple *masnad*. Such a bare setting but powerful. I wondered then if they found the rebirthing of the dead form of Dastangoi challenging and difficult, especially because of the culture of short attention spans these days.

I recalled my meeting with Farooqui earlier at the India International Centre during one of my visits to Delhi. He was not the quintessential dastangoh in his medieval apparel that I had seen in the media. Rather he wore a pair of jeans and looked very modern. He has a thoughtful face and is pleasantly neck-deep in Urdu literature. He must be pretty bohemian, I mused, since he has rejected a formal career and pursues his passions, namely, Dastangoi. Farooqui told me how humanist and realistic writings had displaced gupbaazi (narration of fabricated tales).

I hope that gupbaazi would be back in vogue once again. For the time being, this duo have kept Dastangoi alive.

Farooqui, the modern-day dastangoh, did a bit of homework. He drew lessons from a three-minute precious tape stored in a London library. The recording had the piece of a daastaan narrated by Mir Baqar Ali, perhaps the last great dastangoh of Delhi. Ali would hold weekly mehfils at his residence in Bhojla Pahari near Jama Masjid. The entry fee was one anna (one-sixteenth of a rupee). During the performance, Ali, a thin, spindly man would become an imperial monarch in one instant, a humble beggar in the next. His grasp over lifestyle, culture and language was dazzling. In his book, *Dilli Ki Chand Ajeeb Hastiyan*, Ashraf Subhui says that once during a performance, Mir Baqar Ali mentioned twenty-five types of musical instruments, nineteen kinds of wrestling equipment and forty-three types of wrestling holds among other descriptions. If the story had even a passing anecdote concerning medicines, Ali would consult a hakim on medicinal herbs and diseases. Popular lore has it that one evening his listeners rushed to see a bioscope which had newly arrived in the city. The storyteller's heart broke. He parted company with daastaans and started selling paan. He died in 1928 and the curtain came down on Dastangoi.

It was raised again in 2008 with the publication of *The Adventures of Amir Hamza*, translated by Musharraf Ali Farooqi, a Pakistani-Canadian writer, from a forty-six-volume Urdu edition published in 1855 by Ghalib Lakhnavi and later revised by Abdullah Bilgrami. This English-language edition has 948 pages of high drama, suspense, thrills and enough romance to captivate the imagination of the new generation nurtured on a diet of Western adventures—*Star Trek*, *Lord of the Rings* and the *Harry Potter* series. Free of colonial influence and loaded with unfettered imagination, these fantasies open up alternative worlds without hammering any point home except a subtle humanism and what is known in Urdu as insaan dosti.

Tilism-e-Hoshruba, the great daastaan of all times, was my childhood and adolescent obsession in Lahore. *Bachon ka Baagh*, a Pakistani magazine for children, would print small, sanitized stories from *Hoshruba*. At the age of eleven, my uncle gifted me a *Tilism* version of seven volumes edited by the Urdu writer, Raees Ahmed Jafri. Ustad Allah Bakhsh's paintings would adorn the covers and make these volumes even more spellbinding—a world of fairies, demons, ogres and princes. Only with age I could understand the cumbersome Persianized language of the introductions.

The *Tilism* was my constant companion. I still vividly remember my excitement each time as I would read the part where Hamza's grandson, Asad Sherdil, would enter the Tilism and reach a garden where a white gateway would open 'like the arms of the beloved'. I was overawed by the powers of Hamza as he breathed the Great Name on the corpse of his slain son that turned out to be made of lentil flour! I was riveted by the antics of his companion and trickster, Amar, who could assume any disguise and outmanoeuvre the most powerful wizards with the help of *galeem* and *zambeel*—magical gifts that had been bestowed on him by the prophets.

While undoubtedly the cultural references are mostly Islamic in essence, there is a subtle secular spirit embedded in the tale. It is a pleasure-oriented, almost hedonistic world where there are no barriers and no inhibitions. Endless fantasy allows for cultural mingling where believers and non-believers interact, copulate, and befriend each other in a no-holds-barred fashion.

In the decline of Dastangoi in Delhi, and elsewhere in India, lies a saga of how a timeless yarn lost its appeal because of the circumstances of history, colonial interventions and changed literary conventions. Dastangois are as entertaining and intimate as say, Ramlilas. While during Dussehra, street corners all over north India are abuzz with Ramayana performances, the art of Dastangoi has vanished. Is it because we discard our shared heritage by marking them as exclusive properties of a certain religion? Is the politics of language powerful enough to break down great literature?

After 1857, the reformist ethos of Urdu was contemptuous of the daastaan romances. Later, the progressive writers in the 1930s and '40s also declared them as archaic and decadent. But at the popular level, the daastaans remained in vogue. Partition was to alter the destiny of Urdu and label it as the language of the Muslim Pakistan.

In Pakistan, a reassessment of daastaans took place from the 1950s onwards. Mohammad Hasan Askari, Urdu's leading critic, selected portions of *Tilism-i-Hoshruba* saying that these fantastic fables had layers of meaning and social commentary within their subtexts and dramas. A decade later, a leading Urdu critic, Suhail Ahmad Khan, interpreted daastaans and unlocked their symbolism. Similarly, Frances Pritchett of Columbia University, while researching on daastaans, brought out a summarized version in English of a part of the *Dastan-i-Amir Hamza* with a detailed introduction for the benefit of her Western readers. Musharraf Ali Farooqi's *The Adventures of Amir Hamza* is only the latest. But can a few books resurrect the popularity of the daastaans? This is why the work of Mahmood Farooqui and Danish Husain is so important. They are reinventing the tradition albeit in an innovative and modern way.

Driving or auto-ing back from Shahjahanabad to New Delhi, I always notice how the past is dead and yet so undead, floating like an old ghost between the living and dying. One such ghost floats above the Khooni Darwaza (Gateway of Blood) that stands testimony to history's horrors. Falling right in the middle of Bahadur Shah Zafar Marg that connects New Delhi to Old, almost midway between the ITO crossing and Daryaganj, Khooni Darwaza is one of the thirteen surviving historical gates of Shahjahanabad.

Today when history-immune Delhi-walas drive past it, they can, at best, go back just a few years ago, when a medical student was raped inside its walls. But that was just the most recent terror to be added to the bloodied legend of Khooni Darwaza.

I have heard people saying that blood drips from its ceilings during the monsoons. Some say that dead Mughal princes scurry around like Hamlet's ghosts. Others say that decapitated heads hang there. The last is not merely a story. Built by Sher Shah Suri and originally named Kabuli Darwaza, since caravans coming from Kabul would pass through it, the gateway came to be known as Khooni Darwaza. The Mughals liked to display the heads of executed criminals there. Over time, unwanted princes and other nobles began to be disposed of within the Darwaza, augmenting its notoriety. Khooni Darwaza was particularly convenient in Mughal India since there has hardly been a peaceful accession to the throne—courtiers were murdered, fathers imprisoned and princes exiled. When Jehangir's succession was resisted by a few of Akbar's 'navaratnas' or special courtiers, he promptly dispatched Abdul Rahim Khan-I-Khanan's two sons to this hell's gate. The bodies, left to rot, must have been thrown away after a few days of public viewing. Jehangir's grandson, Aurangzeb proved his invincibility to the people of Delhi by displaying brother Dara's head at the gate.

Early British chroniclers may have scoffed at such barbarities of the Orientals, but their generals did not differ much in cruelty. Khooni Darwaza remained in use. Bahadur Shah Zafar, the last great Mughal, more of a Sufi than a sultan, was spared a violent end, but his four sons and a grandson were killed at the Darwaza during the 1857 Mutiny. Legend has it that the spirits of Zafar's sons scamper around in the grotesque ruins.

However, I do not feel any ghostly presence of Zafar within the compound of Moti Masjid in Mehrauli, not too far away from the Khooni Darwaza. A grave was dug here as his final resting place, but the unlucky emperor was banished after being charged with 'rebellion, treason and murder' by the British, to faraway Rangoon. The defeated emperor, stripped of his kingdom, wealth, palace, sons and dignity, was denied even the spot where he wanted to be buried. An old doddering man, who was more devoted to music and poetry, was unwittingly forced into becoming an official guardian angel of a rebellion he had not started. He was like a Dara Shikoh at a time when what the Mughals needed was another Aurangzeb.

During the riots of 1947, more bloodshed occurred near Khooni Darwaza when several refugees going to the camp established in Purana Quila were killed here. When Sadia and I went to a mosque near the Darwaza, the mullah there told us stories of djinns and ghosts. However, as I walked around the monument, I saw no invisible messengers from the other world. Neither did Sadia. There was just a cop quietly smoking a cigarette in a makeshift police post.

Each time my friends in Lahore and Karachi get wind of my trips to Delhi, they start calling me. Requests pour in. Somebody wants Arundhati Roy's latest book of essays, another wants such-and-such a book which is not available in Pakistan. I happily oblige. So bookshop browsing is an integral part of my trips. In Khan Market, where Delhi's middle and upper classes buy little doses of happiness from upmarket retail stores, a trip to Bahrisons Booksellers is a must. Bahri's is also perhaps the only bookshop in the city where there is a great collection of Pakistani books. Each time I go there, besides buying scores of books, I also occasionally catch up with visiting Pakistani acquaintances whom, ironically, I have not met back home in months.

The cosy Bookshop in nearby and much-quieter Jor Bagh was earlier located in Khan Market but its lease ran out and the owner had to shift here. Now there is a showroom of a luxury watch brand where the old bookshop used to be. In fact, Khan Market is becoming the new mall—a shoe shop replaced a book studio a few years ago and many glitzy shops have sprung up. As I find out, Jor Bagh is a haven for book lovers. A peaceful stillness lurks here. There is no noise, no traffic and no crowds—something that the genteel Sikh owner of The Bookshop must surely not be happy about. But I'm not complaining.

Unfortunately, Delhi's charming bookshops are the victims of the bitter realities of globalization. I am told that smaller, independently owned bookshops are shutting down and being replaced by large corporate bookshop chains. A very popular bookstore in Connaught Place, The Bookworm, decided to close down because they could not compete with the high discounts offered by big retail chains. And yet, when I went to the wonderful shop, Fact and Fiction, in the trendy Vasant Vihar market, it was hard to believe that small shops have no future. Here was the most singular collection of eccentric books in such a tiny space. I have always found it packed with people. Talking about small shops, I always keep some time aside for second-hand bookshops in Paharganj, the hotel district for Western backpackers. In a shop called Jackson's, I once found a book on Jerusalem that bore the seal of a Rawalpindi bookstore. The world is really round!

But perhaps the best bookshop in Delhi, according to my book-obsessed friend Mayank, a Delhi journalist-blogger, is the Daryaganj book bazaar. Each Sunday, booksellers lay out their ware on the mile-long pavement. Browsing there is one of Delhi's rituals. I never came here often enough, but when I did, I have stumbled upon antique copies of classics, as well as other books, which are simply not available, say, in upmarket Bahrisons. For instance, I saw the first edition of Stanley Wolpert's biography of Jinnah, a book which is tough to find in first-hand shops in India. But of course, I did not buy it since I have two copies back home. Needless to say, my Daryaganj excursions always culminate in the legendary Moti Mahal restaurant with its tandoori chicken, a speciality which its founder had invented in Peshawar during pre-Partition days.

And then there is the Urdu bazaar opposite Jama Masjid. Like many other landmarks in the walled city, it carries a depressing aura. But, as in the stories of many Delhi monuments, you just have to wade deep into the squalor to find the jewel. While there are many who mourn the demise of Urdu in India, browsing in the Maktaba Jamia bookshop does not give one that impression. This is a place where I have spent hours browsing and forgetting all the cares of the world. I discovered the shop during my second trip to Delhi and remember buying *Kaf-i-Gul Farosh* (Sleeve of a Flower Seller), a hefty two-volume photo journal by the late Qurratulain Hyder, a project she had completed just before I met her during my first trip to Delhi.

Bahadur Shah Zafar's tutor, Zauq wrote '*Kaun jaaye Zauq, dilli ki galiyan chhodkar?*' ('Who would leave the streets of Delhi, Zauq, and go elsewhere?') A fleeting visitor like me had to perforce leave the streets of Delhi. But the books on Delhi that I collected rarely allow Delhi to make an exit from my inner landscape. Never have I read, or reread as profusely about a city, as I have about Delhi. In a way, once you get to know Delhi, or imagine that to be the case, you cannot let go of it.

Delhi's slippery, sprawling reality lies not only in its physical geography or its seasons but also in how it has been described by its various chroniclers. A large number of writers have focused on its history and its grand past though not in the quantum one would have wished for. A parallel city thus exists in the realm of books. In the face of the dying oral histories and culture of Shahjahanabad and even Lutyens's urbanity, how difficult it would be to understand Delhi's history in all its dimensions without making a note of how the way it is chronicled has changed, or not changed, over centuries.

Listing all those memorable books that I have read would take too much space and may not interest all my readers. However, I would like to touch upon a few that I have particularly enjoyed, without entering into too much descriptions or details about them. *City Improbable*, edited by Khushwant Singh was one of the early acquisitions and since then it has remained by my bedside. Ahmed Ali's timeless novel *Twilight in Delhi* is an evocative compendium of social history. A translated version of Dipty Nazir Ahmad's *The Bride's Mirror: A Tale of Life in Delhi a Hundred Years Ago*, like Janc Austen's miniature portraits, peeps into Shahjahanabad lives and havelis with a progressive message for Muslim women.

Maheshwar Dayal's clippings on Delhi in newspapers later led me to his book, *Rediscovering Delhi*, which is full of little nuggets about the city. Another brilliant book that I found in Bahrisons was *Delhi: The Built Heritage—A Listing* by Ratish Nanda, Narayani Gupta and O.P. Jain which gives us a spatial and aesthetic sense of Delhi covering nearly 1,200 buildings of archaeological and cultural significance. Percival Spear's book, *Delhi: Its Monuments and History*, shows us his fascination with the city. A friend in Delhi gifted me the utterly irresistible Lucy Peck's book, *Delhi: A Thousand Years of Building*, revealing the plans and architectural details of the known and not-so-known monuments.

Going back in time a little, Shama Mitra Chenoy's book, *Shahjahanabad: The City of Delhi, 1638–1857*, is a thoroughly researched account of Shahjahanabad over two centuries about the inner cohesion and cultural unity despite differences within the Walled City. I loved the accounts of havelis in Pawan Varma's book *Havelis of Old Delhi* (1992). This formidable tale of Delhi's lost mansions talks about the atomization of urbanity as opposed to the sharing of living spaces. *Delhi: A Novel* by Khushwant Singh (1990) is a tale with a larger-than-life canvas, erotic in parts, meandering between the modern and the ancient city. In Lahore, I found another delightful book, *Nature Watch*, by Singh on the trees and flowers of Delhi that my friends and I have read several times with awe because of its unmissable similarities with Lahore. Pradip Krishen's *Trees of Delhi* goes beyond a textual exercise. It is a historical compendium and a marker of sorts in an age of the fast-degrading environment.

My prized possession is the *Delhi Omnibus* which collates four classic works on the history of Delhi: Percival Spear's *Delhi: A Historical Sketch* and *Twilight of the Mughals: Studies in Late Mughal Delhi*, Narayani Gupta's *Delhi between Two Empires 1803-1931* and the R.E. Frykenburg-edited anthology, *Delhi Through the Ages: Selected Essays in Urban History, Culture and Society*. It is the last one which always enchants me in the manner in which it deals with empires and the criss-crossing of eras and movements.

William Dalrymple's book, *City of Djinns* can be picked up at any time and hold the reader. Delhi itself emerges as a character, wounded and old, vibrant and fractured and the drama unfolds as a book within the book. Delhi is now his adopted home and his third book, *The Last Mughal: The Fall of a Dynasty, Delhi, 1857*, on the tragic life of Emperor Bahadur Shah Zafar, contains the much-talked-about discoveries of new archival materials that earlier Indian historians may have ignored.

Another gem, *Historic Delhi: An Anthology*, published in 1997, and edited by H.K. Kaul has intimate accounts of Delhi from ancient eras to the twentieth century.

I was lucky to find a reprint of the celebrated 1906 book called *The Seven Cities of Delhi* by a colonial official, Gordon Risley Hearn. And, in recent years, another young writer, Robert Grant Irving, wrote *The Indian Summer: Lutyens, Baker and Imperial Delhi*, a very readable book about the myriad snippets and facets of the Delhi that Lutyens had built. However, R.V. Smith's major contribution towards unearthing the invisible stories of Delhi's past, *The Delhi That No One Knows*, has not received the attention it deserves. A compilation of Smith's newspaper articles, circa 1905, it is a thin volume but lucid in its descriptions that detail the legends and myths connected with Delhi's monuments. He writes, 'I did not refer to any book, did not make notes from dusty volumes in old libraries–I just walked! This is how the book happened.'

Charmaine O'Brien is the Dalrymple of culinary Delhi. She lived in the Nizamuddin Basti, and after observing and tasting the countless flavours of fine cooking, wrote *Flavours of Delhi: A Food Lover's Guide* in 2003, followed by *Recipes from an Urban Village.* Interestingly, when I learnt to cook as a student in London, Madhur Jaffrey's book *Cuisines of Delhi* became my guide. Her culinary odyssey is not just a journey into the past but contemporary too, a peek into Delhi's street food as well as its home cooking.

Nothing is more fascinating than the corpus of Delhi books in Urdu. These are authentic voices and grounded in real time and hearts as opposed to the stylized prose of a researcher or historian. Ghalib's epic *Diwan-i-Ghalib* is arguably the best of all Delhi's poetry. *Gul Feroz Shah* is a slice-of-life portrait of Delhi in Ghalib's time and Ralph Russell's books on Ghalib's poetry and letters are my permanent companions. Delhi also introduced me to the excellent translation, *Zikr-i-Mir: Autobiography of the Eighteenth Century Mughal Poet, Mir Muhammad Taqi 'Mir'* by C.M. Naim. It contains picturesque details of the poet Mir's sad life and even sadder times he lived in. Though expelled from Delhi he could not overcome his fondness for the city.

Partition stories abound in various books. Anees Qidwai's *Azadi ki Chaon Mein,* written immediately after Partition in 1948 is like a melancholic daastaan—stories of violence and the gutter-like refugee camps. Similarly, Shahid Ahmed Dehlvi's *Dilli ki Bipta* (1948) is also a testament of loss and longing. He chooses to move back to his beloved city after a short stint in Pakistan.

Mulla Wahidi's book, *Dilli Jo Aik Sheher Tha* (1929) is a rich mosaic of Delhi life in the early part of the twentieth century.

He writes as a train passenger, moving from station to station, packing and unpacking his luggage and conversing with others on the train. And then that fine book, *Old Delhi: Ten Easy Walks* by Gaynor Barton and Laurraine Malone. I have always wondered why a Delhi-wala could not have written it.

In the years of my distant though distinct intimacy with Delhi, I have often wondered why there is a relative paucity of books and stories on Delhi since Delhi is no ordinary city. It is a long, winding tale of history, power, powerlessness and mysticism that needs more investigation and interpretation now that colonial power is no more driving the Indian destiny. Leaving history aside, there is much in contemporary Delhi that has not been documented. Delhi, for all purposes now, is a Punjabi city. The woes of Partition have been well recorded but what happened to the new residents and their stories of adjustment and realignment? A notable exception to this trend has been Ranjana Sengupta's *Delhi Metropolitan: The Making of an Unlikely City*, but this excellent book raises the need for further inquiries into the hundreds of Delhis that now coexist in twenty-first-century India. For instance, 'urban villages' which are villages no more, 'farmhouses' with no farms, 'community centres' disconnected from the community and 'colonies' which continue to appropriate Delhi have been hardly addressed. The intellectual elite are contemptuous of the nouveau riche classes with the well-known architect Gautam Bhatia coining the term 'Punjabi Baroque'. Going further, rarely does one find a book on the erstwhile India Coffee House or a detailed look at the Jamia Millia, and, lest I forget, the JNU that hugs the Aravalli ranges and its ever-changing ethos. There are empty crevices in the otherwise lovable bookshops of Delhi.

Perhaps today's Delhi displays the ascendancy of money, power and an all-pervasive greed that would rather have a huge mall than a problematic Jama Masjid and a cluster of commerce rather than a heritage enclave. This ambivalence towards 'heritage' is a South Asian curse seeking to wipe out its rather eclectic histories. Forgetting is a fantasy that could easily reincarnate into a haunting dream.

NOTES

1. Syed Ahmed Khan was a modernist reformer in the mid-nineteenth-century India and a founder of the Aligarh Muslim University. Jamaluddin Afghani was a peripatetic pan-Islamist and anti-imperialist who travelled all over the Islamic world in the late nineteenth century. He also spent three years in India during the 1880s. Mohammad Abduh was a disciple of Afghani and a late nineteenth-century modernist reformer of Egypt.
2. *Seminar*, Vol. 516, August 2002.
3. The word Dastangoi refers to the art of storytelling. It is a compound of two Persian words daastaan and goi, which means to tell a daastaan. Daastaans were epics, often oral in nature, which were recited or read aloud and, in essence, were like medieval romances everywhere. Telling tales of adventure, magic and warfare, daastaans mapped new worlds and horizons, encountered the unseen and protected the hero through many travails and lovers as he moved on his quest. The Persian versions of the story narrated the life and adventures of Amir Hamza, supposedly an uncle of the Prophet Mohammad. By the sixteenth century, versions of the Hamza story had begun to circulate in India. http:21dastangoi.blogspot.in/p/dastangoi-lost-art-form-of-urdu.html

Glossary

Aam choor	dried mango powder
Aham Brahmasmi	I am Brahma.
Aloo gosht	mutton curry with potatoes
Ang	style
Badam ki lauz	almond fudge
Bakhar khani	layered bread
Barbat	wooden-topped lute
Bedmi puri	fried puffed bread with a mix of lentils and spices
Beenkari	playing of the been
Chanchal	boisterous
Chang	harp
Charaghan	lighting of lamps
Dai	missionary
Desi	native
Dhadhi	one who sings ballads
Dhak	tree known as flame of the forest

Dhruva-pada	refrain
Dua e roshnai	prayer of the light
Gajak	dried sweet made of sesame seeds cooked in sugar syrup
Galeem	cloak of invisibility
Ghoom tana	literally 'move around'
Gumti	canopy
Hama-oost	all is one
Hamwatan	countrymen
Hujra	small meditation room
Katra	mews
Khanqah	hospices, spiritual retreats
Makhfi	invisible
Markaz	headquarters
Marthiya	elegy
Masnad	divan/high seat
Mathnawi/Masnavi/ Mathnavi	romantic poem based on independent, internally rhyming lines
Milad mehfil	gathering devoted to the recitation of hymns and songs in remembrance of the Holy Prophet (PBUH) of Islam
Murshid	Arabic term for 'guide' or 'teacher'
Naatkhwani	Urdu devotional songs

Namaazee	worshipper
Piste ki lauz	pistachio fudge
Qasida	panegyric
Qaul	utterance
Qirat	Quranic readings and recitation
Ram laddoo	fried lentil balls served with a radish salad
Salariat	salaried
Sema	ceremony of the whirling dance
Shakarkandi	baked sweet potatoes served with spices
Shams	Arabic word for sun
Shereen qand	dessert
Surbahar	bass sitar
Tableeghi Jamat	group formed to propagate the spread of Islam.
Talabwas	pond
Tambur	long-necked lute with wooden soundboard
Tariqa	the Sufi way
Tasawwuf	loving God through the service of mankind
Tazkira	formal Islamic narratives
Tibbi	traditional medicine system

Tucke	turban
Wahdatul Wajud	unity of being
Zambeel	pouch that could contain the entire world

Acknowledgements

This book would not have been possible without the support and active engagement of many friends, colleagues and acquaintances, spread all over the globe. First and foremost, I need to thank Karthika V.K. of HarperCollins who was incredibly encouraging about the idea and helped me overcome my initial fears. My amazing friends, Sadia Dehlvi and Rakhshanda Jalil, provided their inputs as well as critical comments throughout the process of writing it. I also have to express immense gratitude to Mayank Austen Soofi who read all the drafts diligently and helped me find material for the book. I am lucky to have a friend like him. Mention must be made of the editor, Rukmini Sekhar, who did a great job and also filtered several of my sweeping generalizations in the book. I enjoyed several arguments with her, and will always be grateful for her help in bringing a little bit of nuance to my understanding of India and Delhi. Garga Chatterjee read the final draft on a long journey from Kolkata to Delhi and was most helpful. I also have to thank Kabir Altaf, Babar Mirza and Shemrez Nauman, my younger friends in Pakistan, for their last-minute help with the proofreading.

In Pakistan, my parents were excited about my idea of this book. I made my father read all the initial drafts and surprisingly he was very supportive of my underlying argument. As he had been a state official for most of his working life I was afraid my critique of nation state would offend him. Pakistan's leading poet, Fahmida Riaz, gave extraordinary support by reading, commenting on and approving my prose. Thanks are due to Sumaira, who helped me browse through books on Delhi and read the chapters when I was writing them. Irfan Javed reviewed the first few drafts and I must thank him for urging me to finish the manuscript. I am also indebted to the UK-based writer Suhayl Saadi who was kind enough to read the first few chapters and give most creative suggestions. Saadi was Rumi's most gifted mentor (no pun intended!). And the fiery editor Faiza Sultan Khan graciously helped with the titles for the chapters.

It would not be out of place to thank Arjun Goswami, a senior colleague at the Asian Development Bank, who indirectly helped develop the idea of this book when he asked me to join a project based in Delhi. I hope he reads this.

Finally, countless friends and acquaintances in Delhi, even strangers, need to be acknowledged. How could I have known the city without their assistance? The autorickshaw and taxi drivers, the dhaba-walas, dargah keepers and even the hotel's room-service staff were all welcoming and fun to get to know.

Acknowledgements are also due to various institutions such as the Network for Asia Pacific Schools and Institutes of Governance, Foundation of SAARC Writers and Literature, Amarjit Bhagwant Singh Charitable Trust (Attic), Jamia Millia Islamia University, Jawaharlal Nehru University, Sahmat, FICCI, and finally, the Centre for Dialogue and Reconciliation, for inviting me to their events in Delhi during the last few years.